CALIFORNIA

HOME LANDSCAPING

Other titles available in the *Home Landscaping* series:

MID-ATLANTIC

MIDWEST
including South-Central Canada

NORTHEAST
including Southeast Canada

NORTHWEST

SOUTHEAST

SOUTHERN COASTAL

TEXAS

WESTERN

CALIFORNIA
HOME LANDSCAPING

Roger Holmes
Lance Walheim

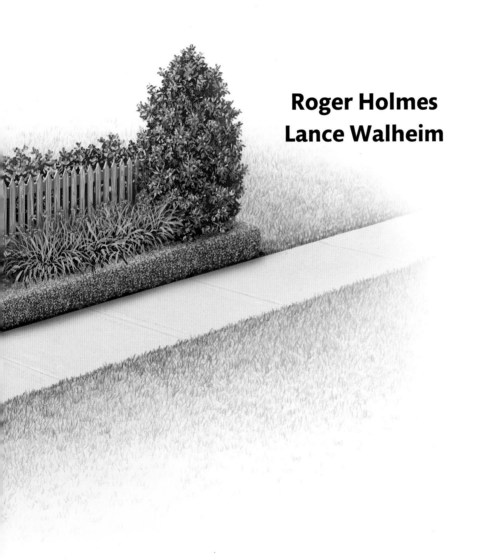

CREATIVE HOMEOWNER®

COPYRIGHT © 2001, 2006, 2010, 2016

CREATIVE HOMEOWNER®

CALIFORNIA HOME LANDSCAPING
WORDWORKS

EDITORS	Roger Holmes, Lance Walheim
EDITORIAL CONSULTANT	Rita Buchanan
ASSISTANT EDITOR	Sarah Disbrow
COPY EDITORS	Nancy J. Stabile, Sarah Disbrow
INTERIOR DESIGN	Deborah Fillion
ILLUSTRATORS	Steve Buchanan (Portfolio of Designs); Michelle Angle Farrar, Lee Hov, Robert LaPointe, Rick Daskam, Teresa Nicole Green (Guide to Installation)

Manufactured in China

Current Printing (last digit)
10 9 8 7

California Home Landscaping, Third Edition
ISBN: 978-1-58011-499-8

We are always looking for talented authors. To submit an idea, please send a brief inquiry to acquisitions@foxchapelpublishing.com.

CREATIVE HOMEOWNER®
www.creativehomeowner.com

Creative Homeowner books are distributed in North America by Fox Chapel Publishing, 903 Square Street, Mount Joy, PA 17552 **www.FoxChapelPublishing.com**, and in the UK by Grantham Book Service, Trent Road, Grantham, Lincolnshire, NG31 7XQ.

About the Authors

Roger Holmes is the founding editor of Fine Gardening magazine. He co-edited the monumental Taylor's **Master Guide to Gardening** and other highly regarded gardening books, and produced the landscaping series of which this book is part. He also co-wrote Creative Homeowner's **Creating Good Gardens**.

Lance Walheim lives in California and has authored or contributed to more than 30 gardening books, including **Lawns for Dummies, Roses for Dummies, The Natural Rose Gardener,** and **Citrus.** He has also been a staff editor at Sunset magazine.

Safety First

Though all concepts and methods in this book have been reviewed for safety, it is not possible to overstate the importance of using the safest working methods possible. What follows are reminders—do's and don'ts for yard work and landscaping. They are not substitutes for your own common sense.

- *Always* use caution, care, and good judgment when following the procedures described in this book.

- *Always* determine locations of underground utility lines before you dig, and then avoid them by a safe distance. Buried lines may be for gas, electricity, communications, or water. Start research by contacting your local building officials. Also contact local utility companies; they will often send a representative free of charge to help you map their lines. In addition, there are private utility locator firms that may be listed in your Yellow Pages. Note: previous owners may have installed underground drainage, sprinkler, and lighting lines without mapping them.

- *Always* read and heed the manufacturer's instructions for using a tool, especially the warnings.

- *Always* ensure that the electrical setup is safe; be sure that no circuit is overloaded and that all power tools and electrical outlets are properly grounded and protected by a ground-fault circuit interrupter (GFCI). Do not use power tools in wet locations.

- *Always* wear eye protection when using chemicals, sawing wood, pruning trees and shrubs, using power tools, and striking metal onto metal or concrete.

- *Always* read labels on chemicals, solvents, and other products; provide ventilation; heed warnings.

- *Always* wear heavy rubber gloves rated for chemicals, not mere household rubber gloves, when handling toxins.

- *Always* wear appropriate gloves in situations in which your hands could be injured by rough surfaces, sharp edges, thorns, or poisonous plants.

- *Always* wear a disposable face mask or a special filtering respirator when creating sawdust or working with toxic gardening substances.

- *Always* keep your hands and other body parts away from the business ends of blades, cutters, and bits.

- *Always* obtain approval from local building officials before undertaking construction of permanent structures.

- *Never* work with power tools when you are tired or under the influence of alcohol or drugs.

- *Never* carry sharp or pointed tools, such as knives or saws, in your pockets. If you carry such tools, use special-purpose tool scabbards.

The Landscape Designers

Michael Buccino has been designing desert landscapes since 1966. A landscape architect and graduate of Cal Poly, Pomona, he and the members of his small Palm Desert firm, Michael Buccino Associates, undertake residential, commercial, and public projects. His designs appear on pp. 32-35 and 88-91.

Susan Romiti and **Ross Holmquist** are the principal landscape designers in the Landscape Design Division of Mike Parker Landscape in Laguna Beach. They work on projects from small beach cottages to large estates and have produced award-winning designs throughout southern California. Their designs appear on pp. 24-27, 40-43, 44-47, and 56-59.

Jana Ruzicka operates her own landscape design business in Laguna Beach, specializing in residential projects. Trained in Czechoslovakia, she has been a landscape architect in California since 1969. Before establishing her own firm in 1980, she worked on residential, public, and commercial projects. She has won several design awards, and her work has appeared in regional publications. Her designs appear on pp. 92-95, 84-87, and 104-107.

Carolyn Singer owns Foothill Cottage Gardens, a nursery she developed from her own gardens in the Sierra foothills near Grass Valley. Since 1980, she has sold perennials and taught gardening classes at the nursery as well as designed landscapes for foothill and valley residents. She lectures widely and has written about gardening for national and regional publications. Her designs appear on pp. 20-23, 36-39, 64-67, and 76-79.

John Valentino and **Bob Truxell** are principals in Truxell and Valentino Landscape Development, Inc., founded in 1979 and located in Clovis, in the central valley. Their work encompasses private, public, and corporate projects, including a number of award-winning designs. It is regularly featured in regional publications. Their designs appear on pp. 16-19, 60-63, 68-71, 72-75, and 108-111.

Jenny Webber is a self-employed landscape architect in Oakland. Also trained in horticulture and fine arts, she specializes in ecologically balanced and creative landscapes. She has won several awards for her designs and has written about gardening and design for national publications. Her designs appear on pp. 48-51, 80-83, and 96-99.

Richard William Wogisch is a landscape architect and founding partner of Oasis Gardens, a landscape design firm in San Francisco. Since 1989, he has concentrated on designing intimate gardens in the Bay Area. His work has been featured in numerous publications. His designs appear on pp. 28-31, 52-55, and 100-103.

Contents

About This Book

Of all the home improvement projects homeowners tackle, few offer greater rewards than landscaping. Paths, patios, fences, arbors, and, most of all, plantings can enhance home life in countless ways, large and small, functional and pleasurable, every day of the year. At the main entrance, an attractive brick walkway flanked by eye-catching shrubs and perennials provides a cheerful send-off in the morning and welcomes you home from work in the evening. A carefully placed grouping of small trees, shrubs, and fence panels creates privacy on the patio or screens a nearby eyesore from view. An island bed showcases your favorite plants, while dividing the backyard into areas for several different activities.

Unlike with some home improvements, the rewards of landscaping can be as much in the activity as in the result. Planting and caring for lovely shrubs, perennials, and other plants can afford years of enjoyment. And for those who like to build things, outdoor construction projects can be especially satisfying.

While the installation and maintenance of plants and outdoor structures are within the means and abilities of most people, few of us are as comfortable determining exactly which plants or structures to use and how best to combine them. It's one thing to decide to dress up the front entrance or patio, another to come up with a design for doing so.

That's where this book comes in. Here, in the Portfolio of Designs, you'll find designs for 24 common home-landscaping situations, created by landscape professionals who live and work in California. Drawing on years of experience, these designers balance functional requirements and aesthetic possibilities, choosing the right plant or structure for the task, confident of its proven performance in similar situations.

Complementing the Portfolio of Designs are the Plant Profiles, the book's second section, which gives information on all the plants used in the designs in the book. The third section, Guide to Installation, will help you install and maintain the plants and structures called for in the designs. The discussions that follow take a closer look at each section; we've also printed representative pages of the sections on pp. 9 and 10 and pointed out their features.

Portfolio of Designs

This section is the heart of the book, providing examples of landscaping situations and solutions that are at once inspiring and accessible. Some are simple, others more complex, but each one can be installed in a few weekends by homeowners with no special training or experience.

For each situation, we present two designs, the second a variation of the first. As the sample pages on the facing page show, the first design is displayed on a two-page spread. A perspective illustration (called a "rendering") depicts what the design will look like several years after installation, when the perennials and many of the shrubs have reached mature size. (For more on how plantings change as they age, see "As Your Landscape Grows," pp. 12–13.) The rendering also shows the planting as it will appear at a particular time of year. A site plan indicates the positions of the plants and structures on a scaled grid. Text introduces the situation and the design, and describes the plants and projects used.

The second design, presented on the second two-page spread, addresses the same situation as the first but differs in one or more important aspects. It might show a planting suited for a shady rather than a sunny site, or it might incorporate different structures or kinds of plants to create a different look. As for the first design, we present a rendering, site plan, and written information, but in briefer form. The second spread also includes photographs of landscapes in situations similar to those featured in the two designs. The photos showcase noteworthy variations or details that you may wish to use in the designs we show or in designs of your own.

Installed exactly as shown here, these designs will provide years of enjoyment. But individual needs and properties will differ, and we encourage you to alter the designs to suit your site and desires. Many types of alterations are easy to make. You can add or remove plants and adjust the sizes of paths, patios, and arbors to accommodate larger or smaller sites. You can rearrange groupings and substitute favorite plants to suit your taste. Or you can integrate the design with your existing landscaping. If you are uncertain about how to solve specific problems or about the effects of changes you'd like to make, consult with staff at a local nursery or with a landscape designer in your area.

PORTFOLIO OF DESIGNS

FIRST DESIGN OPTION

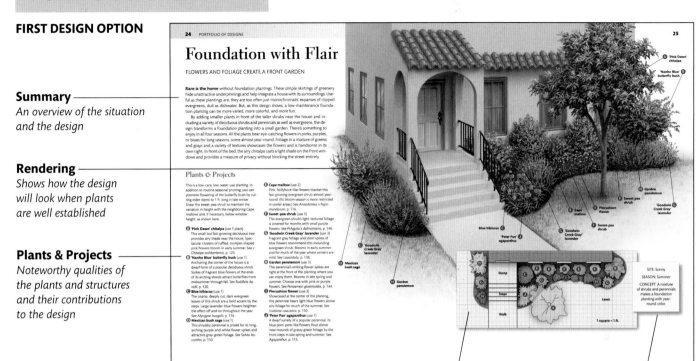

Summary
An overview of the situation and the design

Rendering
Shows how the design will look when plants are well established

Plants & Projects
Noteworthy qualities of the plants and structures and their contributions to the design

Site Plan
Positions all plants and structures on a scaled grid

Concept Box
Summarizes an important aspect of the design; tells whether the site is sunny or shady and what season is depicted in the rendering

SECOND DESIGN OPTION

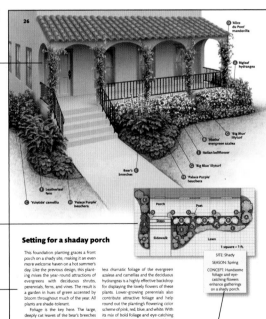

Rendering
Depicts the design when plants are well established

Site Plan
Plants and structures on a scaled grid

Summary
Addressing the same situation as the first design, an overview of differences in design concept, site conditions, or plant selection

Concept Box
Site, season, and design summary

Variations on a Theme
Photos of inspiring designs in similar situations

PLANT PROFILES

Choices
Selections here help you choose from the many varieties of certain popular plants.

Plant Portraits
Photos of selected plants

Detailed Plant Information
Descriptions of each plant's noteworthy qualities and requirements for planting and care

GUIDE TO INSTALLATION

Sidebars
Detailed information on special topics, set within ruled boxes

Step-by-Step
Process illustrations; steps keyed by number to discussion in the main text

Plant Profiles

The final section of the book includes a description of each of the plants featured in the Portfolio. These profiles outline the plants' basic preferences for environmental conditions—such as soil, moisture, and sun or shade—and provide advice about planting and ongoing care.

Working with the book's landscape designers, we selected plants carefully, following a few simple guidelines: every plant should be a proven performer in the region; once established, it should thrive without pampering. All plants should be available from a major local nursery or garden center; if they're not in stock, they could be ordered, or you could ask the nursery staff to recommend suitable substitutes.

In the Portfolio section, you'll note that plants are referred to by their common name but are cross-referenced to the Plant Profiles section by their Latinized scientific name. While common names are familiar to many people, they can be confusing. Distinctly different plants can share the same common name, or one plant can have several different common names. Scientific names, therefore, ensure greatest accuracy and are more appropriate for a reference section such as this. Although you can confidently purchase most of the plants in this book from local nurseries using the common name, knowing the scientific name allows you to ensure that the plant you're ordering is the same one shown in our design.

Guide to Installation

In this section, you'll find detailed instructions and illustrations covering all the techniques you'll need to install any design from start to finish. Here, we explain how to think your way through a landscaping project and anticipate the various steps. Then you'll learn how to do each part of the job: readying the site; laying out the design; choosing materials; addressing basic irrigation needs; building paths, trellises, or other structures; preparing the soil for planting; buying the recommended plants and putting them in place; and caring for the plants to keep them healthy and attractive year after year.

We've taken care to make installation of built elements simple and straightforward. The paths, trellises, and arbors all use basic, readily available materials, and they can be assembled by people who have no special skills or tools beyond those commonly used for home maintenance. The designs can easily be adapted to meet specific needs or to fit in with the style of your house or other landscaping features.

Installing different designs requires different techniques. You can find the techniques that you need by following the cross-references in the Portfolio to pages in the Guide to Installation, or by skimming the Guide. You'll find that many basic techniques are reused from one project to the next. You might want to start with one of the smaller, simpler designs. Gradually you'll develop the skills and confidence to do any project you choose.

Most of the designs in this book can be installed in several weekends; some will take a little longer. Digging planting beds and erecting fences and arbors can be strenuous work. If you lack energy for such tasks, consider hiring a neighborhood teenager to help out; local landscaping services can provide more comprehensive help.

CALIFORNIA HARDINESS ZONES

This map is based on one developed by the U.S. Department of Agriculture. It divides the state according to minimum winter temperatures and assigns "zone" numbers to those temperature bands. California's zones range from winter minimum temperatures of -10°F to 40°F. Most of the plants in this book will survive the lowest temperatures in Zones 8, 9, and 10. Others are hardy to Zone 6. To ensure successful plantings, confirm with a local nursery that plants you choose are reliably hardy in your area.

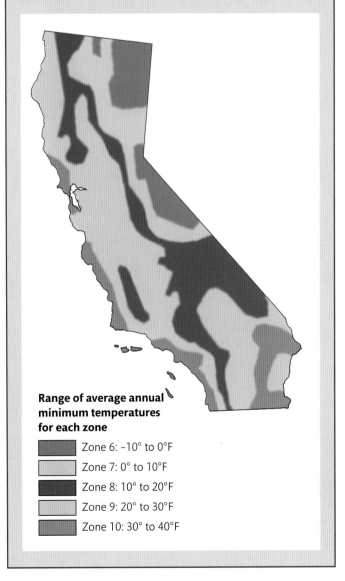

Range of average annual minimum temperatures for each zone

Zone 6: –10° to 0°F
Zone 7: 0° to 10°F
Zone 8: 10° to 20°F
Zone 9: 20° to 30°F
Zone 10: 30° to 40°F

As Your Landscape Grows

AT PLANTING

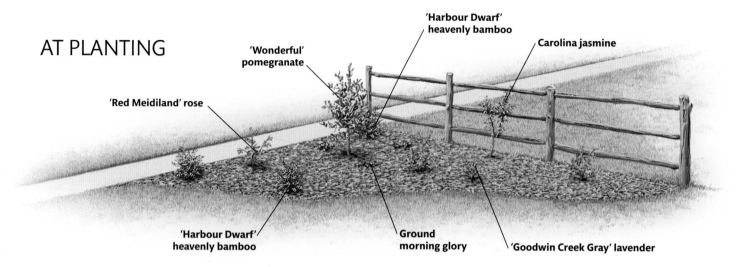

'Wonderful' pomegranate

'Harbour Dwarf' heavenly bamboo

Carolina jasmine

'Red Meidiland' rose

'Harbour Dwarf' heavenly bamboo

Ground morning glory

'Goodwin Creek Gray' lavender

Landscapes change over the years. As plants grow, the overall look evolves from sparse to lush. Trees cast cool shade where the sun used to shine. Shrubs and hedges grow tall and dense enough to provide privacy. Perennials and ground covers spread to form colorful patches of foliage and flowers. Meanwhile, paths, arbors, fences, and other structures gain the comfortable patina of age.

Constant change over the years—sometimes rapid and dramatic, sometimes slow and subtle—is one of the joys of landscaping. It is also one of the challenges. Anticipating how fast plants will grow and how big they will eventually get is difficult, even for professional designers, and was a major concern in formulating the designs for this book.

To illustrate the kinds of changes to expect in a planting, these pages show one of the designs at three different "ages." Even though a new planting may look sparse at first, it will soon fill in. And because of careful spacing, the planting will look as good in 10 to 15 years as it does after 3 to 5. It will, of course, look different, but that's part of the fun.

THREE TO FIVE YEARS

'Wonderful' pomegranate

Carolina jasmine

'Harbour Dwarf' heavenly bamboo

Ground morning glory

'Goodwin Creek Gray' lavender

'Red Meidiland' rose

At Planting–Here's how the corner planting (pp. 40–41) might appear in spring immediately after planting. The branches of the Carolina jasmine, 2 to 3 ft. long, have been tied to the fence. The roses are about 18 in. tall, their canes already beginning to arch. Bought in 1-gal. containers, the lavender and heavenly bamboo have yet to reach a foot in height. The pomegranate is 3 to 4 ft. tall; the ground morning glories are little tufts about 6 in. tall. In addition to mulch, you can fill the spaces between the small plants with some short annuals during the first few growing seasons.

Three to Five Years–As shown here in fall, the planting has filled out nicely. The Carolina jasmine creeps along much of the fence. The roses sprawl, covered now (and for much of the year) with red flowers. The lavender and heavenly bamboo have become bushy plants, with handsome foliage, flowers, and berries. At about 6 to 8 ft. tall, the pomegranate displays colorful foliage and a crop of edible fruits in fall. The ground morning glory has filled in beneath the tree and the planting no longer has space, or need, for annuals.

Ten to Fifteen Years–Shown again in fall, the pomegranate, now 10 to 12 ft. tall, is the focal point of the planting. Its lower limbs have been removed as the tree has grown, making room for the roses, which have been allowed to overtake some of the ground morning glory under the tree as well as the two heavenly bamboos at the corner (which have been replanted elsewhere on the property). The third heavenly bamboo has been removed to allow the ground morning glory to spread. Annual pruning has kept the height of the roses in check and prevented them from overgrowing the lavender. Judicious pruning has also kept some of the fence visible around the vigorous Carolina jasmine.

TEN TO FIFTEEN YEARS

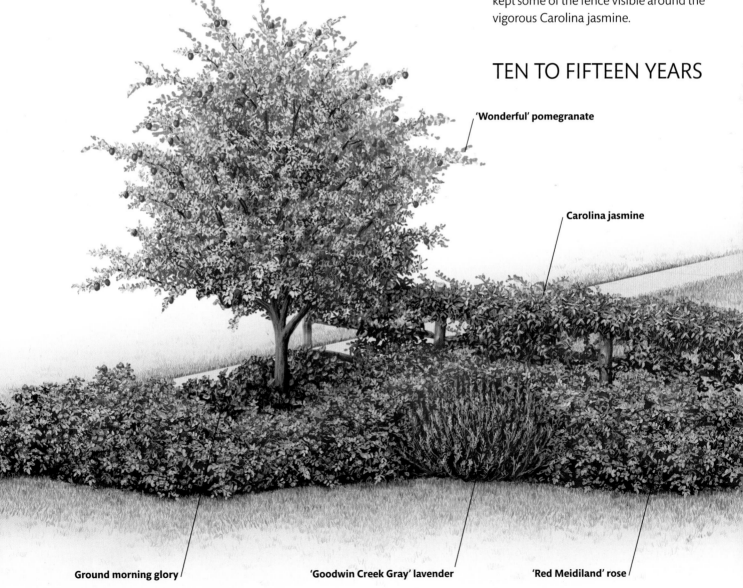

'Wonderful' pomegranate

Carolina jasmine

Ground morning glory

'Goodwin Creek Gray' lavender

'Red Meidiland' rose

Portfolio *of* Designs

This section presents designs for twenty-four situations common in home landscapes. You'll find designs to enhance entrances, decks, and patios. There are gardens of colorful perennials and shrubs, as well as structures and plantings that create shady hideaways, dress up nondescript walls, and even make a centerpiece of a lowly mailbox. Large color illustrations show what the designs will look like, and site plans delineate the layout and planting scheme. Texts explain the designs and describe the plants and projects appearing in them. Installed as shown or adapted to meet your site and personal preferences, these designs can make your property more attractive, more useful, and—most important—more enjoyable for you, your family, and your friends.

An Elegant Entry

GARDEN GEOMETRY TRANSFORMS A SMALL FRONT YARD

Formal gardens have a special appeal. Their simple geometry can be soothing in a hectic world, and the look is timeless, never going out of style. Homes with symmetrical facades are especially suited to formal makeovers, which complement and accent the architecture.

This design enhances both approaches to a front door—from the sidewalk and the driveway—while echoing the symmetry of the house facade when viewed from the street. The result is more playful and unpredictable than a "classic" formal landscape design.

Visitors approaching from street or drive are drawn toward the leafy crape myrtle canopy at the intersection of the two walkways. From

SITE: Sunny

SEASON: Late spring

CONCEPT: Subtle geometry and well-chosen plants create an entry garden of comfortable, low-key formality.

Crape myrtle **A**

Saucer magnolia **B**

Texas privet **G**

Common lilac **C**

Daylily **I**

'Veitchii' gardenia **D**

Dwarf periwinkle **J**

'Winter Gem' boxwood **H**

Walkway extension **K**

'Iceberg' rose **E**

here, you can proceed to the door, or enjoy a few minutes of conversation and relaxation in a grassy semicircular courtyard nearby, with its central birdbath or fountain and bench tucked into an evergreen hedge.

Overcrowded, intricate plantings can make a small space seem smaller. So here, a limited palette of plants is arrayed in bold masses to impart a comfortably spacious feel to a small garden. Flowers are abundant from late winter through fall, and the balance of deciduous and evergreen foliage ensures a year-round presence. For much of the year, fragrant lilacs, gardenias, and roses reward a stroll around the garden.

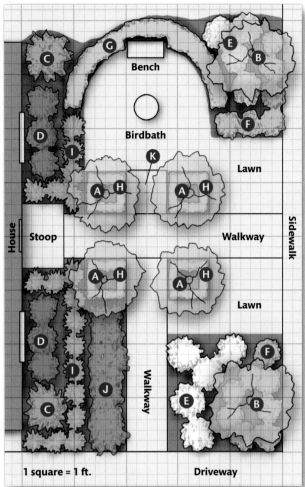

1 square = 1 ft.

Bench

Birdbath

Lawn

House

Stoop

Walkway

Sidewalk

Lawn

Walkway

Driveway

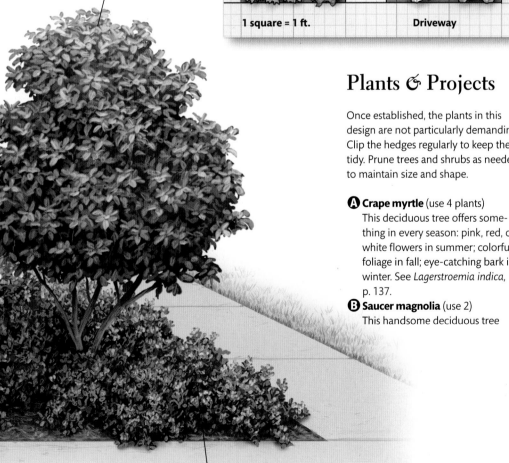

ⓑ Saucer magnolia

ⓕ 'Ballerina' Indian hawthorn

Plants & Projects

Once established, the plants in this design are not particularly demanding. Clip the hedges regularly to keep them tidy. Prune trees and shrubs as needed to maintain size and shape.

ⓐ Crape myrtle (use 4 plants)
This deciduous tree offers something in every season: pink, red, or white flowers in summer; colorful foliage in fall; eye-catching bark in winter. See *Lagerstroemia indica*, p. 137.

ⓑ Saucer magnolia (use 2)
This handsome deciduous tree accents the front corners with bold foliage and striking flowers. Blooms appear in spring on bare branches before the leaves expand. See *Magnolia x soulangiana*, p. 140.

ⓒ Common lilac (use 2)
Marking the corners of the house, this upright deciduous shrub produces sweet-scented flowers in spring. See *Syringa vulgaris*, p. 152.

ⓓ 'Veitchii' gardenia (use 6)
These compact evergreen shrubs won't outgrow the space under the windows. Dark foliage showcases very fragrant white flowers from spring through fall. See *Gardenia jasminoides*, p. 132.

ⓔ 'Iceberg' rose (use 9)
A floribunda rose, it bears clusters of fragrant white flowers all year. It forms upright clumps and makes a fine mid-height ground cover. See *Rosa*, p. 149.

ⓕ 'Ballerina' Indian hawthorn (use 14)
This low evergreen shrub is another excellent ground cover. It bears numerous clusters of pink flowers in spring. See *Rhaphiolepis indica*, p. 147.

ⓖ Texas privet (use 9)
The glossy leaves of this evergreen shrub make a handsome formal hedge. Though clipping as a hedge diminishes their numbers, scented white flowers will draw you to the bench in early summer. See *Ligustrum japonicum* 'Texanum', p. 139.

ⓗ 'Winter Gem' boxwood (use 48)
The small leaves and dense habit of this evergreen shrub are ideal for a small clipped hedge like this. See *Buxus microphylla* var. *japonica*, p. 120.

ⓘ Daylily (use 18)
The grassy foliage of this perennial contrasts pleasantly with the clipped hedges and bushy shrubs nearby. Choose cultivars with flower colors and bloom times to suit your taste. See *Hemerocallis*, p. 134.

ⓙ Dwarf periwinkle (as needed)
The glossy dark green leaves of this low, spreading perennial ground cover are evergreen. Lilac-colored flowers bloom in late spring. Plant 6 in. apart. See *Vinca minor*, p. 154.

ⓚ Walkway extension
Made of precast pavers (see p. 164) or poured concrete, this short extension creates symmetry at the crossing of the two front walkways.

Formal and fresh

In this design, a paved courtyard and a planting of handsome trees, shrubs, and ground covers have transformed a site typically given over to lawn and a concrete walkway. The result is a more dramatic entry, but also one where you can happily linger with guests.

Like the previous design, this one is simple, comprising mass plantings of a limited number of plants. Small trees shade the paving and, with the low hedge and underplanting of shrubs, create a cozy atmosphere in the courtyard without walling out the street. A birdbath garnished with colorful annuals provides

a focal point in the courtyard. A pair of benches offer perches for enjoying the results of your landscaping labors.

Replacing the lawn with an evergreen perennial ground cover completes the transformation from front yard to front garden. While the ground cover will not

stand up to games of touch football, it will look good year-round with less water and maintenance than a turfgrass lawn. The deep green foliage adds an attractive texture to the garden. And, as a bonus, in early spring it becomes a carpet of small white flowers.

SITE: Sunny

SEASON: Late spring

CONCEPT:
A courtyard garden of elegant simplicity complements a home with a symmetrical facade.

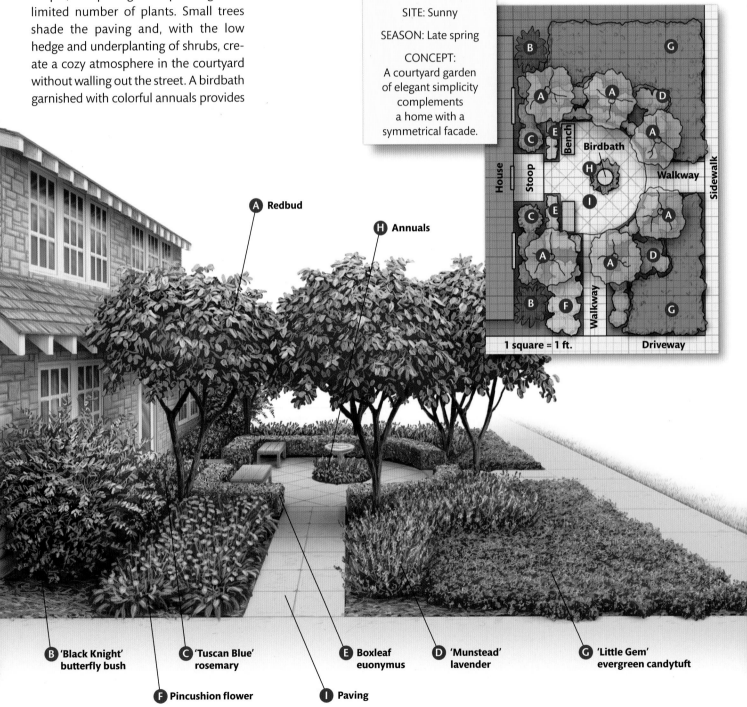

A Redbud

H Annuals

B 'Black Knight' butterfly bush

C 'Tuscan Blue' rosemary

F Pincushion flower

E Boxleaf euonymus

I Paving

D 'Munstead' lavender

G 'Little Gem' evergreen candytuft

House Stoop Bench Birdbath Walkway Sidewalk Walkway Driveway

1 square = 1 ft.

Plants & Projects

Ⓐ Redbud (use 6 plants)
Branches of this small deciduous tree are covered with tiny bright purple flowers in early spring before the leaves appear. The leaves turn gold in fall. Tracery of bare branches is handsome in winter. See *Cercis canadensis*, p. 124.

Ⓑ 'Black Knight' butterfly bush (use 2)
The arching stems of this deciduous shrub bear long spikes of fragrant dark purple flowers from midsummer through fall. Butterflies love them. See *Buddleia davidii*, p. 120.

Ⓒ 'Tuscan Blue' rosemary (use 6)
This evergreen Mediterranean shrub is prized for its aromatic foliage and attractive upright form. It bears small dark blue flowers in spring. See *Rosmarinus officinalis*, p. 149.

Ⓓ 'Munstead' lavender (use 19)
Bushy mounds of silver-gray aromatic foliage make an attractive mid-height ground cover beneath the redbuds. Spikes of lavender-blue flowers scent the air in late spring. See *Lavandula angustifolia*, p. 138.

Ⓔ Boxleaf euonymus (use 23)
Neatly clipped to form a low formal hedge, this evergreen shrub reinforces the geometry of the design. See *Euonymus japonicus* 'Microphyllus', p. 130.

Ⓕ Pincushion flower (use 8)
Planted as a ground cover next to the walkway, this perennial offers airy foliage covered with light blue flowers from late spring through fall. See *Scabiosa caucasica*, p. 150.

Ⓖ 'Little Gem' evergreen candytuft (as needed)
Replacing lawn grass, this perennial ground cover forms a low mat of fine dark green leaves. Bears bright white flowers for a few weeks in early spring. Space plants on 2-ft. centers. Lightly trim plants with a weed whacker after bloom and whenever the foliage needs rejuvenation. See *Iberis sempervirens*, p. 136.

Ⓗ Annuals
Plant seasonal annuals at the foot of the birdbath (or other garden ornament) in the center of the paving. For spring, try combinations of salvia, phlox, snapdragons, alyssum, and purple basil.

Ⓘ Paving
We've shown square precast concrete pavers here. Poured concrete, scored to form the gridwork patterns, is a more expensive but very durable alternative. See p. 164.

VARIATIONS ON A THEME

A formal design can serve intimacy or expansiveness. It may be open, light, and gay, or subdued and contemplative.

This serene courtyard entry is a pleasing combination of simplicity and subtle detail.

In this large, cheerful garden, the lawn forms paths around planting beds of tree roses, shrub roses, and perennials.

This is a formal entryway garden in the classical tradition, complete with a fountain and stone benches.

Front-Door Makeover

ENHANCE YOUR MAIN ENTRY IN A WEEKEND

Sometimes the simplest landscaping projects pack a surprisingly big punch. This design uses only a few plants and can be easily installed in a single weekend. Yet this small investment of time and money can transform one of the most important parts of your property, welcoming visitors to your home as well as presenting a pleasing face to passersby.

Small plantings often suffer from busyness—too many different kinds of plants in too little space. This design makes a bold display with just five different plants. Potted shrubs and upright viburnums with a skirt of candytuft frame the doorway, while low masses of pinks and daylilies border the walkway. There are pretty flowers and a variety of foliage textures to catch the eye, as well as a subtle mix of scents. The planting is enticing to visitors, but not overpowering. And it offers a pleasant spot to chat as guests enter or leave the house.

'Little Gem' evergreen candytuft **B**

D 'Stella d'Oro' daylily

A 'Spring Bouquet' viburnum

Cottage pink **C**

House

B

Stoop

E

A

C

Walkway

D

1 square = 1 ft.

Lawn

SITE: Sunny

SEASON: Late winter

CONCEPT: A few well-chosen plants and a few hours' work can invigorate a nondescript entry.

'Compacta' heavenly bamboo **E**

Cottage pink **C**

'Little Gem' evergreen candytuft **B**

A 'Spring Bouquet' viburnum

D 'Stella d'Oro' daylily

Plants & Projects

This simple planting is easy to maintain. Clip the candytuft after its spring bloom to encourage rebloom in the fall. Deadhead the daylilies and pinks to keep them tidy. As the years pass, you may need to prune the heavenly bamboo and viburnum in spring or fall to keep them an attractive size.

Ⓐ 'Spring Bouquet' viburnum (use 2 plants) This compact evergreen shrub blooms from late fall to spring, bearing white flowers with a rosy pink tinge and light fragrance. Dense, dark green foliage looks good year-round. See *Viburnum tinus*, p. 154.

Ⓑ 'Little Gem' evergreen candytuft (use 6) Forming a solid mass at the feet of the viburnums, the dark leaves of this evergreen perennial are covered with white flowers for several weeks in spring; in some areas they bloom all year. See *Iberis sempervirens*, p. 136.

Ⓒ Cottage pink (use 6) This perennial is prized for its delicious scent. Single or double flowers in shades of white, pink, and red float on wiry stems above a mat of gray-green foliage from late spring into autumn. See *Dianthus plumarius*, p. 128.

Ⓓ 'Stella d'Oro' daylily (use 6) A remarkably long-blooming daylily, it bears cheerful yellow flowers on sturdy stalks from late spring through fall on mounds of grassy foliage. See *Hemerocallis*, p. 134.

Ⓔ 'Compacta' heavenly bamboo (use 2) Planted in containers, this evergreen shrub greets visitors with colorful foliage, fluffy white flowers in summer, and long-lasting red berries. It won't quickly outgrow its pot or its space. See *Nandina domestica*, p. 141.

On the shady side

The concept here is the same as for the preceding design—rejuvenate your home's entrance with a limited number of plants and just a few hours' labor. The difference is that these plants will thrive in shady conditions.

The planting offers flowers for many months of the year, from the early-spring Lenten rose to the last gardenias in the fall. The heavily scented gardenias are an enticement to linger at the doorstep. While the flowers come and go, the foliage is a constant and attractive presence. Providing subtle contrasts and complements in color and texture, all the leaves are evergreen (or nearly so) where winters are mild.

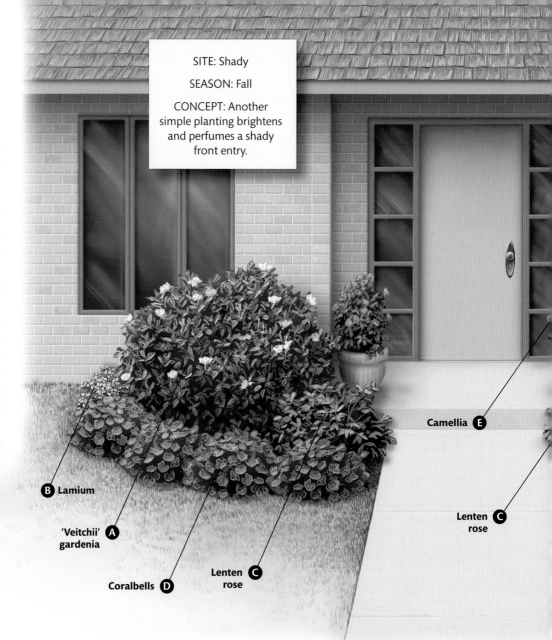

SITE: Shady

SEASON: Fall

CONCEPT: Another simple planting brightens and perfumes a shady front entry.

Camellia **E**

B Lamium

'Veitchii' **A** gardenia

Lenten **C** rose

Coralbells **D**

Lenten **C** rose

Plants & Projects

A **'Veitchii' gardenia**
(use 2 plants)
This evergreen shrub is prized for its intensely fragrant white summer flowers. It blooms from spring through fall where winters are mild. The spreading mound of dark green foliage is an attractive presence by the door all year. See *Gardenia jasminoides*, p. 132.

B **Lamium** (use 6)
Forming a solid mass of silver-white leaves at the feet of the gardenias, this perennial is a durable ground cover. Cultivars offer a choice of pink or white flowers from spring through summer and have silvery green foliage that is evergreen where winters are mild. See *Lamium maculatum*, p. 138.

C **Lenten rose** (use 2)
This perennial makes a handsome clump of shiny evergreen foliage. Distinctive flowers in pink, rose, white, or green bloom for weeks in early spring. See *Helleborus orientalis*, p. 133.

D **Coralbells** (use 8)
Clouds of tiny flowers hover on thin stems above this perennial's foliage from spring into summer. Low clumps of round evergreen leaves are attractive the rest of the year. See *Heuchera*, p. 134.

E **Camellia** (use 2)
Blooming in fall and winter, this evergreen shrub picks up where the gardenias leave off. Many of the smaller sasanqua camellias are ideal for containers. See *Camellia*, p. 120.

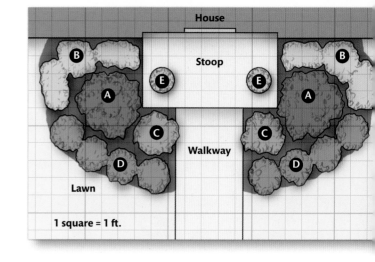

VARIATIONS ON A THEME

The entryway gardens shown here demonstrate the appeal of asymmetrical designs. These plantings are tied into more extensive landscapes but would also look good on their own.

D Coralbells

'Veitchii' **A**
gardenia

Lamium **B**

Roses are a welcome addition to a sunny entry.

*Evergreen shrubs, palms, and ground covers complement this brick path.
A few dashes of bright red deliver a big punch among the greenery.*

Foundation with Flair

FLOWERS AND FOLIAGE CREATE A FRONT GARDEN

Rare is the home without foundation plantings. These simple skirtings of greenery hide unattractive underpinnings and help integrate a house with its surroundings. Useful as these plantings are, they are too often just monochromatic expanses of clipped evergreens, dull as dishwater. But, as this design shows, a low-maintenance foundation planting can be more varied, more colorful, and more fun.

By adding smaller plants in front of the taller shrubs near the house and including a variety of deciduous shrubs and perennials as well as evergreens, the design transforms a foundation planting into a small garden. There's something to enjoy in all four seasons. All the plants bear eye-catching flowers in pinks, purples, or blues for long seasons, some almost year-round. Foliage in a mixture of greens and grays and a variety of textures showcases the flowers and is handsome in its own right. In front of the bed, the airy chitalpa casts a light shade on the front windows and provides a measure of privacy without blocking the street entirely.

Plants & Projects

This is a low-care, low-water-use planting. In addition to routine seasonal pruning, you can promote flowering of the butterfly bush by cutting older stems to 1 ft. long in late winter. Shear the sweet-pea shrub to maintain the variation in height with the neighboring Cape mallows and, if necessary, below window height, as shown here.

Ⓐ 'Pink Dawn' chitalpa (use 1 plant)
This small but fast-growing deciduous tree provides airy shade near the house. Spectacular clusters of ruffled, trumpet-shaped pink flowers bloom in early summer. See x *Chitalpa tashkentensis*, p. 125.

Ⓑ 'Nanho Blue' butterfly bush (use 1)
Anchoring the corner of the house is a dwarf form of a popular deciduous shrub. Spikes of fragrant blue flowers at the ends of its arching shoots attract butterflies from midsummer through fall. See *Buddleia davidii*, p. 120.

Ⓒ Blue hibiscus (use 1)
The coarse, deeply cut, dark evergreen leaves of this shrub are a bold accent by the steps. Large lavender-blue flowers heighten the effect off and on throughout the year. See *Alyogyne huegelii*, p. 116.

Ⓓ Mexican bush sage (use 1)
This shrubby perennial is prized for its long, arching purple-and-white flower spikes and attractive gray-green foliage. See *Salvia leucantha*, p. 150.

Ⓔ Cape mallow (use 2)
Pink, hollyhock-like flowers blanket this fast-growing evergreen shrub almost year- round. (Its bloom season is more restricted in cooler areas.) See *Anisodontea x hypomandarum*, p. 116.

Ⓕ Sweet-pea shrub (use 3)
This evergreen shrub's light-textured foliage is covered for months with small purple flowers. See *Polygala x dalmaisiana*, p. 146.

Ⓖ 'Goodwin Creek Gray' lavender (use 3)
Fragrant gray foliage and short spikes of blue flowers recommend this mounding evergreen shrub. Blooms in early summer and for much of the year where winters are mild. See *Lavandula*, p. 138.

Ⓗ Garden penstemon (use 3)
This perennial's striking flower spikes are right at the front of the planting where you can enjoy them. Blooms in late spring and summer. Choose one with pink or purple flowers. See *Penstemon gloxinioides*, p. 144.

Ⓘ Pincushion flower (use 3)
Showcased at the center of the planting, this perennial bears light blue flowers above airy foliage for much of the summer. See *Scabiosa caucasica*, p. 150.

Ⓙ 'Peter Pan' agapanthus (use 7)
A dwarf variety of a popular perennial, its blue pom-pom-like flowers float above neat mounds of grassy green foliage by the front steps in late spring and summer. See *Agapanthus*, p. 115.

Ⓖ 'Goodwin Creek Gray' lavender

Ⓓ Mexican bush sage

Ⓗ Garden penstemon

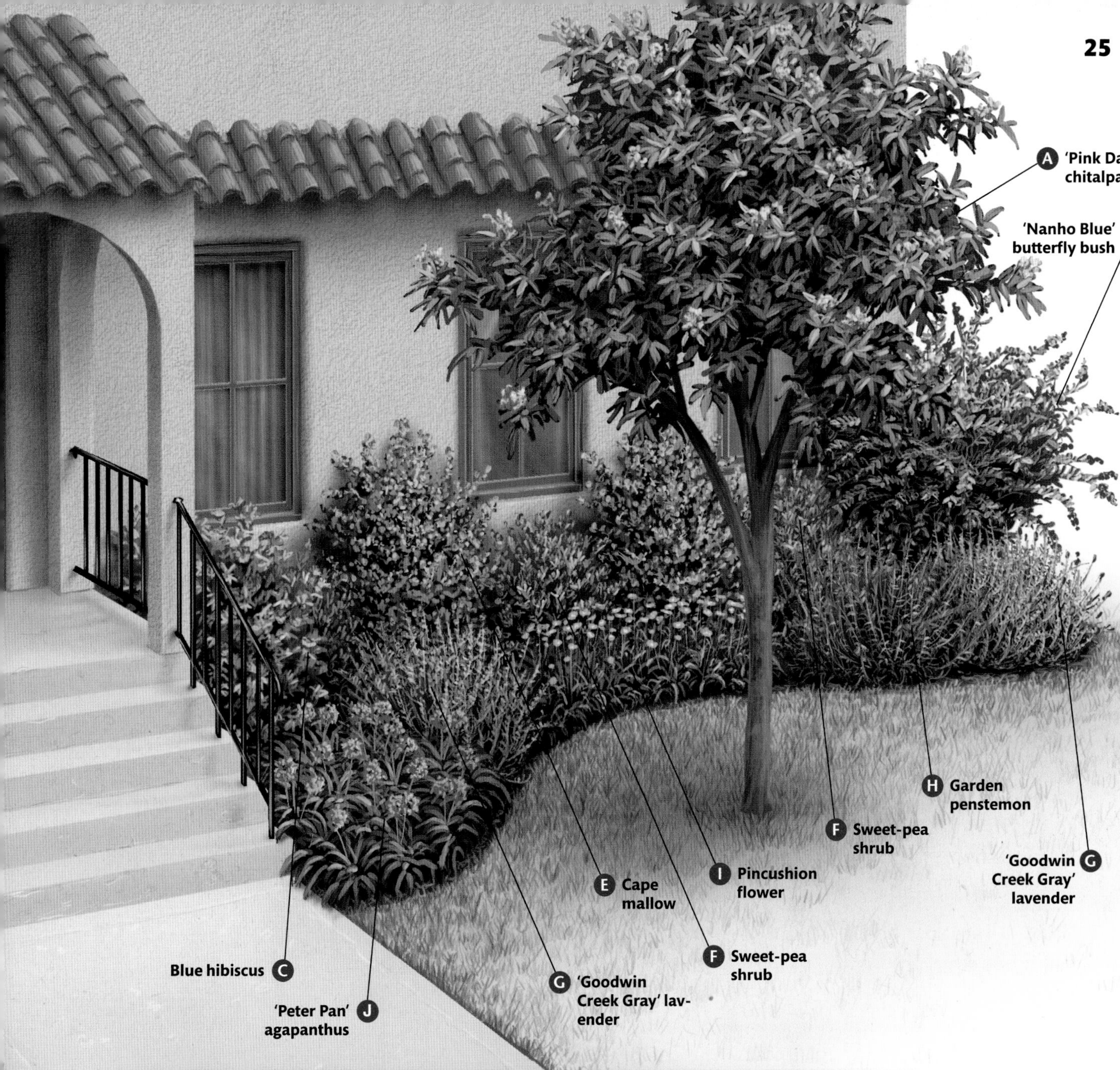

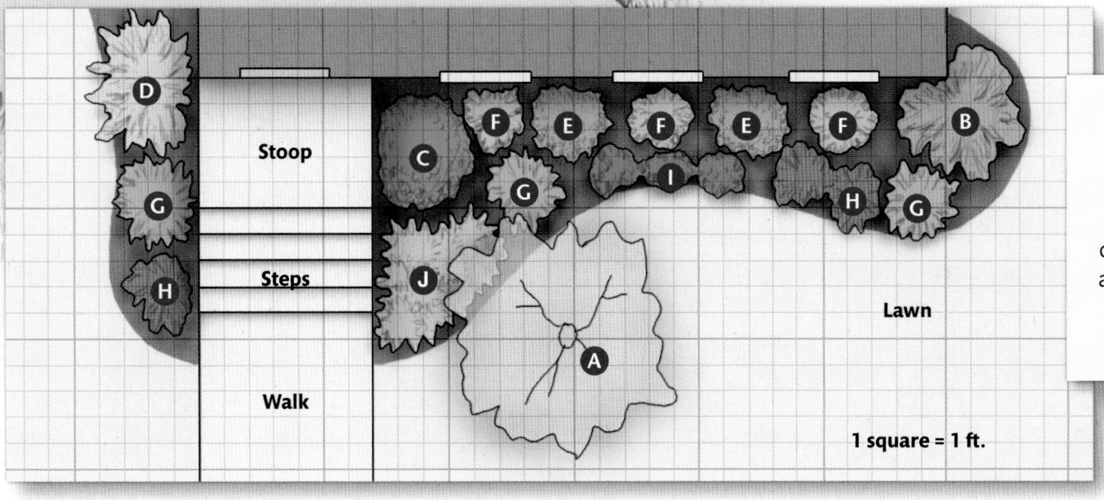

A 'Pink Dawn' chitalpa

B 'Nanho Blue' butterfly bush

H Garden penstemon

F Sweet-pea shrub

G 'Goodwin Creek Gray' lavender

I Pincushion flower

E Cape mallow

F Sweet-pea shrub

G 'Goodwin Creek Gray' lavender

Blue hibiscus **C**

J 'Peter Pan' agapanthus

Stoop

Steps

Walk

Lawn

1 square = 1 ft.

SITE: Sunny

SEASON: Summer

CONCEPT: A mixture of shrubs and perennials makes a foundation planting with year-round color.

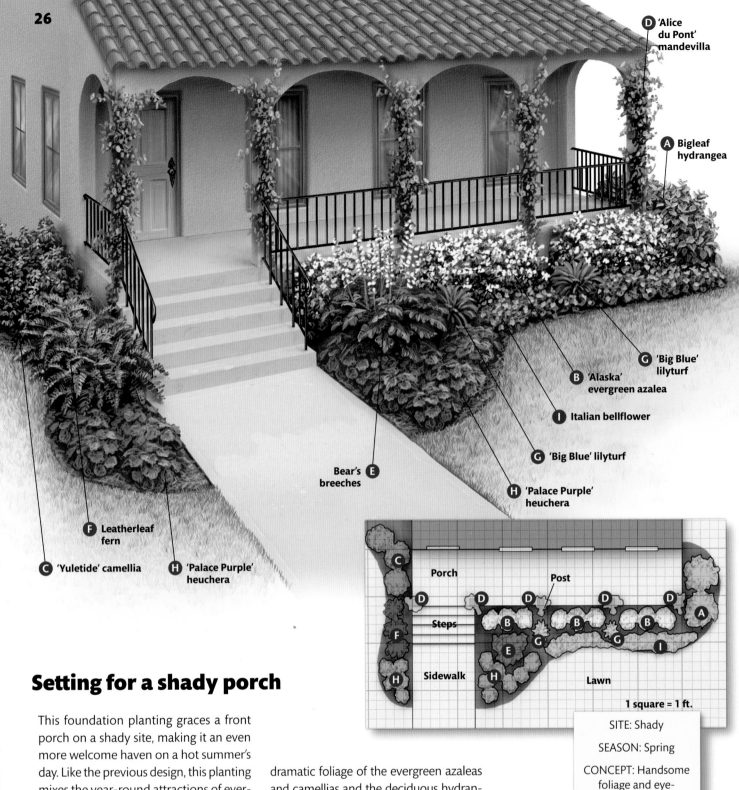

D 'Alice du Pont' mandevilla

A Bigleaf hydrangea

G 'Big Blue' lilyturf

B 'Alaska' evergreen azalea

I Italian bellflower

G 'Big Blue' lilyturf

H 'Palace Purple' heuchera

Bear's breeches **E**

F Leatherleaf fern

C 'Yuletide' camellia

H 'Palace Purple' heuchera

Porch

Post

Steps

Sidewalk

Lawn

1 square = 1 ft.

SITE: Shady

SEASON: Spring

CONCEPT: Handsome foliage and eye-catching flowers enhance gatherings on a shady porch.

Setting for a shady porch

This foundation planting graces a front porch on a shady site, making it an even more welcome haven on a hot summer's day. Like the previous design, this planting mixes the year-round attractions of evergreens with deciduous shrubs, perennials, ferns, and vines. The result is a garden in hues of green accented by bloom throughout much of the year. All plants are shade-tolerant.

Foliage is the key here. The large, deeply cut leaves of the bear's breeches and the more delicately cut fronds of the leatherleaf fern are striking accents. The less dramatic foliage of the evergreen azaleas and camellias and the deciduous hydrangeas is a highly effective backdrop for displaying the lovely flowers of these plants. Lower-growing perennials also contribute attractive foliage and help round out the planting's flowering color scheme of pink, red, blue, and white. With its mix of bold foliage and eye-catching flowers, this planting can be enjoyed from the street as well as from the porch.

Plants & Projects

ⒶBigleaf hydrangea (use 2 plants)
This deciduous shrub displays showy clusters of papery-textured blue, pink, or white flowers for months in summer. See *Hydrangea macrophylla*, p. 136.

Ⓑ'Alaska' evergreen azalea (use 9)
Spectacular in bloom, a handsome foliage presence the rest of the year, these evergreen shrubs bear snow white flowers with chartreuse markings in spring and sometimes intermittently thereafter. See *Rhododendron*, p. 149.

Ⓒ'Yuletide' camellia (use 3)
The red flowers of this distinctive evergreen shrub stand out against the dark glossy foliage in late fall and winter. See *Camellia sasanqua*, p. 120.

Ⓓ'Alice du Pont' mandevilla (use 5)
This vine bears striking ruby-pink flowers from spring through fall on light-textured, glossy evergreen foliage. See *Mandevilla*, p. 140.

ⒺBear's breeches (use 1)
An eye-catching perennial with tall spikes of white flowers that rise in spring above the large, deeply lobed leaves. See *Acanthus mollis*, p. 114.

ⒻLeatherleaf fern (use 3)
The finely cut, glossy foliage of this evergreen fern contrasts effectively with the acanthus across the walkway. See Ferns: *Rumohra adiantiformis*, p. 131.

Ⓖ'Big Blue' lilyturf (use 2)
An evergreen perennial, its grassy mounds of arching dark green leaves bear spikes of blue flowers in summer. See *Liriope muscari*, p. 139.

Ⓗ'Palace Purple' heuchera (use 12)
A perennial grown primarily for its attractively marked brownish purple foliage. Bears tiny white flowers on slender stalks in late spring and summer. See *Heuchera*, p. 134.

ⒾItalian bellflower (use 12)
This low-growing, spreading perennial forms a carpet of soft blue flowers in late summer and fall. See *Campanula isophylla*, p. 122.

VARIATIONS ON A THEME

Four very different foundation plantings are shown here, each one a complementary addition to the home.

This foundation planting plays off the symmetrical features of this house and its white louvered windows. Subtle contrasts in color and texture add interest to the overall repetition.

A simple palette of plants can create dramatic effect. This striking threesome enhances the spare facade of a stucco home.

This bold planting is achieved simply. A row of variegated grasses is coupled with bright impatiens. Ferns add height and texture at the back.

A more varied approach to a stucco facade, this design takes its cue from the mix of cactus, yuccas, and wildflowers found in southwestern gardens.

A Welcoming Entry

MAKE A PLEASANT PASSAGE TO YOUR FRONT DOOR

Why wait until a visitor reaches the front door to extend a cordial greeting? An entryway landscape of well-chosen plants and a revamped walkway not only make the short journey a pleasant one, they can also enhance your home's most public face and help settle it comfortably in its surroundings.

The flagstone paving here creates a walkway with the feel of a cozy courtyard, an atmosphere enhanced by the small trees and bench. Extending along the driveway, the paving makes it easier for passengers to get in and out of a car. A semicircular garden makes the stroll to the door inviting, while providing interest to viewers inside the house and on the street.

Flowering trees and shrubs bloom throughout the spring and summer in pinks and lavenders. Attractive foliage, much of it evergreen, and striking bark ensure interest all year.

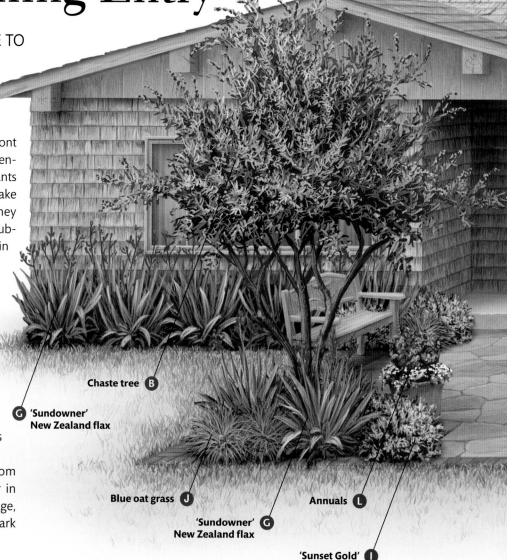

Chaste tree **B**

G 'Sundowner' New Zealand flax

Blue oat grass **J**

'Sundowner' **G** New Zealand flax

Annuals **L**

'Sunset Gold' **I** pink breath of heaven

Plants & Projects

Preparing the planting beds and laying the flagstone walkway are the main tasks in this design. With low-water-use plants, this design requires only seasonal cleanup and pruning once plants are established.

Ⓐ 'Marina' arbutus (use 3 plants)
These small trees provide interest year-round, with pink flowers in fall, red berries, and shiny evergreen leaves. Prune to show off the colorful bark and handsome multi-trunk form. See *Arbutus* 'Marina', p. 117.

Ⓑ Chaste tree (use 1)
This deciduous tree arches beautifully over the walk, displaying airy foliage and, in summer and fall, long spikes of violet flowers. See *Vitex agnus-castus*, p. 154.

Ⓒ 'Zuni' crape myrtle (use 1)
A deciduous multitrunked tree with striking clusters of papery flowers in summer and colorful fall foliage. Flaking bark provides winter interest. See *Lagerstroemia indica*, p. 137.

Ⓓ Dwarf Indian hawthorn (use 6)
Low masses of glossy dark evergreen foliage show off spring flowers and blue berries from summer into fall. Choose a pink cultivar. See *Rhaphiolepis indica*, p. 147.

Ⓔ 'Winter Gem' boxwood (use 8)
These evergreen shrubs form a loosely trimmed low hedge that contrasts with the flowing grasses near the house. See *Buxus microphylla* var. *japonica*, p. 120.

Ⓕ Purple fountain grass (use 7)
This smallish ornamental grass features eye-catching reddish brown leaves that turn gold or tan in fall. Fluffy bronze seed heads arch above the foliage from midsummer to fall. See *Pennisetum setaceum* 'Rubrum', p. 142.

Ⓖ 'Sundowner' New Zealand flax (as needed)
The swordlike, colorfully striped foliage of this evergreen perennial provides bold accents as you approach the door. Tall, airy flower spikes heighten the effect in summer. See *Phormium tenax*, p. 144.

Ⓗ 'Otto Quast' Spanish lavender (use 17)
Spikes of blue flowers cover these mounding shrubs in early summer. Fragrant silver-gray foliage is evergreen and looks good all year. See *Lavandula stoechas*, p. 138.

Ⓘ 'Sunset Gold' pink breath of heaven (use 5)
A loose, airy evergreen shrub, it has colorful fragrant foliage and tiny pink flowers for months in winter and spring. Shear to maintain a compact shape near the walkway. See *Coleonema pulchrum*, p. 127.

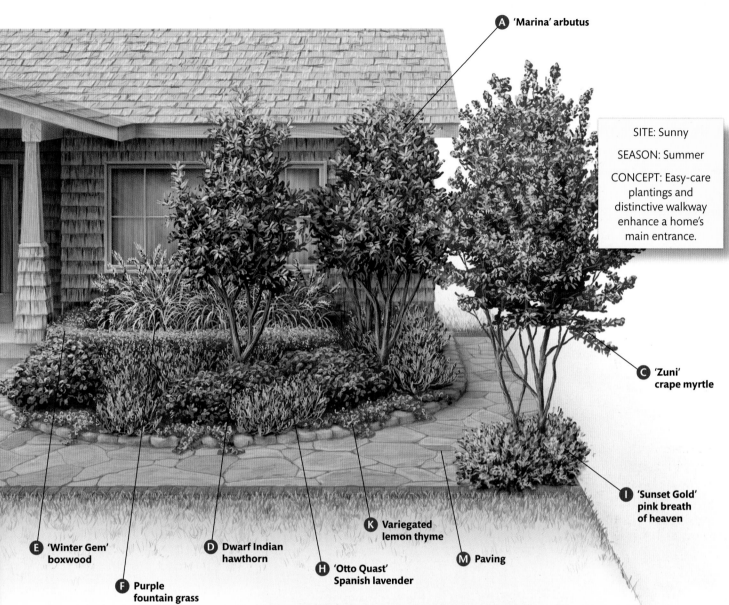

A 'Marina' arbutus

SITE: Sunny

SEASON: Summer

CONCEPT: Easy-care plantings and distinctive walkway enhance a home's main entrance.

C 'Zuni' crape myrtle

I 'Sunset Gold' pink breath of heaven

K Variegated lemon thyme

M Paving

H 'Otto Quast' Spanish lavender

D Dwarf Indian hawthorn

E 'Winter Gem' boxwood

F Purple fountain grass

J Blue oat grass (use 8)
Fine-textured blue foliage of this mounding ornamental grass complements the colors and forms of nearby plants. See *Helictotrichon sempervirens*, p. 142.

K Variegated lemon thyme (use 10)
A low-growing perennial ground cover, its attractive yellow-and-green foliage sprawls out over the edge of the walkway. See *Thymus* x *citriodorus* 'Aureus', p. 153.

L Annuals (as needed)
A large pot of colorful annuals marks the walkway's turn toward the front door. Try a pink, blue, and white mix of annual salvia, lobelia, annual phlox, alyssum, and zinnia.

M Paving
Irregular flagstones are edged by brick next to the lawn, while cobblestones outline the semicircular planting bed. See p. 164.

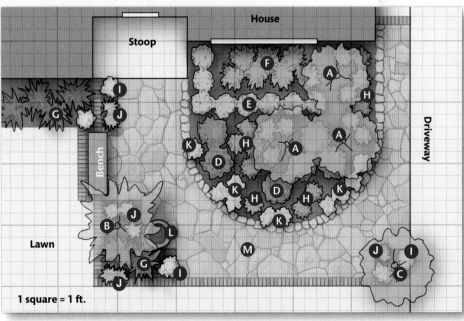

1 square = 1 ft.

VARIATIONS ON A THEME

In addition to extending a splendid welcome to your home, each of these plantings can be enjoyed as a garden.

In this design, a flagstone path set in gravel leads through the yard to the front door. Lined with ornamental grasses and other foliage plants, the design is at once natural and tastefully composed.

Here, a small front yard accommodates a richly planted entry garden. The wide flagstone walkway and colorful foliage complement this bungalow-style home.

A picket fence, brick path, poppies, and other gaily colored perennials create a charming entry to this home.

A shadier welcome

If your entry is lightly shaded, getting less than six hours of sun a day, try this planting scheme. The configuration remains the same as that of the previous design, but here we've used plants that do well in shadier conditions. Overall, the emphasis is still on year-round good looks.

Near the drive, the walkway is framed by a columnar yew pine and the semicircular garden bed. At the opposite corner, a Japanese maple shelters a bench where you can sit and enjoy the plantings. Shrubs and perennials provide flowers in spring and summer as well as attractive foliage throughout the year. The Tasmanian tree ferns add an exotic flavor, with distinctive arching foliage that is echoed by grasses and perennials elsewhere in the planting.

Plants & Projects

Ⓐ Coralbark maple (use 1 plant)
An eye-catching accent for many months, this small deciduous tree has fine-textured foliage that is light green in summer and yellow in fall. Bright red twigs stand out in winter. See *Acer palmatum* 'Sango Kaku', p. 114.

Ⓑ Shrubby yew pine (use 1)
This evergreen tree is a sentinel at the beginning of the walk. Needlelike leaves give it a fine texture. See *Podocarpus macrophyllus* 'Maki', p. 146.

Ⓒ Tasmanian tree fern (use 3)
These Australian natives will eventually form an exotic grove of small "trees" with long, arching fronds and thick, fuzzy trunks. See Ferns: *Dicksonia antarctica*, p. 131.

Ⓓ 'Gumpo White' evergreen azalea (use 7)
Low, spreading mounds of dark evergreen foliage are a handsome backdrop for a late-spring display of striking large white flowers. Foliage is attractive for the remainder of the year. See *Rhododendron*, p. 149.

Ⓔ Dwarf heavenly bamboo (use 7)
Airy and upright, this shrub provides a leafy accent and companion for nearby plants. Evergreen foliage changes color with the seasons. See *Nandina domestica* 'Gulf Stream', p. 141.

Ⓕ Variegated eulalia grass (use 4)
Graceful clumps of long, arching, white-and-green striped leaves rustle in the breeze beneath the window. Tall, fluffy

Shrubby yew pine **B**

Coralbark maple **A**

G Agapanthus

Bloody cranesbill **I**

Annuals **L**

N Paving

H Japanese anemone

F Variegated eulalia grass

J Ajuga

C Tasmanian tree fern

Agapanthus **G**

Lilyturf **K**

Dwarf heavenly bamboo **E**

E Dwarf heavenly bamboo

M 'Winter Gem' boxwood

D 'Gumpo White' evergreen azalea

seed heads last from fall through winter. See *Miscanthus sinensis* 'Variegatus', p. 142.

G **Agapanthus** (as needed)
Tall stalks bearing ball-shaped clusters of small blue flowers strike a welcoming note near the door in late spring and summer. This perennial's straplike foliage is attractive year-round. See *Agapanthus orientalis*, p. 115.

H **Japanese anemone** (use 21)
This perennial's airy white flowers add color in late summer and fall. Soft-textured foliage contrasts nicely with nearby azaleas. See *Anemone* x *hybrida*, p. 116.

I **Bloody cranesbill** (use 5)
A low-growing perennial with finely cut leaves and small pink flowers from spring into summer. A nice accent plant. See *Geranium sanguineum* var. *striatum*, p. 133.

J **Ajuga** (as needed)
Use this perennial evergreen ground cover to fill in open spaces; maturing shrubs will shade some out. See *Ajuga reptans* 'Bronze Beauty', p. 115.

K **Lilyturf** (use 13)
The grassy, white-striped evergreen leaves of this perennial edge the walkway and echo the larger ornamental grasses in the planting. See *Liriope muscari* 'Silver Dragon', p. 139.

L **Annuals** (as needed)
A pot of pink annual vinca brightens the walkway here.

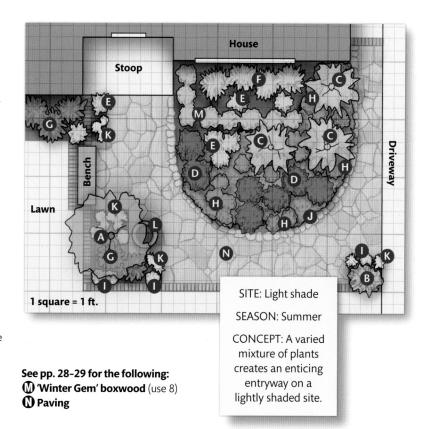

1 square = 1 ft.

House

Stoop

Bench

Lawn

Driveway

See pp. 28–29 for the following:
M 'Winter Gem' boxwood (use 8)
N Paving

SITE: Light shade

SEASON: Summer

CONCEPT: A varied mixture of plants creates an enticing entryway on a lightly shaded site.

An Entry Oasis

EXTEND A FRIENDLY DESERT WELCOME

A trend in new suburban developments is to crowd larger homes onto smaller and smaller lots. As a consequence, homeowners enjoy spaciousness inside the house but not outside. Making the most of limited space for outdoor living requires expanding the uses of some traditional areas.

This design transforms the entrance of a desert home from a corridor linking the front door and the driveway into a courtyard garden that invites gathering or relaxing outdoors. Shaded by the canopy of a small tree, enclosed by a wall low enough to allow breezes in, and soothed by the trickle of a small fountain, the courtyard can be enjoyed by family and friends year-round.

The design celebrates the desert environment and low-maintenance, low-water use principles. Local materials such as gravel, granite, and boulders provide natural surfaces to showcase striking desert plants. To fully integrate the design with the yard and house, you may want to cover the entire yard in gravel as we've shown here. It makes a water-efficient surface that is comfortable for both plants and people. Note the mounded undulating surface around the wall, indicated on the plan by broken lines.

The desert-loving plants featured here contribute distinctive forms, textures, and colors. Grouped together they create a dramatic composition. Spiky agave and ocotillo are boldly paired with the loosely arching bougainvillea and low-spreading lantana. The flowers in the planting bloom in spring, and they are a spectacular sight.

SITE: Sunny

SEASON: Spring

CONCEPT: A host of desert plants and a shady courtyard make an inviting entry to a desert home.

Plants & Projects

Installing the paving, wall, and fountain are the biggest jobs here, though not beyond the means of a resourceful do-it-yourselfer. Once established, the plants will thrive with occasional watering and just seasonal care.

A Desert willow (use 1)
From spring to fall this tree's willowy gray-green leaves are decorated with orchid-like flowers in shades of red, purple, pink, and white. The flowers are followed by long dangling seedpods. Leaves drop in winter, exposing attractive twisting branches. See *Chilopsis linearis*, p. 125.

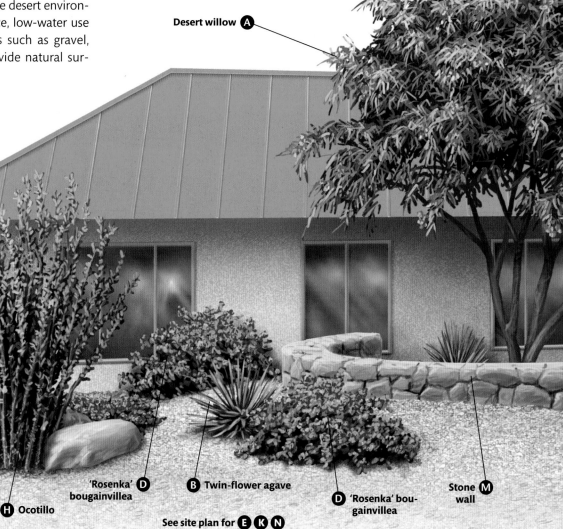

Desert willow **A**

B Twin-flower agave

H Ocotillo

D 'Rosenka' bougainvillea

B Twin-flower agave

D 'Rosenka' bougainvillea

Stone **M** wall

See site plan for **E** **K** **N**

B Twin-flower agave (use 4)
An unusually fine-textured agave, with narrow succulent leaves that form a perfect rosette 2 to 3 ft. in diameter. In spring, it sends up double spikes of large, pale yellow, bell-shaped flowers. See *Agave geminiflora*, p. 115.

C 'New Gold' bougainvillea (use 1)
Trained on a trellis, this evergreen vine's lavish display of gold flowers will be eye-catching from the street or drive. Blooms spring and summer. See *Bougainvillea*, p. 119.

D 'Rosenka' bougainvillea (use 2)
This bougainvillea's arching branches are festooned with papery gold and pink flowers for a long time in spring and summer. It makes a lush green mound in winter. See *Bougainvillea*, p. 119.

E Damianita (use 2)
Fragrant yellow daisies blanket this small shrub in spring and fall. Needlelike leaves have a pungent but pleasant aroma. Evergreen. See *Chrysactinia mexicana*, p. 125.

F Mexican grass tree (use 1)
This unusual shrub creates a fountain of succulent evergreen foliage. As it matures, it forms a central trunk capable of reaching 10 ft. tall, and produces long dense clusters of bell-shaped white flowers in summer. See *Dasylirion longissima*, p. 128.

G Euphorbia hybrid (use 2)
Greatly admired for their large, showy blossoms, euphorbias have been hybridized into dozens of varieties. Pick a compact one for this entry. Shown here is crown of thorns (*E. milii*), which has bright red flowers all year. See *Euphorbia* hybrids, p. 130.

H Ocotillo (use 1)
This desert shrub is noted for its burst of brilliant orange-red blossoms in spring. Leaves are small, gray-green, and deciduous in dry spells. See *Fouquieria splendens*, p. 130.

I Madagascar palm (use 1)
An eye stopper by the door, this exotic tree looks like a cross between a cactus and a palm; its plump, spiny trunk is crowned with straplike deep green leaves. See *Pachypodium lamerei*, p. 143.

J Lantana (use 2)
Small lavender flowers brighten this low-spreading perennial's dark green leaves. Evergreen and ever-blooming where winters are mild. See *Lantana montevidensis*, p. 138.

K Annuals (as needed)
A collection of colorful pansies, snapdragons, and marigolds adds a festive look to this desert entry.

L Paving
Flagstones in muted desert tones provide an attractive and level surface for the patio and paths. See p. 164.

M Stone wall
Choose your favorite stone. Shown here is a colorfully veined granite.

N Water feature
Water is a wonderful focal point for a courtyard. Incorporate a small fountain or pool into the wall or have it stand alone. See p. 172.

O Gravel
Gravel emulates a desert surface in lieu of a lawn. Shown here is Desert Tan birdseye gravel.

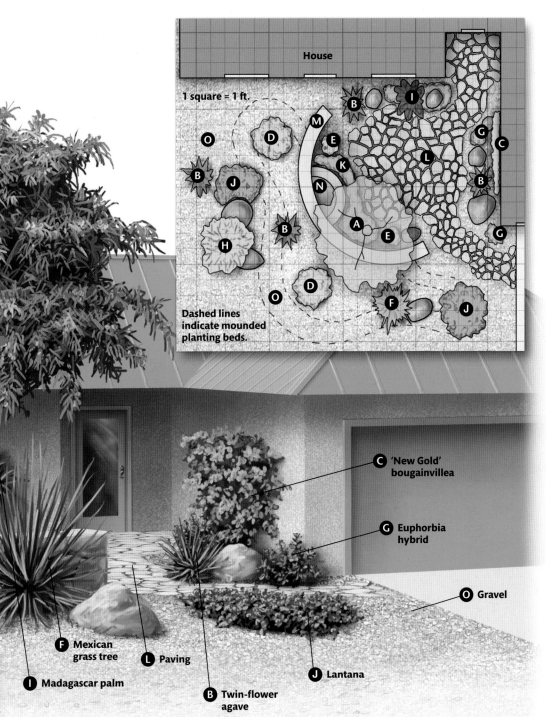

House

1 square = 1 ft.

Dashed lines indicate mounded planting beds.

C 'New Gold' bougainvillea

G Euphorbia hybrid

O Gravel

F Mexican grass tree

L Paving

I Madagascar palm

B Twin-flower agave

J Lantana

VARIATIONS ON A THEME

Here, three different planting styles produce striking entry gardens for Southwestern-style homes.

Loose mounds of foliage and a liberal sprinkling of flowers flank a gravel walk in this "cottage" garden.

This eye-catching front door garden is largely a mix of foliage plants. A few colorful impatiens tucked in here and there add bright accents.

A desert garden is an ideal setting for this modern version of an adobe-style home.

Tropical hello

This design creates a front yard entertainment area with a different look and less installation expense—there's no wall and it accommodates an existing walkway. The plants require little maintenance but more (low to moderate) supplemental watering than those in the previous design.

This flagstone courtyard is defined by mounded, sweeping planting beds mulched with gravel. A small pool of water adds an oasis-like touch. Under the protective umbrella of the tipu tree, the plants will produce luxuriant foliage all year and a profusion of blossoms in many vibrant colors, sometimes on a single plant. Brunfelsia bears purple, lavender, and white blossoms, and each of Ixora's huge flowers makes an exquisite bouquet of its own.

Plants & Projects

Ⓐ Tipu tree (use 1)
This lovely tree has light green, divided leaves and yellow to apricot flowers in late spring. Woody seedpods follow in fall. See *Tipuana tipu*, p. 153.

Ⓑ Pygmy date palm (use 1)
Crowned with dark green, fine-textured fronds, this is an at-tractive palm for a small space. Reaches about 6 ft. tall. See *Phoenix roebelenii*, p. 143.

Ⓒ Yesterday-today-and-tomorrow (use 2)
From spring to summer the dark glossy leaves of this bushy evergreen shrub are smothered in pansy-like flowers that age from purple to lavender to white. See *Brunfelsia pauciflora* 'Floribunda Compacta', p. 119.

Ⓓ 'Thai Dwarf' ixora (use 4)
A fine ever-blooming tropical shrub. Huge flower clusters in red, orange, pink, or gold are displayed against dark green and glossy leaves. See *Ixora* 'Thai Dwarf', p. 137.

Ⓔ Arabian jasmine (use 1)
Wonderfully fragrant white flowers bloom among this climbing vine's deep green leaves throughout the summer. See *Jasminum sambac*, p. 137.

Ⓕ 'Flower Carpet Pink' rose (use 12)
This rose spreads into a beautiful low mat of small glossy leaves topped with clusters of everblooming pink rosettes. See *Rosa*, p. 149.

See p. 33 for the following:

Ⓖ Annuals

Ⓗ Mexican grass tree

Ⓘ Paving

Ⓙ Water feature

Ⓚ Gravel mulch

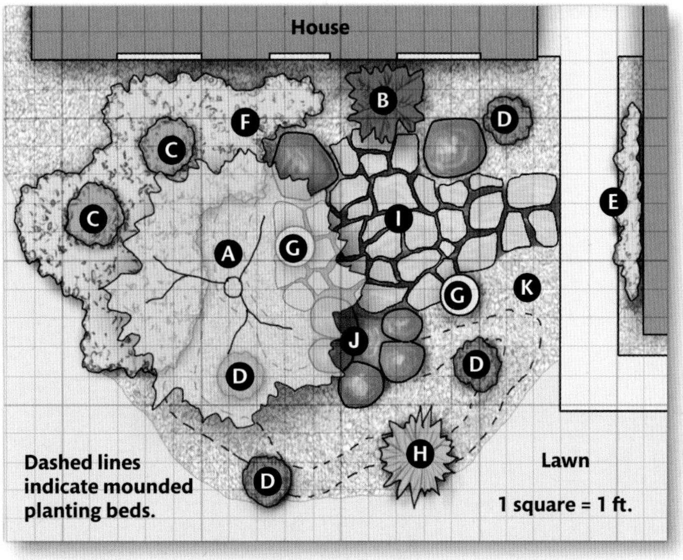

House

Dashed lines indicate mounded planting beds.

Lawn

1 square = 1 ft.

SITE: Sunny

SEASON: Spring

CONCEPT: Fragrant flowers and lush foliage grace this desert oasis.

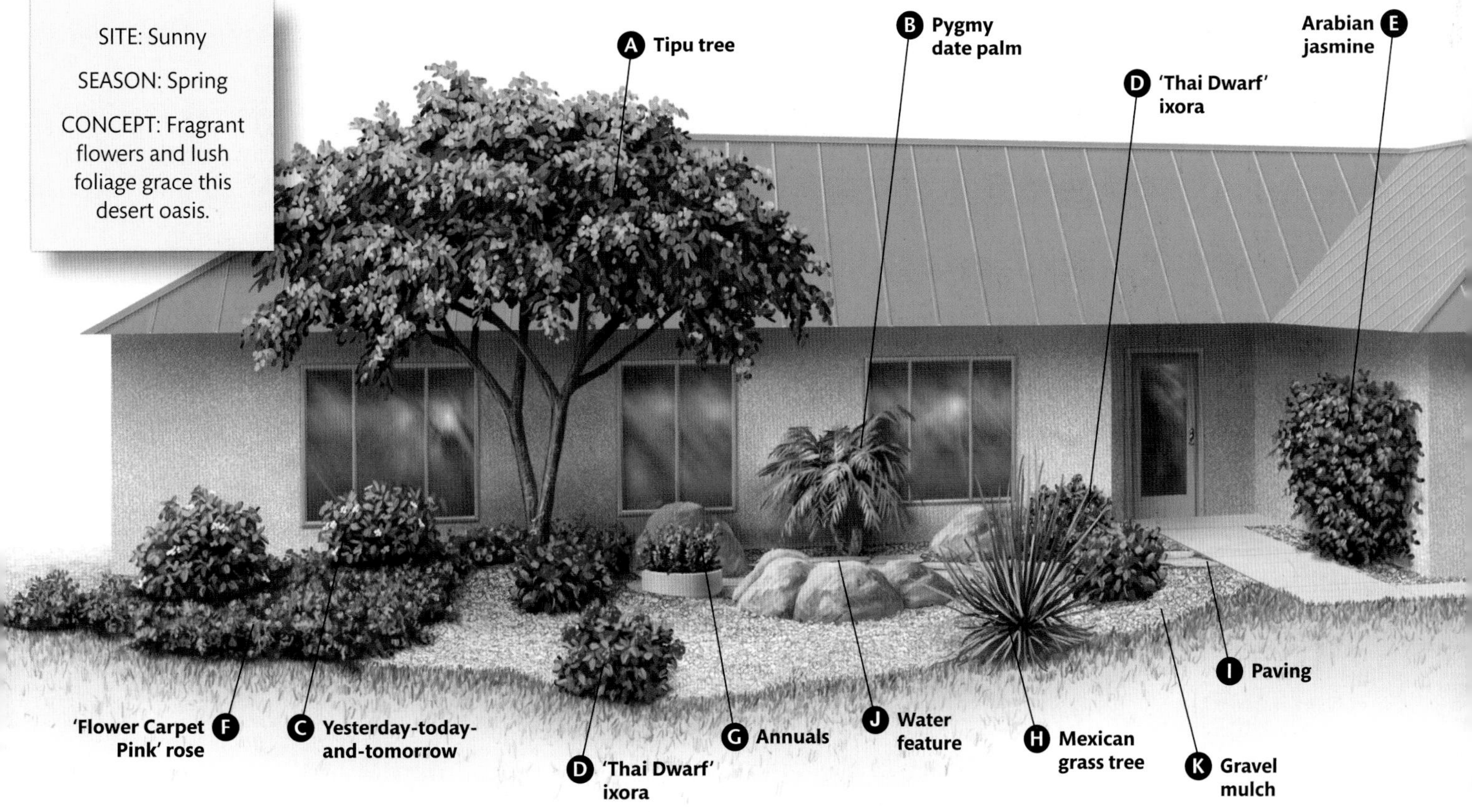

Ⓐ Tipu tree

Ⓑ Pygmy date palm

Ⓓ 'Thai Dwarf' ixora

Ⓔ Arabian jasmine

Ⓘ Paving

Ⓕ 'Flower Carpet Pink' rose

Ⓒ Yesterday-today-and-tomorrow

Ⓓ 'Thai Dwarf' ixora

Ⓖ Annuals

Ⓙ Water feature

Ⓗ Mexican grass tree

Ⓚ Gravel mulch

On the Street

GIVE YOUR CURBSIDE STRIP A NEW LOOK

Homeowners seldom give a thought to the part of their property adjacent to the street. Often bounded by a sidewalk, this area is at best a tidy patch of lawn and at worst a weed-choked eyesore. Yet this is one of the most public parts of many properties. Filling this strip with attractive plants and paths from street to walkway can give pleasure to passersby and visitors who park next to the curb, as well as enhancing the streetscape you view from the house. (Curbside strips are usually city-owned, so check local ordinances for restrictions before you start a remake.)

This can be a difficult site, subject to summer drought and heat, pedestrian and car traffic, and errant dogs. Plants need to be tough and drought-tolerant to perform well here. (Water-conserving plantings in curbside areas are encouraged by many towns and cities.)

The plants in this design meet both criteria. And they look good, too. Though there are many flowers from late winter to early summer, foliage is the main event here. In shades of silver, gray, green, blue, and striking purple and an equal variety of textures, the foliage provides interest throughout the year. Two paths afford access from cars parked on the street. If your curbside property doesn't include a sidewalk, you can extend the planting farther into the yard and connect the paths to the walkway to your front door.

> SITE: Sunny
>
> SEASON: Spring
>
> CONCEPT: Plants with striking foliage transform an often-neglected area and treat visitors and passersby to a colorful display.

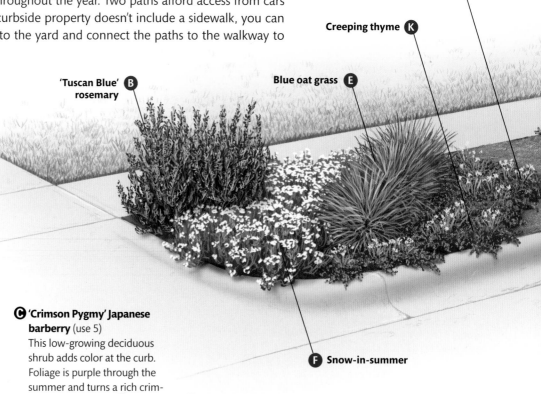

Dwarf daffodil **I**

Creeping thyme **K**

'Tuscan Blue' rosemary **B**

Blue oat grass **E**

Snow-in-summer **F**

Plants & Projects

Once established, these plants require very little care. You can lightly shear the Russian sage and rosemary after bloom and the ground morning glory in midwinter. Trim the thyme to keep it out of the path. In late winter, cut the Russian sage to short stubs and run your fingers through the blue oat grass to remove dead leaves.

A Feathery cassia (use 1 plant)
This evergreen shrub forms an airy clump of gray needlelike foliage. Bears small sulphur yellow flowers from late winter through spring. See *Cassia artemisioides*, p. 123.

B 'Tuscan Blue' rosemary (use 4)
An upright evergreen shrub with aromatic gray-green foliage marks two corners of the planting. Deep blue flowers bloom in late winter. See *Rosmarinus officinalis*, p. 149.

C 'Crimson Pygmy' Japanese barberry (use 5)
This low-growing deciduous shrub adds color at the curb. Foliage is purple through the summer and turns a rich crimson in fall. See *Berberis thunbergii*, p. 118.

D Russian sage (use 6)
With straight stems and small, light gray leaves, this perennial is a wispy presence. Its delicate lavender-blue flowers complement the form and foliage perfectly all summer. See *Perovskia atriplicifolia*, p. 144.

E Blue oat grass (use 6)
This evergreen perennial's spiky mounds of thin blue leaves look striking next to nearby foliage. See *Helictotrichon sempervirens*, p. 142.

F Snow-in-summer (use 16)
A perennial ground cover, its silvery leaves are covered with small white flowers in late spring to early summer. See *Cerastium tomentosum*, p. 124.

G Ground morning glory (use 7)
Edging the sidewalk, this perennial spreads to form a cushion of soft gray-green leaves. Bears pretty lavender-blue flowers from summer into fall. See *Convolvulus mauritanicus*, p. 127.

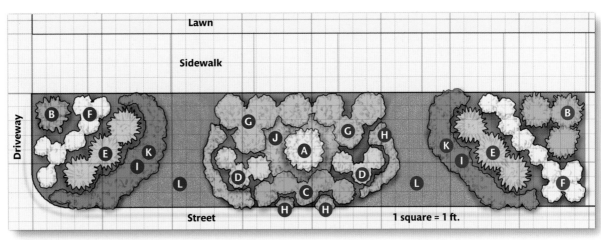

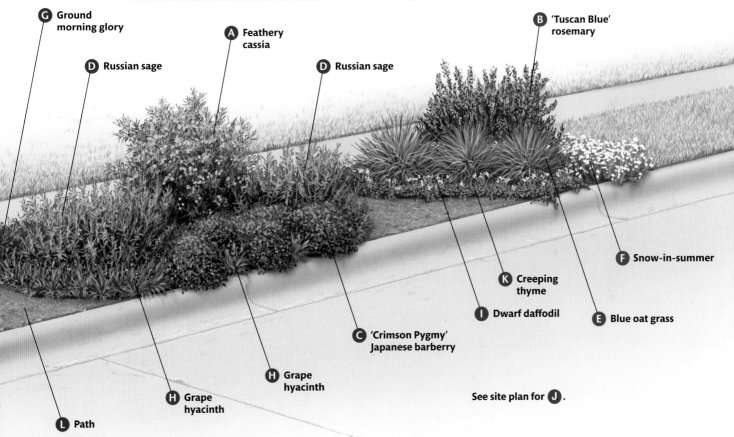

G Ground morning glory

A Feathery cassia

D Russian sage

D Russian sage

B 'Tuscan Blue' rosemary

F Snow-in-summer

K Creeping thyme

I Dwarf daffodil

E Blue oat grass

C 'Crimson Pygmy' Japanese barberry

H Grape hyacinth

See site plan for **J**.

H Grape hyacinth

H Grape hyacinth

L Path

H Grape hyacinth (use 180)
The fragrant blue flowers of this little bulb edge the path in spring. Grassy leaves are dormant in summer and appear again in fall. See Bulbs: *Muscari armeniacum*, p. 121.

I Dwarf daffodil (use 120)
A small version of the popular bulb, these perky flowers enliven the path in spring. Choose from a variety of dwarf cultivars, such as the yellow 'Tête-à-Tête' shown here. Foliage will grow through the thyme planted in the same space and die back after bloom. See Bulbs: *Narcissus*, p. 121.

J Blue allium (use 28)
Blooming in June, after the daffodils, these bulbs produce balls of blue flowers held on erect stems above grassy foliage. See Bulbs: *Allium caeruleum*, p. 121.

K Creeping thyme (use 20)
This perennial herb spreads to form low-growing mats of pun-gent dark green foliage along the path. It can bear light foot traffic. See *Thymus praecox* ssp. *arcticus*, p. 153.

L Path
Decomposed granite or crushed rock laid on a sand-and-gravel base makes a durable, easily maintained surface. See p. 164.

A curbside stroll garden

In this design, paths and steppingstones allow visitors emerging from a car to move directly to the sidewalk or to meander and enjoy the planting. As in the previous design, the evergreen and long-lasting deciduous foliage of small shrubs and perennials is attractive year-round, mixing shades of green, gray, and red. From spring through fall, there are colorful flowers. Those of the English lavender are fragrant and, with its aromatic leaves, will encourage lingering along the path.

This is also a low-maintenance, low-water-use planting, requiring little more than shearing off spent flowers. Or, better yet, cut and dry the flowers and seed heads of yarrow, lavender, and fountain grass for long-lasting arrangements.

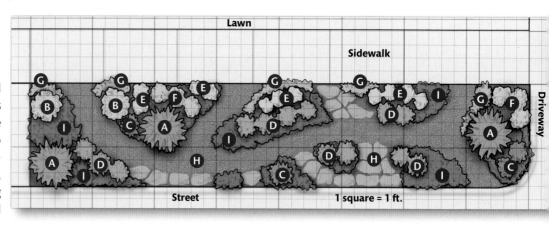

Plants & Projects

A Purple fountain grass (use 3 plants)
This ornamental grass offers reddish brown leaves that turn gold or tan in fall. Bronze seed heads arch above the foliage from midsummer. See *Pennisetum setaceum* 'Rubrum', p. 142.

B 'Moonshine' yarrow (use 2)
Attractive clumps of silvery green foliage give this perennial a year-round interest. Flat clusters of tiny golden yellow flowers top the foliage in summer. See *Achillea*, p. 115.

C 'Otto Quast' Spanish lavender (use 4)
An evergreen shrub with fragrant gray-green foliage and showy spikes of dark lavender flowers in early summer. See *Lavandula stoechas*, p. 138.

D 'Munstead' English lavender (use 13)
Shorter than its nearby relative, this lavender produces spikes of wonderfully fragrant dark blue flowers in early summer. See *Lavandula angustifolia*, p. 138.

E Santa Barbara daisy (use 11)
A perennial with airy low-growing foliage, it bears small whitish pink daisylike flowers from spring through fall. See *Erigeron karvinskianus*, p. 130.

F 'Nana' heavenly bamboo (use 6)
The fine-textured evergreen foliage of this dwarf shrub changes colors with the seasons; its fiery red leaves are particularly striking in winter. See *Nandina domestica*, p. 141.

G Golden garlic (use 68)
Ball-shaped yellow flowers brighten the edges of the sidewalk in spring. This little bulb's grassy foliage looks good long after the flowers are gone. See Bulbs: *Allium moly*, p. 121.

H Walkway
Flagstone steppingstones and a path of decomposed granite or crushed rock provide several avenues from street to sidewalk. See p. 164.

See p. 37 for the following:
I Creeping thyme (use 49)

SITE: Sunny

SEASON: Early summer

CONCEPT: Meandering paths encourage more leisurely enjoyment of the curbside planting.

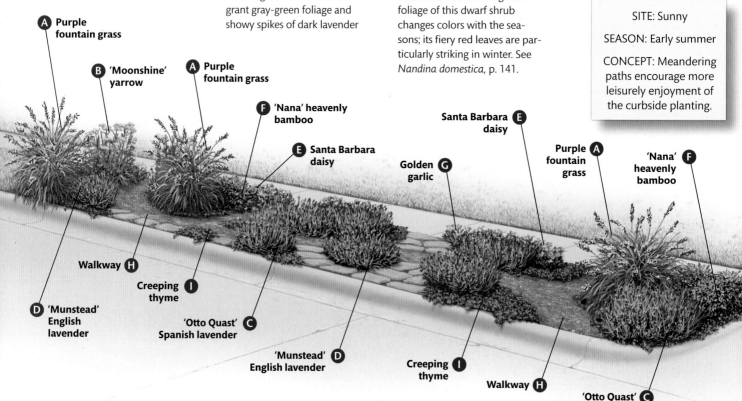

VARIATIONS ON A THEME

An attractive selection of readily available low-growing shrubs and perennials is tough enough to thrive in demanding streetside conditions.

Clump-forming ornamental grasses highlight this durable and colorful planting at the curb.

These brightly colored perennials and shrubs are as easy to appreciate when you're going 35 miles per hour as they are at a stroll.

Here, a single planting is split by a sidewalk. Low-growing perennials and spreading shrubs keep sight lines open between the sidewalk and street.

An Eye-Catching Corner

BEAUTIFY A BOUNDARY WITH EASY-CARE PLANTS

The corner where your property meets your neighbor's and the sidewalk is often a kind of grassy no-man's-land. This design defines that boundary with a planting that can be enjoyed by both property owners, as well as by passersby. Good gardens make good neighbors, so we've used well-behaved, low-maintenance plants that won't make extra work for the person next door—or for you.

Because of its exposed location, remote from the house and close to the street, this is a less personal planting than those in more private and frequently used parts of your property. It is meant to be appreciated from a distance. Anchored by a small multitrunked tree, the planting is a bold patchwork of leaf colors and bright flowers. An existing fence provides scaffolding for a vigorous vine. While not intended as a barrier, the planting also provides a modest psychological, if not physical, screen from activity on the sidewalk and street.

Something is in bloom almost every month, producing flowers in red, orange, yellow, blue, or lavender. The foliage is nearly as colorful, with yellows, maroon, reds, and grays as well as green. Scented flowers and tasty fruit make a stroll to the planting worthwhile, too.

'Wonderful' pomegranate **A**

'Red Meidiland' rose **C**

'Harbour Dwarf' heavenly bamboo **E**

'Harbour Dwarf' heavenly bamboo **E**

Ground morning glory **F**

C 'Red Meidiland' rose

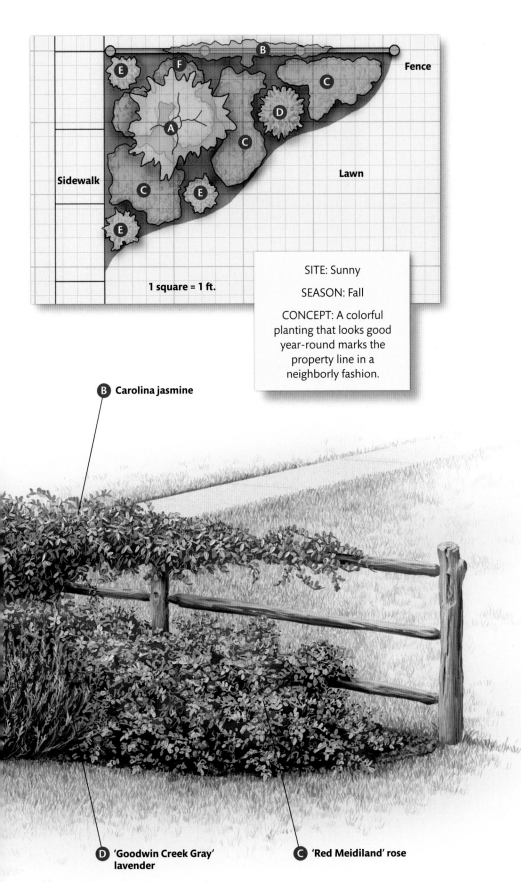

Fence

Lawn

Sidewalk

1 square = 1 ft.

SITE: Sunny

SEASON: Fall

CONCEPT: A colorful planting that looks good year-round marks the property line in a neighborly fashion.

B Carolina jasmine

D 'Goodwin Creek Gray' lavender

C 'Red Meidiland' rose

Plants & Projects

As befits a planting some distance from the house, these durable, reliable plants require little care beyond seasonal pruning. Shear the morning glory and lavender after bloom to keep plants neat and compact. Trim the Carolina jasmine to control its size. Remove spent flowers from the roses. The plants withstand dry spells but do best with regular watering.

A **'Wonderful' pomegranate** (use 1 plant)
This popular deciduous fruit tree provides months of enjoyment. Spring's eye-catching orange-red flowers produce bright red edible fruits in fall. The fine-textured green foliage of summer turns yellow in autumn. The tree's multitrunked fountain shape is handsome in winter. See *Punica granatum*, p. 146.

B **Carolina jasmine** (use 1)
Draped over the fence, the evergreen leaves of this vigorous vine form a shiny dark green backdrop in summer, turning maroon in winter. Fragrant yellow flowers bloom in early spring. See *Gelsemium sempervirens*, p. 132.

C **'Red Meidiland' rose** (use 3)
This sprawling shrub rose makes an effective and colorful ground cover. It bears white-centered red flowers in profusion for much of the year. See *Rosa*, p. 149.

D **'Goodwin Creek Gray' lavender** (use 1)
The gray-green leaves of this evergreen shrub are set off handsomely by the surrounding roses. In summer and fall, the foliage bristles with spikes of deep blue flowers. See *Lavandula*, p. 138.

E **'Harbour Dwarf' heavenly bamboo** (use 3)
This evergreen shrub bears fine-textured leaves that change from gold, to green, to red from spring through fall. Fluffy white flowers appear in summer, followed by a long-lasting crop of red berries. See *Nandina domestica*, p. 141.

F **Ground morning glory** (use 3)
A perennial ground cover, its soft gray-green leaves echo those of the lavender. It's sprinkled with cheerful lavender-blue flowers from summer through fall. See *Convolvulus mauritanicus*, p. 127.

VARIATIONS ON A THEME

These photos show a few of the numerous ways a planting, or an element in a planting, can catch the eye.

Large masses of brightly colored flowers don't so much catch the eye as grab it.

Set among fuzzy lamb's ears and fine-textured eulalia grass, a large terra-cotta pot makes a handsome accent.

A white picket fence is an ideal backdrop for the play of foliage color and texture in this planting.

Roses set the tone

The backbone of this planting is the popular 'Iceberg' rose, which provides clusters of beautiful and fragrant white flowers for months. Backed by an evergreen vine on the fence, the roses are at the center of a selection of colorful and durable perennials.

Once again, there are flowers for many months. Panicles of pinkish purple blossoms drape the vine-covered fence in late winter. The summer offers the most variety. Blanketflowers, daylilies, and salvias combine bold oranges, reds, yellows, and blues—a display that is eye-catching whether viewed at a distance or close up.

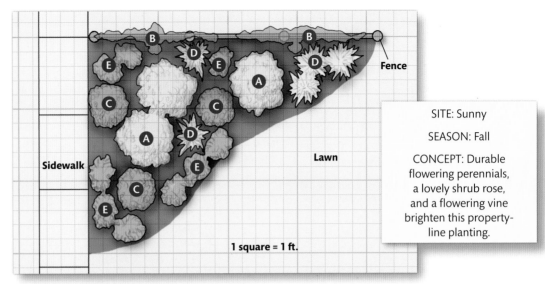

SITE: Sunny

SEASON: Fall

CONCEPT: Durable flowering perennials, a lovely shrub rose, and a flowering vine brighten this property-line planting.

Plants & Projects

Ⓐ 'Iceberg' rose (use 3 plants) Fragrant white flowers are displayed against mounds of light green foliage. Blooms from spring through fall; off and on throughout the year in warm-winter areas. See *Rosa*, p. 149.

Ⓑ 'Happy Wanderer' hardenbergia (use 2) This vigorous vine engulfs the fence in fine-textured evergreen foliage. Bears pinkish purple flowers in late winter and early spring. See *Hardenbergia violacea*, p. 133.

Ⓒ Blanketflower (use 3) The cheerful red-and-orange daisylike blooms of this perennial wildflower accent the planting all summer. See *Gaillardia* x *grandiflora*, p. 131.

Ⓓ Daylily (use 5) Distinctive flowers rise on tall stems above the grassy foliage

of these popular perennials. Choose varieties that bloom at different times to extend the season. Foliage is attractive when the plants aren't blooming. See *Hemerocallis*, p. 134.

Ⓔ Salvia (use 9) This perennial forms a patch of upright, dark green, leafy stems topped all summer with spikes of dark bluish purple flowers. See *Salvia* x *superba*, p. 150.

Gateway Garden

ARBOR, FENCE, AND PLANTINGS MAKE A HANDSOME ENTRY

Entrances are an important part of any landscape. They can welcome visitors onto your property; highlight a special feature, such as a rose garden; or mark the passage between two areas that have different characteristics or functions. The design shown here can serve in any of these situations.

A picket fence set amid shrubs and perennials creates a friendly and attractive barrier, just enough to signal the confines of the front yard or contain the family dog. The simple vine-covered arbor provides welcoming access.

The design combines uncomplicated elements imaginatively, creating interesting details to catch the eye and a slightly formal but comfortable overall effect. Picketed enclosures flank the arbor and help showcase long-blooming roses whose fragrance wafts over the walkway. Tiers of shrubs and perennials ranked alongside the fence offer contrasts in foliage texture as well as pretty flowers and colorful berries from spring through fall.

SITE: Sunny

SEASON: Early summer

CONCEPT: Shrubs, perennials, and flowering vines accent a traditional picket fence and simple entry arbor.

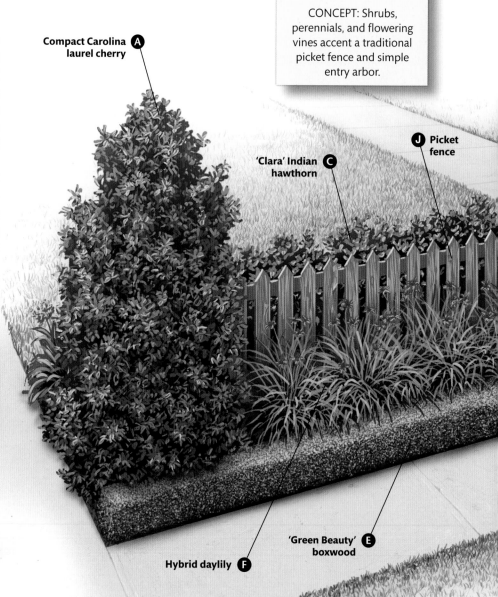

Compact Carolina laurel cherry **A**

'Clara' Indian hawthorn **C**

J Picket fence

E 'Green Beauty' boxwood

Hybrid daylily **F**

Plants & Projects

For many people, a picket fence and vine-covered arbor represent old-fashioned neighborly virtues. The structures and plantings are easy to install. You can extend the fence and plantings as needed. The plants do best with regular water. The shrubs require seasonal pruning to maintain size and shape.

A **Compact Carolina laurel cherry** (use 2 plants)
Marking the ends of the planting, this evergreen shrub showcases spikes of small white flowers against glossy green foliage in spring. Black berries follow. Trim to enhance the plant's naturally loose conical shape. See *Prunus caroliniana* 'Compacta', p. 146.

B **'Iceberg' rose** (use 2)
This popular rose bears fragrant white flowers nearly all year on a mound of dark green foliage. See *Rosa*, p. 149.

C **'Clara' Indian hawthorn** (use 8)
A low, spreading shrub, it forms a neat but informal hedge alongside the fence. In spring it bears small white flowers; blue berries follow in summer and fall. See *Rhaphiolepis indica*, p. 147.

D **'Alice du Pont' mandevilla** (use 2)
This twining evergreen vine sprawls over the arbor. Clusters of pink flowers are sprinkled among the glossy leaves from late spring through fall. See *Mandevilla*, p. 140.

E **'Green Beauty' boxwood** (use 32)
Neatly clipped to form a hedge next to the sidewalk, this evergreen shrub has small leaves and a dense, compact habit. Plant 1 ft. on center. See *Buxus microphylla* var. *japonica*, p. 120.

F **Hybrid daylily** (use 12)
The arching grassy foliage of this perennial contrasts nicely with the nearby hedge. Mix

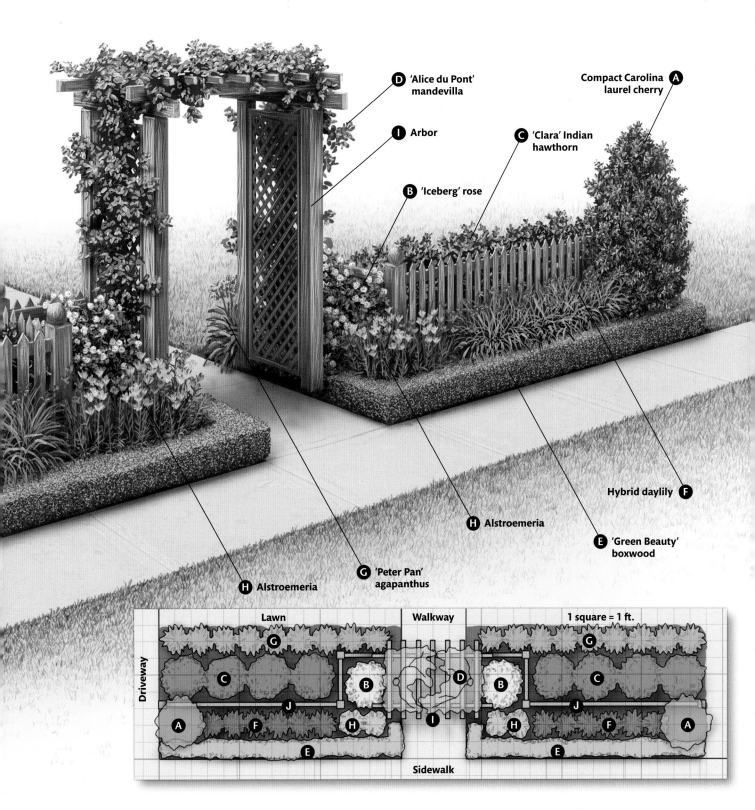

D 'Alice du Pont' mandevilla

I Arbor

C 'Clara' Indian hawthorn

Compact Carolina laurel cherry A

B 'Iceberg' rose

H Alstroemeria

Hybrid daylily F

E 'Green Beauty' boxwood

G 'Peter Pan' agapanthus

H Alstroemeria

Lawn | Walkway | 1 square = 1 ft.

Driveway

Sidewalk

---

cultivars with deep pink flowers and differing bloom times to ensure flowers all summer. See *Hemerocallis*, p. 134.

G 'Peter Pan' agapanthus (use 18)
A dwarf form of a popular perennial, it produces neat mounds of straplike foliage. In late spring and summer, ball-shaped clusters of blue flowers rise above the leaves on long stalks. See *Agapanthus*, p. 115.

H Alstroemeria (use 4)
This perennial is prized for its strikingly colorful flowers borne on upright leafy stalks from spring to midsummer. Choose from the long-blooming evergreen Meyer hybrids. See *Alstroemeria*, p. 116.

I Arbor
Thick posts give this simple structure a sturdy visual presence. You can paint or

stain it, or make it of cedar or redwood and let the weather age it as shown here. See p. 190.

J Picket fence
A low picket fence adds character to the planting. Choose materials and a finish that match or complement those of the arbor. See p. 190.

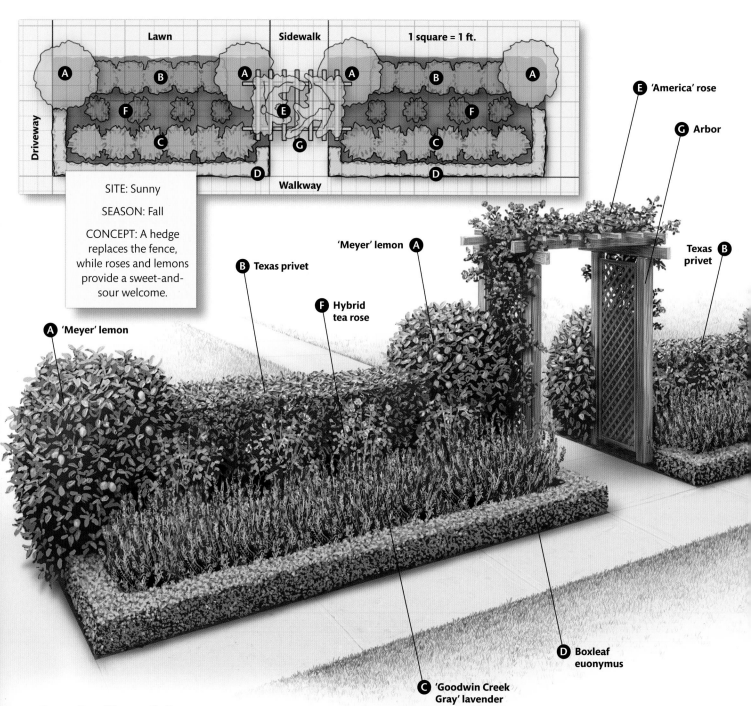

Lawn   Sidewalk   1 square = 1 ft.

A   B   A   A   B   A

F   E   F

Driveway   C   G   C

D   Walkway   D

SITE: Sunny

SEASON: Fall

CONCEPT: A hedge replaces the fence, while roses and lemons provide a sweet-and-sour welcome.

E 'America' rose

G Arbor

'Meyer' lemon A

B Texas privet

F Hybrid tea rose

Texas B
privet

A 'Meyer' lemon

D Boxleaf euonymus

C 'Goodwin Creek Gray' lavender

Say hello with roses

Not every entry calls for a fence. In this simple design, a waist-high clipped hedge serves as a barrier on either side of a rose-covered entry arbor. The hedge is also an excellent backdrop for a display of fragrant hybrid tea roses. A skirt of gray-leaved lavender edged by a low hedge (elements often found in traditional rose gardens) completes the showcase. Small lemon trees add flavor (literally as well as figuratively) at the corners. The roses bloom for many months, and an abundance of evergreen foliage ensures that the planting looks good year-round.

The planting will take a few years to fill in. Once established, the hedges will require regular shearing to look their best. The lemon trees, lavender, and climbing rose will need seasonal care. Rather than pruning the lemon trees to make room for the Texas privet hedge, let the hedge grow right into the trees' foliage. Hybrid tea roses are less difficult than many people fear, but they do require regular attention. (Step over the low hedge at the ends of the beds for access.) If tea roses aren't your passion, plant low-care shrub roses instead.

Plants & Projects

Ⓐ 'Meyer' lemon (use 4 plants)
This small tree offers handsome evergreen foliage, fragrant flowers in spring, and attractive edible fruits in fall and winter. Prune to form a rounded crown. See *Citrus*, p. 126.

Ⓑ Texas privet (use 10)
Trained here as a formal hedge, this evergreen shrub has dense, glossy foliage. Bears scented white flowers in early summer (if buds aren't sheared off). See *Ligustrum japonicum* 'Texanum', p. 139.

Ⓒ 'Goodwin Creek Gray' lavender (use 12)
The light gray-green foliage of this evergreen shrub is an effective color accent here. Bears spikes of blue flowers summer into fall. See *Lavandula*, p. 138.

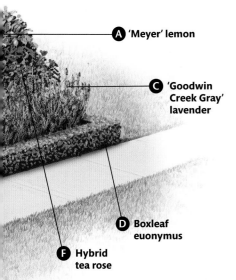

Ⓐ 'Meyer' lemon

Ⓒ 'Goodwin Creek Gray' lavender

Ⓓ Boxleaf euonymus

Ⓕ Hybrid tea rose

Ⓓ Boxleaf euonymus (use 40)
This evergreen shrub has small leaves and a dense, compact habit well suited for a low clipped hedge. See *Euonymus japonicus* 'Microphyllus', p. 130.

Ⓔ 'America' rose (use 2)
The fragrant orange-red flowers of this climbing rose will cover the arbor from late spring to early winter. See *Rosa*, p. 149.

Ⓕ Hybrid tea rose (use 8)
For the planting's showcase, choose your favorite tea roses. We've shown two each of the following varieties (one on each side), which produce fragrant double roses all summer: 'Mister Lincoln', with red flowers; 'Double Delight', with red-and- white flowers; 'Tiffany', with pink flowers; and 'Papa Meilland', with dark crimson flowers. See *Rosa*, p. 149.

See p. 45 for the following:

Ⓖ Arbor

VARIATIONS ON A THEME

A gateway can be an imposing structure with attendant plantings or simply a gap in a fence.

In this entryway garden, a split-rail fence and a colorful arrangement of shrubs and perennials take the place of an arbor. The entrance passes in front of the dark barberry in the foreground.

This wisteria-covered arbor couldn't be simpler or more effective.

An arched arbor, a white picket fence, and roses give an old-fashioned greeting.

A Pleasant Passage

RECLAIM A NARROW SIDE YARD FOR A STROLL GARDEN

Many residential lots include a slim strip of land between the house and a property line. Usually overlooked by everyone except children and dogs racing between the front yard and the back, this often-shady corridor can become a valued addition to the landscape. In this design, a lovely little stroll garden invites adults, and even children, to linger as they move from one part of the property to another.

The wall of the house and a tall, opaque fence on the property line shade the space most of the day and give it a closed-in feeling, like a long empty hallway or a narrow room. The path and

plantings create a cozy passage, and, like the furnishings of a room, they make a small space seem bigger than it is.

As is common on many residential properties, a gated fence closes off one end of the corridor. At the other, a simple vine-covered arch and low plants mark the transition to a front yard or backyard. In between, small Japanese maples form a graceful arching canopy over a gently curving path. On either side, shrubs, perennials, vines, ferns, and ground covers delight the eye with a mixture of foliage textures and colors, as well as flowers from late winter through the summer.

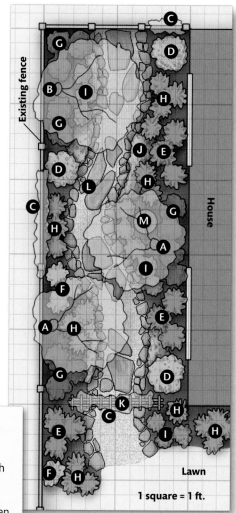

SITE: Shady

SEASON: Summer

CONCEPT: Plants with colorful foliage and pretty flowers make an enticing stroll garden in a frequently neglected area.

Plants & Projects

Lay out and install the path and edging, the arbor, and the irrigation system. Then prepare and plant the beds. As the maples grow, you'll need to prune them so they arch over the path yet provide headroom for strollers. Once established, the plants require seasonal care as well as pruning to maintain size and shape.

Ⓐ Coralbark maple (use 2 plants)
The fine-textured leaves of this small deciduous tree are light green in summer and yellow in fall. In winter and spring, the bright red twigs accent the planting. See *Acer palmatum* 'Sango Kaku', p. 114.

Ⓑ 'Oshio-Beni' Japanese maple (use 1)
Similar to coralbark maple in many respects, this small tree has dark red leaves on its arching branches in summer and fall. See *Acer palmatum*, p. 114.

Ⓒ 'Happy Wanderer' hardenbergia (use 4)
Trained on the arbor and fence, this evergreen vine bears pink-

ish purple flowers in late winter and early spring. The foliage is attractive all year. See *Hardenbergia violacea*, p. 133.

Ⓓ 'Nikko Blue' hydrangea (use 3)
This is a smaller form of the popular deciduous shrub. Big clusters of blue flowers are displayed against its bold foliage for months in summer. See *Hydrangea macrophylla*, p. 136.

Ⓔ Sword fern (use 9)
The shiny dark green fronds of this native fern add interesting form and texture to the planting. See Ferns: *Polystichum munitum*, p. 131.

Ⓕ Mother fern (use 4)
This fern forms an airy mound of light green fronds that are evergreen where winters are mild. See Ferns: *Asplenium bulbiferum*, p. 131.

Ⓖ Lenten rose (use 12)
In early spring, pink, rose, green, or white flowers rise on branched stems above this perennial's attractive toothed evergreen leaves. See *Helleborus orientalis*, p. 133.

Ⓗ 'Big Blue' lilyturf (use 20)
This perennial makes mounds of grassy, dark green foliage. In summer, spikes of small blue flowers float above the leaves. See *Liriope muscari*, p. 139.

Ⓘ 'Palace Purple' heuchera (use 11)
A perennial, it is grown primarily for its distinctive purple foliage. Slender stalks bear tiny white flowers in late spring. See *Heuchera*, p. 134.

Ⓙ Ground covers (as needed)
Along the edges of the beds, plant bellflowers and ajuga. Both bloom in late spring and early summer. Serbian bellflower has dark green foliage and spikes of purple flowers (see *Campanula poscharskyana*, p. 122). 'Bronze Beauty' ajuga

has purple-bronze foliage and bears short spikes of small bluish flowers (see *Ajuga reptans*, p. 115). Between pavers and edging stones try annual lobelia, which self-seeds readily.

Ⓚ Arbor
This shallow arbor can be built easily in an afternoon or two. See p. 187.

Ⓛ Path
Edged with fieldstones, the path comprises a few large flagstone stepping-stones set in crushed rock or decomposed granite. See p. 164.

Ⓜ Decorative urn
Filled with water (you might use a recycling pump), this makes an effective focal point in the center of the planting.

B 'Oshio-Beni' Japanese maple

'Happy Wanderer' C hardenbergia

K Arbor

A Coralbark maple

D 'Nikko Blue' hydrangea

G Lenten rose

E Sword fern

Path

L

M Decorative urn

Ground covers J

'Palace Purple' heuchera I

H 'Big Blue' lilyturf

F Mother fern

H 'Big Blue' lilyturf

H 'Big Blue' lilyturf

A sunny corridor

If the side of your house has a sunny exposure and your taste runs to the formal and fragrant, try this design. Here, sun-loving vines, shrubs, and perennials are arrayed symmetrically along the passage. A flagstone walkway passes through a vine-draped arch at each end. Neat bushes covered nearly year-round with white roses line the walk, accented by the silvery gray foliage of lavender and snow-in-summer that cascades onto the paving. At the center of the planting, a small courtyard is framed by vine-covered trellises attached to the house and fence.

Enticing scents are supplied by star jasmine on the center trellises, as well as by the roses, lavender, and evergreen clematis. The color scheme is elegantly simple, with flowers in blues, purples, and white, and foliage in shades of green and silvery gray.

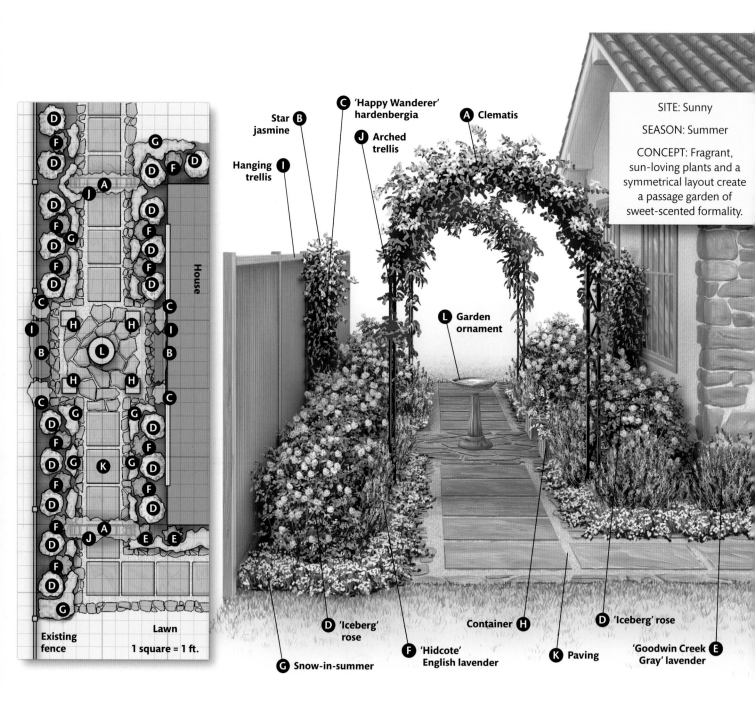

SITE: Sunny

SEASON: Summer

CONCEPT: Fragrant, sun-loving plants and a symmetrical layout create a passage garden of sweet-scented formality.

B Star jasmine

C 'Happy Wanderer' hardenbergia

A Clematis

J Arched trellis

I Hanging trellis

L Garden ornament

D 'Iceberg' rose

F 'Hidcote' English lavender

G Snow-in-summer

H Container

D 'Iceberg' rose

K Paving

E 'Goodwin Creek Gray' lavender

Existing fence

Lawn

1 square = 1 ft.

House

Plants & Projects

Ⓐ Clematis (use 4 plants)
Two different types are used here, one on each arching trellis at the ends of the planting. Evergreen clematis (*Clematis armandii*) bears large clusters of fragrant white flowers in spring against a backdrop of glossy green leaves. C. 'Mme. Le Coultre' is deciduous and produces large white flowers from midsummer through fall. See *Clematis*, p. 126.

Ⓑ Star jasmine (use 6)
Trained up the trellises attached to the house and fence, this evergreen vine offers shiny leaves and clusters of fragrant cream-colored flowers in early summer. See *Trachelospermum jasminoides*, p. 154.

Ⓒ 'Happy Wanderer' hardenbergia (use 4)
Plant this evergreen vine at the ends of the house and fence trellises. Pinkish purple flowers dot the dark foliage in late winter and early spring. See *Hardenbergia violacea*, p. 133.

Ⓓ 'Iceberg' rose (use 18)
A mounded deciduous shrub, it is covered nearly year-round with clusters of fragrant white flowers. See *Rosa*, p. 149.

Ⓔ 'Goodwin Creek Gray' lavender (use 2)
This perennial herb forms a large mound of gray-green foliage topped in summer and fall with short spikes of blue flowers. See *Lavandula*, p. 138.

Ⓕ 'Hidcote' English lavender (use 12)
This lavender makes smaller mounds of gray foliage at the feet of the roses. Bears dark purple flowers in summer. See *Lavandula angustifolia*, p. 138.

Ⓖ Snow-in-summer (as needed)
The silvery evergreen foliage of this perennial ground cover will sprawl into the path from the edges of the beds. It is blanketed with small white flowers in early summer. Plant 12 in. apart. See *Cerastium tomentosum*, p. 124.

Ⓗ Containers
Placed at the corners of the little courtyard, these pots or wooden boxes can be planted with seasonal annuals and bulbs. Here we show two with lavender and white stocks and two with white freesias. All four are underplanted with alyssum.

Ⓘ Hanging trellises
Attached to the house and the fence, these trellises can be built or bought ready-made. See p. 186.

Ⓙ Arched trellises
Framing the entrances, these metal trellises can be purchased in a variety of styles from garden centers.

Ⓚ Paving
Paths of square flagstones lead to a small courtyard of irregular flagstones (see p. 164). Edge the beds with small fieldstones. In the gaps between stones, you can plant creeping thyme (see *Thymus praecox* ssp. *arcticus*, p. 153) and self-seeding annuals such as lobelia and alyssum.

Ⓛ Garden ornament
Place a copper birdbath (as shown), statue, or other ornament as a focal point at the center of the courtyard.

VARIATIONS ON A THEME

A narrow passage is a real design challenge. These examples succeed in creating spaces you want to, rather than have to, walk through.

This side-yard garden features an array of tropical plants, including bird-of-paradise and New Zealand flax.

A geometrical path of cut flagstones set in crushed rock lends an air of formality to this side-yard garden, as does the repetition of plants along the path.

A narrow path overgrown with evergreen plants and accented with playful lighting creates a magical garden in a small space.

Down to Earth

HARMONIZE YOUR DECK WITH ITS SURROUNDINGS

A backyard deck is a perfect spot for enjoying the outdoors. Too often, however, the deck offers little connection to the outdoor life we most enjoy. Perched on skinny posts above a patch of lawn, it is a lonely outpost rather than an inviting gateway to the world of plants and wildlife.

In the design shown here, a low deck nestles in a planting of trees, shrubs, and perennials. The plants provide shade and privacy as well as lovely flowers and foliage and the birds and other wildlife attracted to them. Conceived for a dry foothills site with a backyard that slopes down from the deck, the planting makes effective use of terrain where play areas are impractical and a manicured lawn or traditional garden beds are difficult to maintain. (The planting can easily be adapted for sites that are steeper or more level than the gradual slope shown here.)

The plants are chosen for their ability to thrive in the hot, dry conditions often found on sloping sites. California natives such as western redbud, manzanita, and ceanothus are joined by tough plants from other semiarid regions. There are flowers for much of the year, and a mixture of evergreen and deciduous foliage provides delightful colors and textures year-round. The planting makes a seamless transition to the surrounding cover of native grasses and wildflowers that naturally colonize such hillsides. Mow a path through this "volunteer" ground cover and extend the planting as far as you wish down the hill.

Western redbud **B**

'Twin Peaks' dwarf coyote brush **L**

Mexican bush sage **H**

Autumn sage **J**

Plants & Projects

You'll need to water young plants to get them established. But after a year or two, these durable perennials, trees, and shrubs will require infrequent supplemental watering and a minimum of care. Prune the shrubs (particularly the hop bushes and the butterfly bush) to keep them from overgrowing their neighbors. Shear the dwarf coyote brush each spring. Divide any perennials that become crowded.

A **Chitalpa** (use 1 plant)
This attractive deciduous tree has a wide crown of airy foliage and bears eye-catching clusters of ruffled pink or white flowers in early summer. See x *Chitalpa tashkentensis*, p. 125.

B **Western redbud** (use 3)
Tiny magenta flowers line the bare branches of this small multitrunked deciduous tree in spring. Bright green summer foliage turns yellow in fall. See *Cercis occidentalis*, p. 124.

C **Purple hop bush** (use 3)
Native to the Southwest, this tough evergreen shrub has bronze-green foliage that turns purple in winter. See *Dodonaea viscosa* 'Purpurea', p. 129.

D **'Julia Phelps' ceanothus** (use 4)
This popular evergreen shrub displays clusters of blue flowers against deep green foliage in spring. See *Ceanothus*, p. 123.

E **'Howard McMinn' manzanita** (use 7)
Lining the path, this evergreen shrub forms mounds of shiny dark green foliage. Small white to pink spring flowers produce red berries. See *Arctostaphylos densiflora*, p. 117.

F **'Black Knight' butterfly bush** (use 1)
This deciduous shrub makes a fountain-shaped clump of long arching stems. Clusters of dark purple flowers form at the ends of the stems from midsummer through fall. See *Buddleia davidii*, p. 120.

G **'Happy Wanderer' hardenbergia** (use 1)
The stems and distinctive bright green foliage of this evergreen vine twine around the deck railing. Bears pinkish purple flowers in late winter and early spring. See *Hardenbergia violacea*, p. 133.

H **Mexican bush sage** (use 8)
A shrubby perennial, its gray-green foliage contrasts nicely with the dark evergreen leaves of nearby plants. Long spikes of purple-and-white flowers bloom from late spring to fall. See *Salvia leucantha*, p. 150.

I **'Tuscan Blue' rosemary** (use 4)
The needlelike dark green leaves of this evergreen shrub add interesting texture to the planting. Small deep blue flowers appear in late winter and early spring. See *Rosmarinus officinalis*, p. 149.

J **Autumn sage** (use 11)
This bushy perennial's medium green leaves are topped from spring to fall with airy spikes of red flowers. Place two plants in each of the planters on the wide steps leading up to the deck. See *Salvia greggii*, p. 150.

K **'Yellow Wave' New Zealand flax** (use 4)
This evergreen perennial's colorful spray of swordlike leaves is topped in summer by tubular red flowers on tall stalks. See *Phormium tenax*, p. 144.

L **'Twin Peaks' dwarf coyote brush** (use 10)
The dense foliage of this low, spreading evergreen shrub makes a fine ground cover. See *Baccharis pilularis*, p. 118.

M **Path**
A path mowed through the native grasses and wildflowers on the hillside will be easier to maintain than a path of wood chips or other loose material.

Chitalpa **A**

'Black Knight' **F**
butterfly bush

'Happy **G**
Wanderer'
hardenbergia

'Yellow Wave' **K**
New Zealand flax

Purple **C**
hop bush

H Mexican
bush sage

E 'Howard McMinn'
manzanita

J Autumn sage

M Path

D 'Julia Phelps'
ceanothus

'Tuscan Blue' **I**
rosemary

'Howard McMinn' **E**
manzanita

SITE: Sunny

SEASON: Early summer

CONCEPT: A pleasing
mix of durable plants
integrates a low deck
with its hillside
surroundings.

House

Deck

J

J

Planters

C

C

G

K

H

B

I

L

D

A

F

I

K

B

I

J

E

H

M

D

L

B

H

E

J

1 square = 1 ft.

Native grasses
and wildflowers

VARIATIONS ON A THEME

Imaginative plantings completely integrate each of these decks with their surroundings.

This marvelous deck appears to hover above a lush forest glade. Evergreen shrubs create the illusion of a natural setting.

A successful deck-side planting is a treat when viewed from the deck.

Skirting a shady deck

This design also integrates the deck with its surroundings, but it does so in a shadier environment, produced perhaps by large trees nearby. Small western redbud trees and native toyon shrubs create privacy and a comforting sense of enclosure on the deck. Lower-growing shrubs and ferns form an evergreen understory beneath the trees and look good viewed from the deck or the path. Open ground between the massed shrubs, mulched and planted with a scattering of native island alumroot, gives the planting an open, airy feel.

Peak bloom is in spring, but the varied foliage is attractive year-round. As for the preceding design, these plants are chosen for their durability and low water needs once established. (The container plantings will need regular watering.)

Plants & Projects

Ⓐ Toyon (use 4 plants)
This upright evergreen shrub or small tree displays clusters of small white flowers against its glossy deep green foliage in early summer. Bright red berries follow and attract birds. See *Heteromeles arbutifolia*, p. 134.

Ⓑ Oregon grape (use 7)
The distinctive coarse foliage of this evergreen shrub is tinged red when new and turns purplish in cold winters. Clusters of yellow early-spring flowers produce edible blue berries. See *Mahonia aquifolium*, p. 140.

Ⓒ 'Yankee Point' Carmel creeper (use 9)
This evergreen shrub forms a low, spreading mound of dark green foliage. Bears small clusters of blue flowers in spring. See *Ceanothus griseus* var. *horizontalis*, p. 123.

Ⓓ Sword fern (use 10)
An evergreen fern, its dark green fronds are coarsely divided and glossy. They're an effective screen for the space under the deck. See Ferns: *Polystichum munitum*, p. 131.

Ⓔ Feather reed grass (use 10)
This grass forms leafy upright clumps that are evergreen in areas where winters are mild and turn beige in cold weather. Tall stalks are topped by flowers and seeds from late spring on. Planted when the toyon are young, the clumps of grass will die out as the shrubs expand. See *Calamagrostis* x *acutiflora* 'Stricta', p. 142.

Ⓕ Island alumroot (use 21)
This evergreen perennial forms spreading mounds of distinctive foliage. In summer, clusters of small flowers float above the foliage on narrow stalks. Look for a California native cultivar, such as 'Wendy'. See *Heuchera maxima*, p. 134.

Ⓖ 'Palace Purple' heuchera (use 5)
A popular cultivar, its attraction is striking purple-bronze maple-like leaves rather than its tiny flowers. See *Heuchera*, p. 134.

Ⓗ Planters
Large wooden containers on the pads leading up to the deck are planted with small shrubs and perennials. 'Alaska' azalea offers white flowers and evergreen foliage (1 per box; see *Rhododendron*, p. 149). 'Gulf Stream' heavenly bamboo is an upright shrub with lacy colorful evergreen foliage (1 per box; see *Nandina domestica*, p. 141). For color and texture at the feet of these shrubs, plant 'Palace Purple' heuchera in open spaces.

See p. 52 for the following:

Ⓘ Western redbud (use 2)

Ⓙ Path

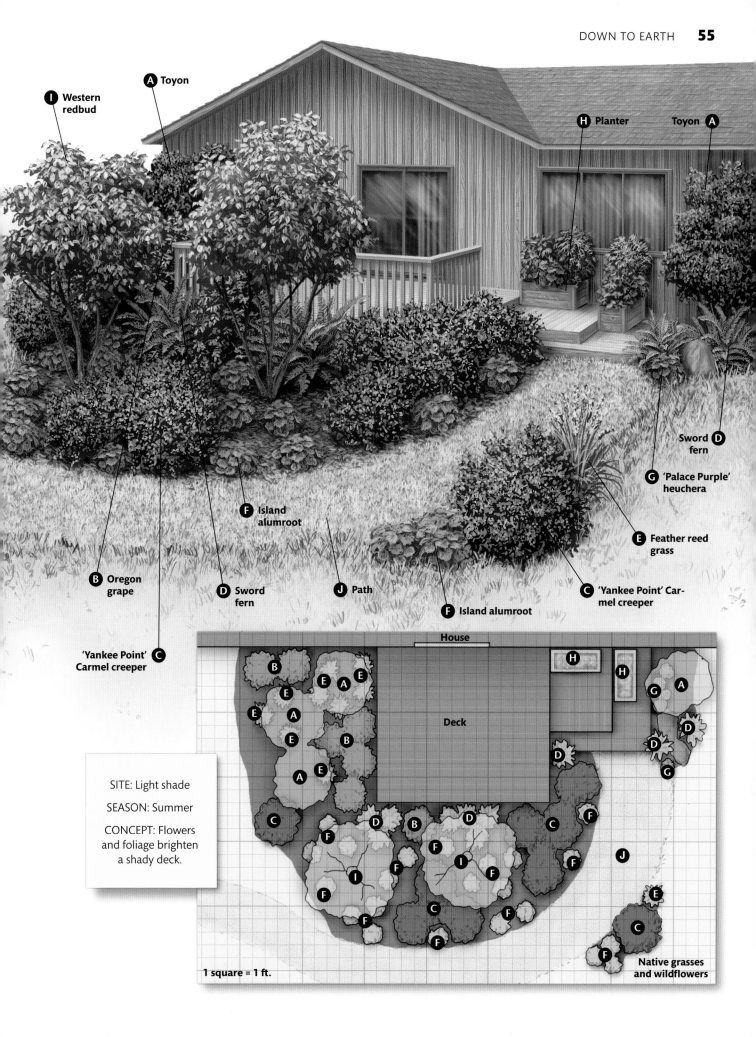

I Western redbud

A Toyon

H Planter

Toyon **A**

Sword fern **D**

G 'Palace Purple' heuchera

E Feather reed grass

F Island alumroot

D Sword fern

J Path

F Island alumroot

C 'Yankee Point' Carmel creeper

B Oregon grape

C 'Yankee Point' Carmel creeper

SITE: Light shade

SEASON: Summer

CONCEPT: Flowers and foliage brighten a shady deck.

House

Deck

1 square = 1 ft.

Native grasses and wildflowers

Garden in the Round

CREATE A PLANTING WITH SEVERAL ATTRACTIVE FACES

In domestic landscapes, plantings are often meant to be viewed from the front, rather like a wall-mounted sculpture in raised relief. However, the planting shown here forms a peninsula jutting into the lawn. Because you can walk around most of the bed, plants can be displayed "in the round," presenting different scenes from several vantage points. This is an excellent option for those who want to squeeze more gardening space from a small lot, add a touch of interest to a rectangular plot, or break up a large, open area into smaller "outdoor rooms."

A bed like this (or its close cousin, the island bed, which floats free of any anchors) requires a sensitivity to scale. To be successful, the bed must neither dominate its surroundings nor be lost in them. The plants here, with their bold forms and textures, have presence when viewed from a distance, while also providing pleasure upon closer inspection. We've shown a patio, but the planting on its own could easily fit into another landscape scheme.

Plants & Projects

Palms set a tropical tone here, reinforced by the saucer-size flowers of the hibiscus. The planting offers flowers and foliage that look good year-round. Where winters are colder, you could substitute rose-of-Sharon (*Hibiscus syriacus*) for the tropical hibiscus and cut-leaf Japanese maples (*Acer* species) for the palms, training one as a low-growing shrub.

Ⓐ King palm (use 1 plant)
This stately palm has distinctive arching, feathery fronds. Choose a multitrunked specimen. See Palms: *Archontophoenix cunninghamiana*, p. 143.

Ⓑ Pygmy date palm (use 1)
Echoing its taller relative, this palm has softer fronds. Choose a multitrunked plant to complement the king palm. See Palms: *Phoenix roebelinii*, p. 143.

Ⓒ 'Barbara Karst' bougainvillea (use 1)
This evergreen vine showcases striking bright red flowers against dense green foliage from late spring into winter. For support, tie stems to wires attached to the fence. See *Bougainvillea*, p. 119.

Ⓓ Tropical hibiscus (use 3)
This upright evergreen shrub displays large flowers against dark green leaves. Choose a compact cultivar with coral or salmon flowers, such as 'Santa Ana', shown here. See *Hibiscus rosa-sinensis*, p. 135.

Ⓔ 'Harbour Dwarf' heavenly bamboo (use 6)
The fine-textured evergreen leaves of this dwarf shrub change color each season. Fluffy clusters of white flowers in spring produce red berries that last into the winter. See *Nandina domestica*, p. 141.

Ⓕ Evergreen daylily (use 5)
This popular perennial produces a fresh batch of lovely flowers daily in summer. Leaves look good throughout the year. A dwarf cultivar with orange flowers suits this planting. See *Hemerocallis*, p. 134.

Ⓖ Dwarf plumbago (use 15)
With its wiry, spreading dark green foliage, this perennial makes a fine ground cover. Leaves are evergreen in mild-winter climates; they turn crimson after frost. Plant bears light blue flowers in summer and fall. See *Ceratostigma plumbaginoides*, p. 124.

Ⓗ Thrift (as needed)
Plant this perennial in the gaps between flagstones, out of traffic areas. Pink pom-pom-like flowers float above the grassy foliage from spring to fall. See *Armeria maritima*, p. 118.

Ⓘ Paving
Irregular flagstones set on a sand-and-gravel base make an informal patio. See p. 169.

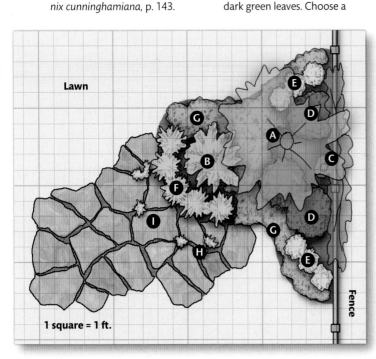

Lawn

1 square = 1 ft.

Fence

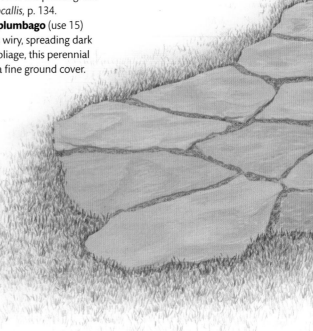

King palm **A**

Pygmy
date palm **B**

C 'Barbara Karst'
bougainvillea

SITE: Sunny

SEASON: Early fall

CONCEPT: Palms
accent a peninsular
planting offering lush
foliage and flowers.

E 'Harbour Dwarf'
heavenly bamboo

D Tropical
hibiscus

F Evergreen
daylily

I Paving

H Thrift

G Dwarf plumbago

VARIATIONS ON A THEME

Whether it is large or small, a garden you can stroll around offers multiple attractions.

A low, neatly trimmed hedge gives a formal feel to this garden-in-the-round. Placed in the center, a potted tree provides a surprising, but effective, focal point.

This peninsula garden makes imaginative use of different paving materials. A brick edging gives way to crushed gravel and wood. At the intersection of all three is a design created out of pebbles.

This walk-around island bed and the plants in it are just the right scale to fit comfortably in a small backyard.

A leafy peninsula

Displaying a range of striking grassy leaves, this planting has a semiarid or Mediterranean feel. Like the previous design, this one affords a variety of attractive views and can serve several ways in the landscape. With minor changes, for example, it could stand alone on a larger property as an island bed.

Foliage is the centerpiece of this garden, with purple, blue, and bronze leaves lending year-round color as well as vibrant textures. But there are knockout flowers, too. The exotic bird-of-paradise and striking bougainvillea blooms are on display for many months.

In keeping with the Mediterranean theme, and with today's water consciousness, these plants require little water beyond what nature provides.

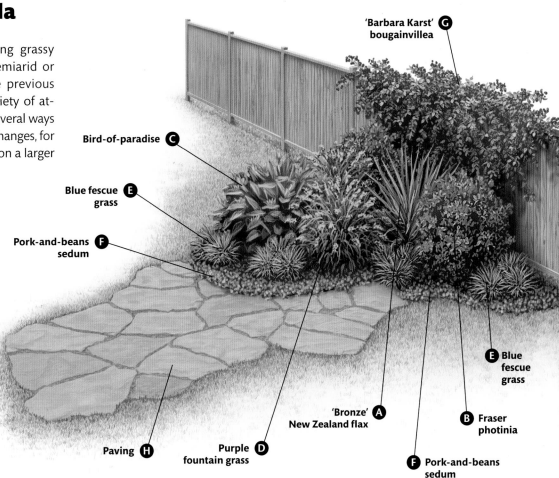

'Barbara Karst' **G** bougainvillea

Bird-of-paradise **C**

Blue fescue **E** grass

Pork-and-beans **F** sedum

E Blue fescue grass

'Bronze' **A** New Zealand flax

B Fraser photinia

Purple **D** fountain grass

Paving **H**

F Pork-and-beans sedum

Plants & Projects

A **'Bronze' New Zealand flax**
(use 1 plant)
This evergreen perennial forms an eye-catching clump of stiff, sword-shaped bronze leaves. In summer, tall stems bear clusters of red or yellow flowers. See *Phormium tenax*, p. 144.

B **Fraser photinia** (use 2)
White spring flowers and colorful foliage recommend this evergreen shrub. New leaves are bronze to bright red and appear all summer. Mature foliage is shiny deep green. See *Photinia x fraseri*, p. 145.

C **Bird-of-paradise** (use 1)
Known for its exotic flowers, this evergreen perennial also produces an attractive clump of stiff leathery leaves. Blooms year-round, heaviest in spring. See *Strelitzia reginae*, p. 152.

D **Purple fountain grass** (use 2)
This perennial forms a fine-textured clump of arching

reddish leaves topped in summer and fall by fluffy spikes of purple flowers and seeds. See *Pennisetum setaceum* 'Rubrum', p. 142.

E **Blue fescue grass** (use 18)
Tufts of thin blue-green leaves make a neat edging along the the front of the planting. This perennial grass sends up narrow spikes of flowers in early summer. See *Festuca ovina* var. *glauca*, p. 142.

F **Pork-and-beans sedum**
(as needed)
This low-growing evergreen perennial ground cover forms a mat of small succulent reddish bronze leaves that look like jelly beans. Bears reddish yellow flowers in late winter. See *Sedum rubrotinctum*, p. 151.

See p. 56 for the following:

G **'Barbara Karst' bougainvillea**
(use 1)

H **Paving**

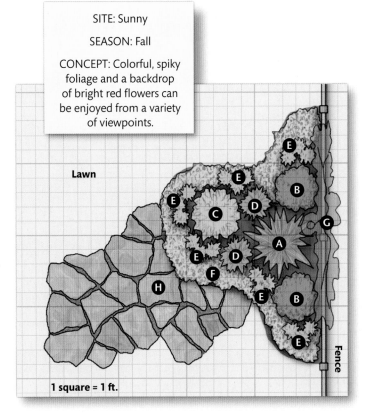

SITE: Sunny

SEASON: Fall

CONCEPT: Colorful, spiky foliage and a backdrop of bright red flowers can be enjoyed from a variety of viewpoints.

Lawn

1 square = 1 ft.

Fence

Landscape a Low Wall

A TWO-TIER GARDEN AND PATIO REPLACE A BLAND SLOPE

Some things may not love a wall, but plants and gardeners do. For plants, walls offer warmth for an early start in spring and good drainage for roots. Gardeners appreciate the rich visual potential of composing a garden on two levels, as well as the practical advantage of working on two relatively flat surfaces instead of a single sloping one.

This design places a mixed border of shrubs and perennials above a paved, informal patio and niche plantings. The upper bed presents a colorful array of flowers and foliage when viewed from the patio or from the house. (You can easily extend the planting along the wall.) Rapidly growing chitalpas will knit a shady canopy of branches and foliage over much of the patio. Fragrant gardenias will draw visitors to the patio if the shade doesn't. The planting niches, one formed by the wall, two others notched into the corners of the patio, help tie the entire design together. (To provide a better view, we have omitted one corner niche from the rendering. It is indicated on the site plan by the canopy of its tree.)

Building the wall that makes this impressive sight possible doesn't require the time or skill it once did. Nor is it necessary to scour the countryside for tons of fieldstone or to hire an expensive contractor. Thanks to precast retaining-wall systems, anyone with a healthy back (or access to energetic teenagers) can install a knee-high do-it-yourself wall in as little as a weekend or two.

1 square = 1 ft.

Lawn

Lawn

Corner niche

Note: This tree canopy represents another corner niche, planted same as the one at left.

SITE: Sunny

SEASON: Late spring

CONCEPT: A low retaining wall, a patio, and two-level plantings turn a sloped area into an outdoor living room.

Purple coneflower F

Annuals I

Plants & Projects

This planting offers months of flowers in pinks, blues, and whites, with splashes of golden yellow. Annuals complement and extend the flowering display, and there's handsome foliage all year. Water regularly for best results.

A 'Pink Dawn' chitalpa (use 3 plants)
This fast-growing deciduous tree casts a cooling shade on the patio. Beginning in late spring, large clusters of pink flowers bloom for weeks at the tips of the branches. See x *Chitalpa tashkentensis*, p. 125.

B 'Veitchii' gardenia (use 5)
This evergreen shrub is covered from spring to fall with fragrant white flowers. Space plants closely to form a solid mass of foliage in the niche. See *Gardenia jasminoides*, p. 132.

C 'China Doll' rose (use 6)
Rounded mounds of leathery green leaves display lovely clusters of small pink double flowers from spring to autumn. See *Rosa*, p. 149.

D 'Nana' heavenly bamboo (use 4)
The fine-textured leaves of this dwarf evergreen shrub change colors with the seasons and turn fiery red in fall and winter. Fluffy white summer flowers are followed by red berries. See *Nandina domestica*, p. 141.

A 'Pink Dawn' chitalpa

A 'Pink Dawn' chitalpa

See site plan for H.

'China Doll' rose C

D 'Nana' heavenly bamboo

Daylily E

J Retaining wall and steps

K Patio

I Annuals

'Peter Pan' G agapanthus

I Annuals

B 'Veitchii' gardenia

E Daylily (use 7)

A durable perennial with grassy foliage and cheerful flowers. Choose a low-growing, long-blooming cultivar like 'Stella d'Oro', shown here. See *Hemerocallis*, p. 134.

F Purple coneflower (use 8)

This perennial's large purple flowers rise on stiff leafy stalks for weeks in late summer. See *Echinacea purpurea*, p. 129.

G 'Peter Pan' agapanthus (use 5)

Clumps of arching foliage are topped by dis-

tinctive ball-shaped clusters from late spring into summer. A perennial, it is evergreen in warm-winter areas. See *Agapanthus*, p. 115.

H Thrift (use 17)

The fine-textured grassy foliage of this evergreen perennial edges the upper bed. Bears spherical pink flowers in spring. See *Armeria maritima*, p. 118.

I Annuals

Planted in the ground and in pots, colorful annuals brighten the patio. Replant season-

ally for year-round variety. We've shown a mixture of pansies and snapdragons here.

J Retaining wall and steps

The low, precast retaining wall shown here is typical of those available at home and garden centers and local landscaping suppliers. See p. 176.

K Patio

Brick (shown here), interlocking pavers, or flagstones can all complement the wall and form a durable surface. See p. 170.

VARIATIONS ON A THEME

A low wall provides all sorts of gardening opportunities as well as eliminating the need to push a mower up and down a sloped lawn.

A small patio is incorporated into this retaining wall.

A Japanese maple

H Coralbells

A flagstone seat beckons from this foliage-covered wall.

It takes skill (or a great deal of patience) to make a flat wall with rounded fieldstones. A mix of roses, catmint, and New Zealand flax decorate the top bed, and yellow flowers add contrast below.

Plants & Projects

Ⓐ Japanese maple (use 3 plants)
This small deciduous tree is valued for its attractive form and delicate, deeply lobed leaves. We've shown the species (called a "seedling") rather than a cultivar. Many have reddish leaves in early spring that later turn green, and then bright red, orange, or yellow in autumn. See *Acer palmatum*, p. 114.

Ⓑ Bigleaf hydrangea (use 4)
Large, very showy clusters of blue, pink, or white flowers cover this deciduous shrub in summer. Cut back in late winter to control its size. See *Hydrangea macrophylla*, p. 136.

Ⓒ 'Alaska' evergreen azalea (use 5)
This evergreen shrub bears masses of white flowers in spring. Bushy plants are attractive when not in bloom. See *Rhododendron*, p. 149.

Ⓓ Variegated gardenia (use 4)
A low, spreading variety of the popular evergreen shrub. Gray-green leaves are tinged with white. Bears small white, very fragrant flowers in summer. See *Gardenia jasminoides* 'Radicans Variegata', p. 132.

Ⓔ Leatherleaf fern (use 7)
Lush and green, but with airy foliage, this evergreen fern contrasts handsomely with

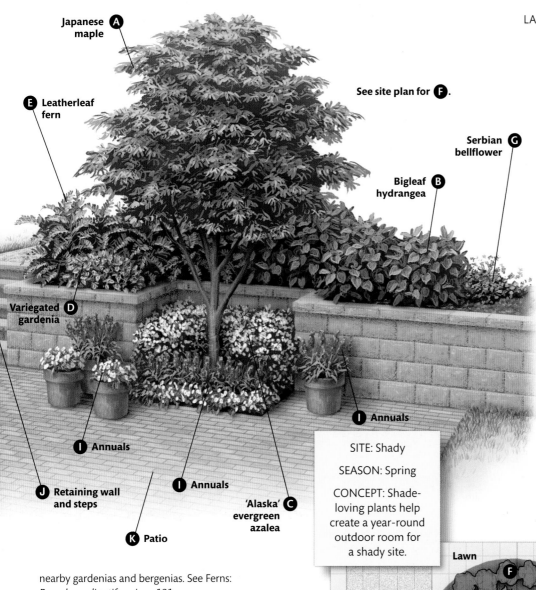

Japanese maple **A**

E Leatherleaf fern

See site plan for **F**.

Serbian bellflower **G**

Bigleaf hydrangea **B**

Variegated gardenia **D**

I Annuals

I Annuals

J Retaining wall and steps

I Annuals

'Alaska' evergreen azalea **C**

K Patio

SITE: Shady

SEASON: Spring

CONCEPT: Shade-loving plants help create a year-round outdoor room for a shady site.

Two tiers in the shade

A retaining wall and patio garden can be equally alluring in a shady backyard. This design echoes the one on the preceding pages, but with shade-tolerant trees, shrubs, and perennials instead of sun lovers. With no need to produce shade, the trees are smaller, providing interesting forms draped in colorful foliage. There are flowers nearly year-round, highlighted by the striking displays of evergreen azaleas in spring and hydrangeas in summer. The intensely fragrant gardenias are less flamboyant but equally compelling. As in the previous design, evergreen foliage and seasonal plantings of annuals make the patio an attractive spot all year.

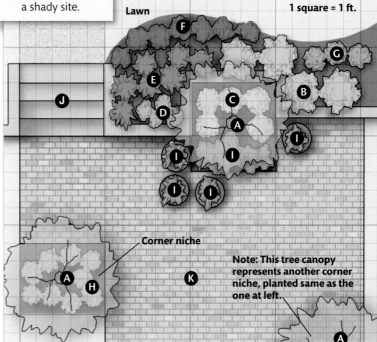

Lawn

1 square = 1 ft.

Corner niche

Note: This tree canopy represents another corner niche, planted same as the one at left.

nearby gardenias and bergenias. See Ferns: *Rumohra adiantiformis*, p. 131.

F **Winter-blooming bergenia** (use 7)

This low-growing evergreen perennial's large dark green leaves edge the upper bed year-round. Stalks bearing spikes of pink flowers rise above the leaves in January and February. See *Bergenia crassifolia*, p. 119.

G **Serbian bellflower** (use 3)

A perennial, this forms a low-growing mat of small heart-shaped leaves. Spikes of star-shaped lavender-blue flowers float above the foliage in spring. See *Campanula poscharskyana*, p. 122.

H **Coralbells** (use 18)

Planted beneath maples in the two corner niches, these perennials offer attractive evergreen foliage. In spring, pink flowers dangle above the foliage from wiry stems. See *Heuchera*, p. 134.

I **Annuals**

Planted in the ground and in pots to add color. Here we show stocks in mixed colors, edged with violas.

See p. 61 for the following:

J **Retaining wall and steps**

K **Patio**

Beautify a Blank Wall

A VERTICAL GARDEN MAKES THE MOST OF A NARROW SITE

Just as you can enhance a wall in your home with a painting, you can decorate a blank wall outdoors with plants. The design shown here transforms a nondescript front entrance by showcasing perennials, ferns, shrubs, and a small tree against an adjacent garage wall. Such entrances are common in suburban homes, but a vertical garden like this is ideal for other spots where yard space is limited.

Selected for a shady site, these plants offer something in every season. Most are evergreen, with foliage that looks fresh year-round. In fall, the maple's yellow leaves brighten the entrance.

The garden is at its flowering peak in early spring. The fragrant white flowers of tobira in spring and gardenia in summer greet visitors by the corner of the garage and at the front door. Adorning the wall are lovely camellias. The wall also serves as a backdrop for the striking red twigs of the coralbark maple, which highlight the graceful patterns of the tree's branches.

Camellia Ⓑ

'**Cream de Mint**' Ⓓ
tobira

Plants & Projects

Training the coralbark maple and the camellia are the most demanding aspects of this planting. As the maple grows, select horizontal branches that grow parallel to the wall and arch over the other plants. Prune to restrict growth toward the walk until the tree is tall enough that you can select branches to arch over the walkway. Train the camellia by attaching it to wire supports fixed to the wall. Prune the foliage so that it extends about 18 in. from the wall.

Ⓐ **Coralbark maple** (use 1 plant)
The fine-textured foliage of this small deciduous tree is light green in summer and yellow in fall. Its bright red twigs are eye-catching in winter and spring before the tree leafs out. See *Acer palmatum* 'Sango Kaku', p. 114.

Ⓑ **Camellia** (use 1)
Trained flat against the wall, the glossy foliage of this popular evergreen shrub is an ideal backdrop for its lovely flowers. Choose a cultivar with flower color and bloom time you like. Here, we've shown the pink-flowered, early-spring-blooming 'Debutante'. See *Camellia japonica*, p. 120.

Ⓒ '**August Beauty' gardenia** (use 1)
This evergreen shrub's intensely fragrant white flowers perfume the entry in summer. Its shiny dark green foliage looks good year-round. See *Gardenia jasminoides*, p. 132.

Ⓓ '**Cream de Mint' tobira** (use 3)
Low-growing, with white-edged leaves, this dwarf evergreen shrub bears small clusters of fragrant creamy white flowers in early spring. See *Pittosporum tobira*, p. 146.

Ⓔ **Sword fern** (use 2)
A native of redwood forests, this evergreen fern forms a neat mound of shiny dark green fronds, just right for this narrow space. See Ferns: *Polystichum munitum*, p. 131.

Ⓕ **Hosta** (use 3)
Prized for its handsome foliage, this perennial also produces lavender, purple, or white flowers in summer. For this spot, choose a small cultivar with green or variegated foliage. See *Hosta*, p. 135.

Ⓖ **Lenten rose** (use 1)
This perennial has attractive toothed evergreen leaves and bears pink, rose, green, or white flowers on branched stems in early spring. See *Helleborus orientalis*, p. 133.

Ⓗ **Lamium** (use 21)
Two cultivars of this perennial ground cover are used here. Both have green-and-white foliage that is evergreen where winters are mild. 'White Nancy', with white flowers in

SITE: Shady

SEASON: Early spring

CONCEPT: Handsome plants arrayed against a blank wall make a picture that pleases year-round.

summer, edges the front and end of the bed. 'Roseum' is planted at the back, between the sword ferns, where its rose-colored flowers catch the eye from late winter through fall. See *Lamium maculatum*, p. 138.

H Lamium

C 'August Beauty' gardenia

G Lenten rose

A Coralbark maple

E Sword fern

H Lamium

F Hosta

Driveway

Garage

B

H

H

E

E

A

C

H

D

H

F

H

G

H

House

Front door

1 square = 1 ft.

Walkway

Lawn

VARIATIONS ON A THEME

Running out of garden space? Here are some ideas to help you garden up as well as out.

Some climbing roses are capable of scaling great heights with the help of a trellis. Notice how the trellis continues above the windows. The roses will soon follow.

A giant stand of sunflowers is a playful way to decorate a wall. And birds can feast on the sunflower seeds in the fall.

Climbing pink and red roses produce a colorful abstract pattern on a clapboard wall.

Dressing up a sunny wall

A sunnier, hotter site, such as a south- or west-facing wall, calls for a different palette of plants. The basic idea of this design remains the same as before: incorporate wall space to make the best use of a narrow plot.

Arrayed on a handsome wooden trellis, the star of this planting is a vigorous bougainvillea. From spring through summer its hot pink flowers glow against the dense green foliage. The supporting cast of plants holds its own with a summer-long display of flowers in yellow, lilac, purple, and white. In spring and fall a dwarf pomegranate takes center stage with bright orange flowers and yellow foliage. After all this color, the planting offers enough foliage that is evergreen, or nearly evergreen, to make a handsome display in winter.

Plants & Projects

Ⓐ Fortnight lily (use 3 plants)
This striking perennial forms a clump of straplike evergreen leaves. Wiry stems bear white flowers with colorful markings from spring through fall. See *Dietes vegeta*, p. 129.

Ⓑ Dwarf pomegranate (use 1)
A dwarf deciduous tree, it makes a mound of shiny green leaves that turn yellow in autumn. Bright orange flowers in spring produce small inedible red fruits. See *Punica granatum* 'Nana', p. 146.

Ⓒ Bougainvillea (use 1)
A vigorous vine with hot pink flowers against a dense backdrop of evergreen. Train a vining type to a trellis. (In colder areas, substitute *Clematis montana*.) See *Bougainvillea*, p. 119.

Ⓓ Garden penstemon (use 3)
This perennial forms a patch of leafy upright stems topped from late spring to frost by distinctive tubular flowers that are available in a wide range of colors; coordinate your choice with the color of your wall. (In colder areas, substitute *Echium fatuosum*.) See *Penstemon gloxinioides*, p. 144.

Garden penstemon **D**

F Snow-in-summer

Fortnight lily **A**

See site plan for **H**.

I Trellis

G Star of Persia

C Bougainvillea

B Dwarf pomegranate

'Moonbeam' **E** coreopsis

E **'Moonbeam' coreopsis** (use 8)
A perennial, its neat mound of fine-textured, dark green foliage is covered for months in summer and fall with small bright yellow flowers. See *Coreopsis verticillata*, p. 127.

F **Snow-in-summer** (use 11)
The silvery evergreen foliage of this perennial will brighten the corner by the door. In early summer, small white flowers completely cover the low-growing foliage. See *Cerastium tomentosum*, p. 124.

G **Star of Persia** (use 12)
Eye-catching spherical clusters of rich lilac flowers hover above this bulb's straplike leaves in early summer. See Bulbs: *Allium christophii*, p. 121.

H **Round-headed garlic** (use 72)
With long, thin leaves and smaller clusters of red-purple flowers, this bulb is attractive but less spectacular than star of Persia. See Bulbs: *Allium sphaerocephalum*, p. 121.

I **Trellis**
You can support the bougainvillea with the homemade trellis shown here, or buy one at a garden center. See p. 186.

SITE: Sunny

SEASON: Summer

CONCEPT: Basking against a sunny wall, a vine, perennials, and shrubs offer a warm welcome at the front door.

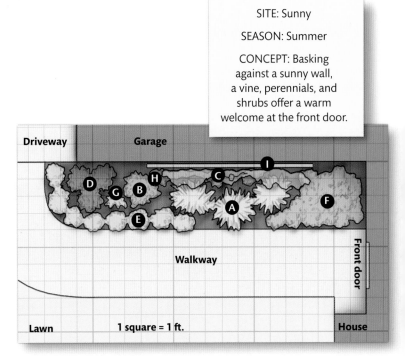

Driveway   Garage

D   H   C   I

G   B

A   F

E

Walkway

Front door

Lawn   1 square = 1 ft.   House

A No-Mow Slope

A TERRACED PLANTING TRANSFORMS A STEEP SITE

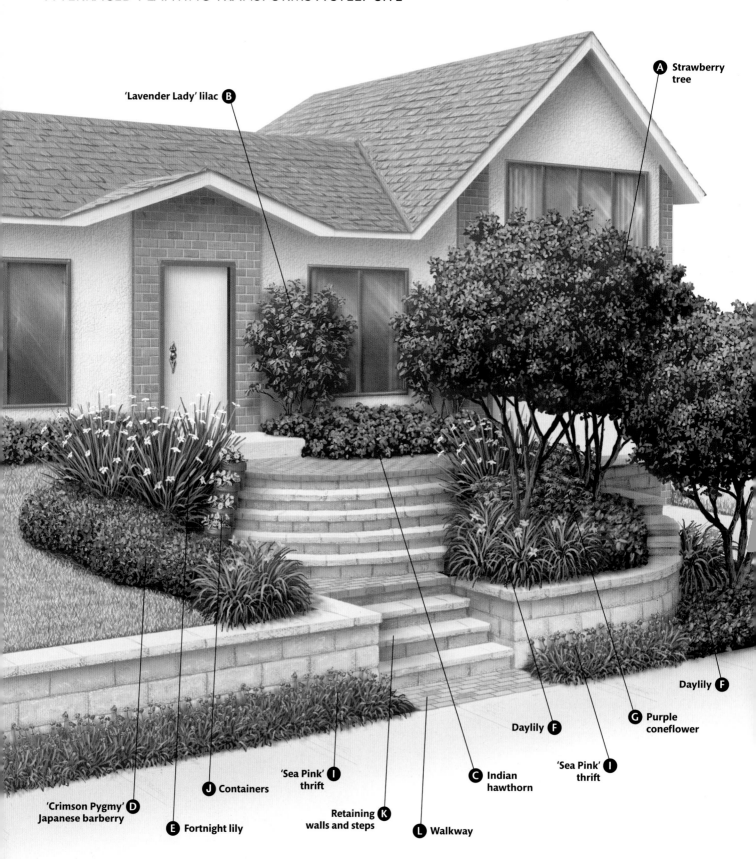

A Strawberry tree

'Lavender Lady' lilac B

D 'Crimson Pygmy' Japanese barberry

E Fortnight lily

J Containers

I 'Sea Pink' thrift

K Retaining walls and steps

L Walkway

C Indian hawthorn

F Daylily

I 'Sea Pink' thrift

G Purple coneflower

F Daylily

Steep slopes can be a landscaping headache. Planted with lawn grass, they're a chore to mow, and they can present problems of erosion and maintenance if you try to establish other ground covers or plantings. One solution is shown here—tame the slope with low retaining walls and steps, and plant the resulting flat (or flatter) beds with attractive trees, shrubs, and perennials.

Steep slopes near the house are common in many California hillside communities. Here, a narrow, steeply sloping front yard has been terraced with low retaining walls and wide steps, creating extra space for plants. The result transforms the home's

public face and creates an enticing path to the front door.

Visitors approaching from the sidewalk pass through colorful plantings. A set of wide curving steps framed by landings above and below encourages a slow passage, offering time to enjoy the nearby plants. The walk from the drive to the front door is more direct, but no less pleasant. Near the house, you can extend the foundation shrubs along the house or tie them into existing plantings. For houses with steep backyards, the lawn can provide a play area. Or, you might replace the lawn with an easy-care alternative ground cover.

Plants & Projects

Reshaping the slope and building the hardscape (retaining walls, steps, and walkways) is a big job. Even if you plan to do much of the work yourself, it is prudent to consult a landscape contractor for advice. Once the plants are established, this design will provide years of enjoyment with little more than seasonal pruning and cleanup.

Ⓐ Strawberry tree (use 3 plants) This multitrunked evergreen tree with gnarly branches offers shiny leaves and attractive bark. Small bell-shaped white flowers are followed by red fruits in autumn and winter. See *Arbutus unedo*, p. 117.

Ⓑ 'Lavender Lady' lilac (use 2) Bred to bloom well in mild-winter areas, this deciduous shrub bears sweetly fragrant lavender flowers in spring. See *Syringa vulgaris*, p. 152.

Ⓒ Indian hawthorn (use 10) From fall to spring, this evergreen shrub showcases small flowers against rich green foliage. Pick a low-growing cultivar such as 'Jack Evans', which bears light pink flowers. See *Rhaphiolepis indica*, p. 147.

Ⓓ 'Crimson Pygmy' Japanese barberry (use 5) The purple foliage of this low, spreading deciduous shrub turns crimson in fall, making a colorful edge to the planting. See *Berberis thunbergii*, p. 118.

Ⓔ Fortnight lily (use 4) This perennial forms an eye-catching clump of straplike evergreen leaves. Colorfully marked white flowers top wiry stems from spring through fall. See *Dietes vegeta*, p. 129.

Ⓕ Daylily (use 10) The cheerful, fresh flowers of this perennial greet visitors. Choose a long-blooming yellow-flowered cultivar such as 'Stella d'Oro'. See *Hemerocallis*, p. 134.

Ⓖ Purple coneflower (use 4) With coarse green foliage and bold purple daisylike flowers, this perennial is a good companion for the nearby daylilies and fortnight lilies. Blooms many weeks in summer. See

Echinacea purpurea, p. 129.

Ⓗ Dwarf plumbago (use 7) A sprawling perennial ground cover, its light green foliage turns maroon after a frost. Bears indigo blue flowers in summer. See *Ceratostigma plumbaginoides*, p. 124.

Ⓘ 'Sea Pink' thrift (use 15) This perennial forms tufts of grassy evergreen foliage. It produces a spring display of pink flowers and scattered bloom into fall. You can extend the planting along the wall. See *Armeria maritima*, p. 118.

Ⓙ Containers Make seasonal plantings in four 12-in. terra-cotta pots, one on each curved step. Yellow and blue pansies are shown here for spring.

Ⓚ Retaining walls and steps The walls and steps are made with a pre-cast concrete retaining-wall system available at garden centers. See p. 176.

Ⓛ Walkway Choose a surface that complements your house. Here a brick walkway echoes brick details on the house. See p. 164.

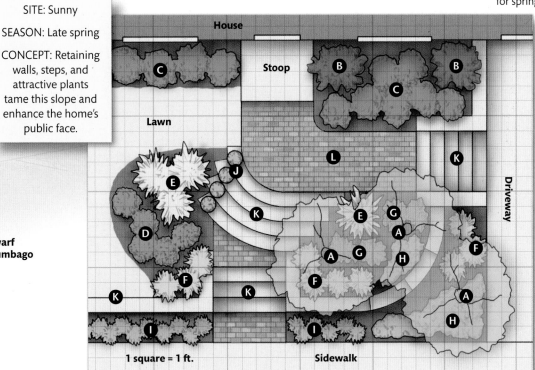

SITE: Sunny

SEASON: Late spring

CONCEPT: Retaining walls, steps, and attractive plants tame this slope and enhance the home's public face.

Ⓗ Dwarf plumbago

House

Stoop

Lawn

Driveway

1 square = 1 ft.

Sidewalk

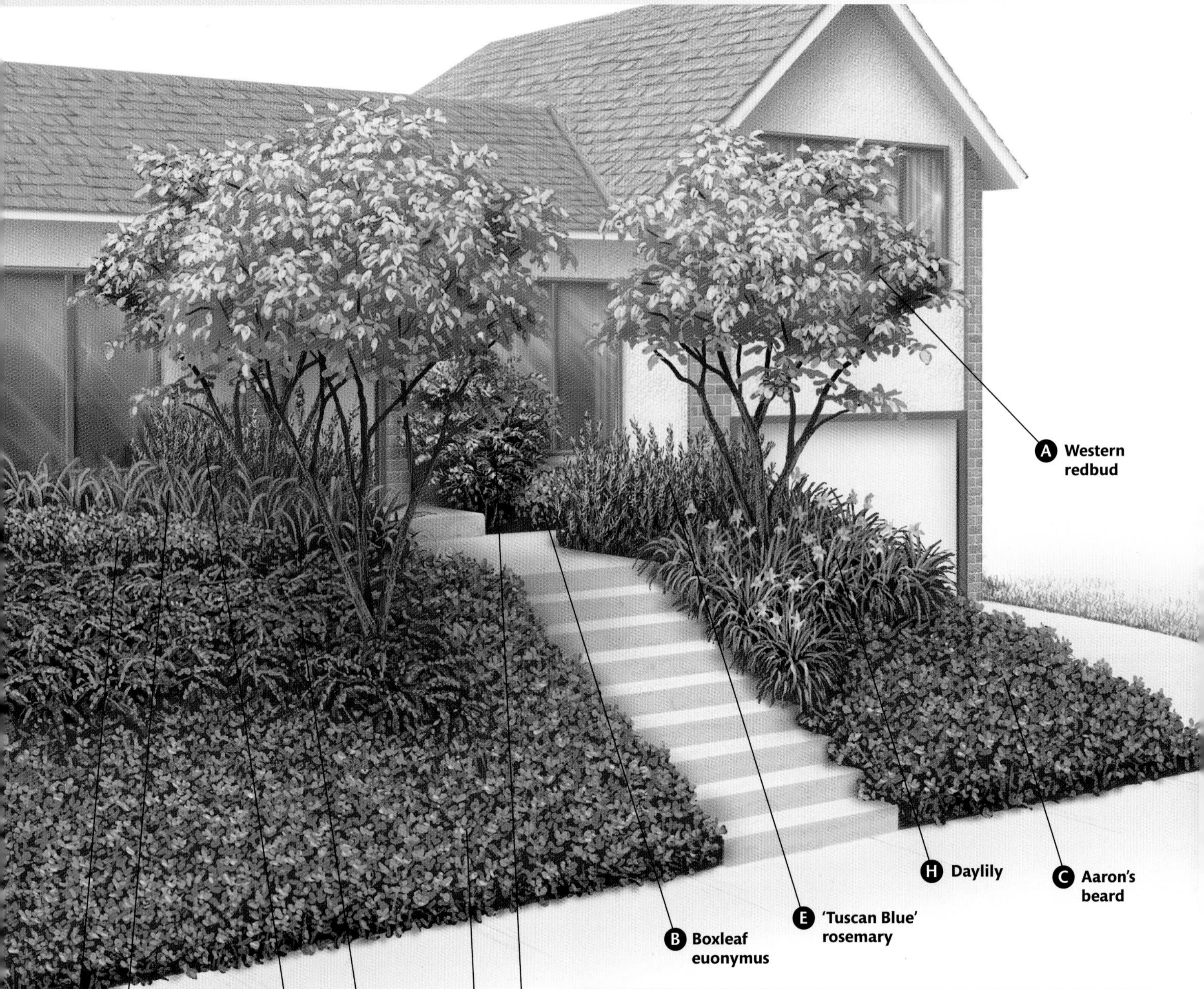

A Western redbud

H Daylily

C Aaron's beard

E 'Tuscan Blue' rosemary

B Boxleaf euonymus

'Tuscan Blue' E rosemary

Aaron's C beard

Rock D cotoneaster

'Nanho Blue' F butterfly bush

G Agapanthus

B Boxleaf euonymus

SITE: Sunny

SEASON: Fall

CONCEPT: Tough but attractive plants make a colorful, easy-care front yard on a sloping site.

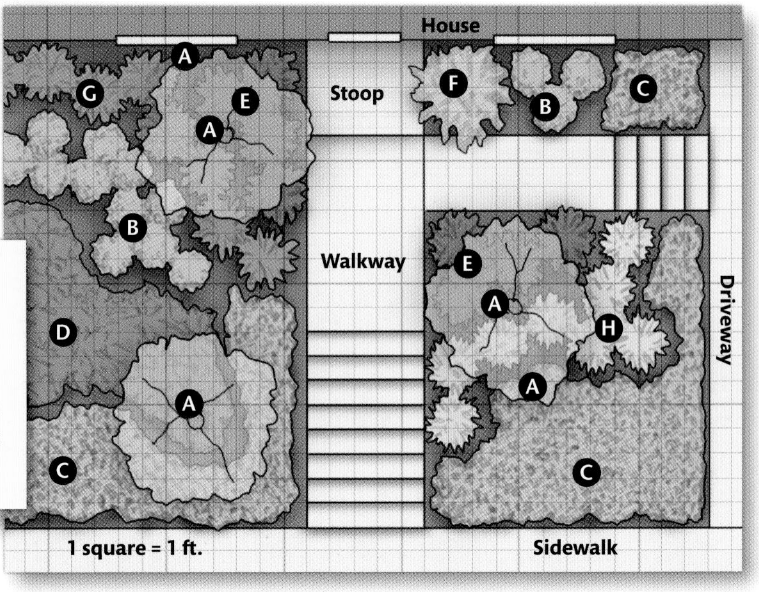

House

Stoop

Walkway

Driveway

Sidewalk

1 square = 1 ft.

Working with a hillside

If terracing a steep slope with retaining walls and steps does not appeal to you, or is beyond your budget, consider this design. Here we've worked with the existing hillside, replacing turfgrass with tough, easy-care ground covers. Small trees provide dappled shade as well as a modest level of privacy from street and sidewalk traffic.

These plants thrive in the poor, dry soil and the heat often found on slopes. Their tenacious root systems, particularly those of Aaron's beard and rock cotoneaster, will hold the soil in place. With the exception of the butterfly bush by the door, these plants require infrequent supplemental watering once they're established.

The planting is as attractive as it is durable. Flowers bloom almost year-round, beginning with the tiny reddish flowers of the redbuds and extending through a late-winter display of deep blue rosemary blossoms. Butterflies hovering over the butterfly bush are an added treat. The varied textures of the foliage are pleasing year-round. And the fall colors of the redbuds and rock cotoneaster are a delight.

Plants & Projects

Ⓐ Western redbud (use 3 plants)
This small California native deciduous tree is well suited to dry hillside conditions. In spring, leafless branches bear small magenta flowers. Foliage is yellow in fall. See *Cercis occidentalis*, p. 124.

Ⓑ Boxleaf euonymus (use 14)
This compact evergreen shrub has small, glossy green leaves. See *Euonymus japonicus* 'Microphyllus', p. 130.

Ⓒ Aaron's beard (as needed)
A low, vigorously spreading ground cover, this evergreen shrub bears large, bright yellow flowers in summer. Space plants 1½ ft. apart for solid coverage. See *Hypericum calycinum*, p. 136.

Ⓓ Rock cotoneaster (as needed)
This wiry deciduous shrub is another tough ground cover. Dark green leaves turn orange and red in fall. New leaves appear quickly. Bears white to pink flowers in spring. Showy red berries follow. Plant 5 ft.

apart, or closer for quicker coverage. See *Cotoneaster horizontalis*, p. 128.

Ⓔ 'Tuscan Blue' rosemary (use 8)
An upright evergreen shrub, it offers fragrant foliage and deep blue flowers in late winter and early spring. See *Rosmarinus officinalis*, p. 149.

Ⓕ 'Nanho Blue' butterfly bush (use 1)
A compact form of the popular deciduous shrub, ideal next to the door. Its arching stems bear spikes of fragrant blue flowers from midsummer to fall. See *Buddleia davidii*, p. 120.

Ⓖ Agapanthus (use 7)
This perennial makes a handsome clump of straplike evergreen leaves topped in late spring and summer with ball-shaped clusters of small blue or white flowers. See *Agapanthus orientalis*, p. 115.

See p. 69 for the following:

Ⓗ Daylily (use 8)

VARIATIONS ON A THEME

The possibilities for attractive plantings on a slope are endless. Similar in approach to the designs shown in the renderings, those shown below employ different plants and hardscape just as effectively.

Low-growing shrubs in shades of gray, green, and purple cover the hillside in this large-scale rock garden. Lavender, santolina, and rosemary are shown here. Narrow evergreen trees provide a vertical accent near the house.

Intermingled with mounding plants, these long, low steps suit the site perfectly.

Poolside Pleasures

PRIVACY PLANTINGS ENHANCE YOUR SWIMMING POOL

Californians love being in and around water, and swimming pools are an increasingly common backyard amenity. On a suburban lot, a pool is often the dominant backyard presence. Too often, however, the backyard pool is little more than an aquatic gym surrounded by a slab of concrete and lawn.

This design shows that a planting of trees, shrubs, and perennials and a little hardscaping can work magic to enhance all your outdoor activities, whether you're escaping with a book, entertaining friends, working in the garden, or playing in the pool. (The rendering shows the design as seen from the house, which is indicated on the plan.)

Tall shrubs on the perimeter heighten the sense of enclosure and privacy provided by the fence, which building codes usually require around a pool. The paving surrounding the pool extends at each end to accommodate a table and chairs for entertaining and recliners for relaxing. An arbor creates a little niche along one side. Low-growing plants lining the surround add color and texture to the setting. And there's still ample lawn for playing games and lounging.

Plants & Projects

The plants in this design are chosen not only for their year-round good looks, but also because they are well-behaved around a pool. All are low-maintenance evergreens that hold on to their foliage throughout the year, producing as little litter as possible. You won't be fishing leaves out of the water as you would with deciduous trees and shrubs.

Ⓐ 'Majestic Beauty' Indian hawthorne (use 5) Trimmed into small trees with overlapping crowns, these evergreen shrubs are decorated with huge clusters of fragrant pearl-pink flowers in spring. Choose single-trunked shrubs for this planting. See *Rhaphiolepis indica* 'Majestic Beauty', p. 147.

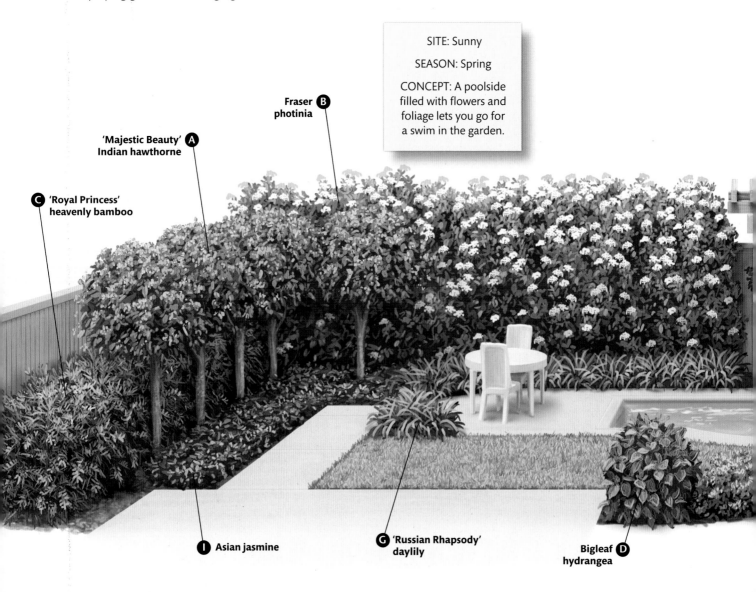

SITE: Sunny

SEASON: Spring

CONCEPT: A poolside filled with flowers and foliage lets you go for a swim in the garden.

Fraser photinia **Ⓑ**

Ⓐ 'Majestic Beauty' Indian hawthorne

Ⓒ 'Royal Princess' heavenly bamboo

Ⓘ Asian jasmine

Ⓖ 'Russian Rhapsody' daylily

Bigleaf **Ⓓ** hydrangea

B **Fraser photinia** (use 15)
Growing 8 ft. tall and 6 ft. wide, these naturally rounded shrubs overlap to form a coarse dark-leafed hedge. In spring, they form a solid bank of white flowers. Note that one is trained flat to the wall as a decorative backdrop for the arbor. See *Photinia x fraseri*, p. 145.

C **'Royal Princess' heavenly bamboo** (use 19)
Airy reddish green foliage covers this narrow, upright evergreen shrub. It bears small pink flowers in spring and summer. See *Nandina domestica*, p. 141.

D **Bigleaf hydrangea** (use 2)
A rounded deciduous shrub clothed in large, deep green, leaves and huge, ball-shaped flowers through summer. Varieties abound in blue, pink, or white flowers. See *Hydrangea macrophylla*, p. 136.

E **Sasanqua camellia** (use 3)
This evergreen shrub produces lovely flowers from late fall into winter. Choose from a range of colors. See *Camellia sasanqua*, p. 120.

F **Pink azaleas** (use 7)
Masses of pink flowers cover this compact slightly spreading shrub in spring. Small dark green leaves are attractive all year. See *Rhododendron*, p. 149.

G **'Russian Rhapsody' daylily** (as needed)
This grassy perennial is bright green and topped with showy purple flowers in summer. Plant about 12 in. apart for a seamless poolside fringe. See *Hemerocallis*, p. 134.

H **Winter-blooming bergenia** (as needed)
Large round leaves with wavy margins distinguish this evergreen perennial. Pink flowers form on short thick spikes in winter. Plant the clumps 18 in. apart for a continuous border. See *Bergenia crassifolia*, p. 119.

I **Asian jasmine** (as needed)
A dense, sprawling ground cover with small, dull green leaves and star-shaped white flowers. For complete coverage in a season, plant on 12 in. centers. See *Trachelospermum asiaticum*, p. 153.

J **Arbor**
Easily built, this attractive structure provides a central focal point and a welcome sun screen by the pool. See p. 188.

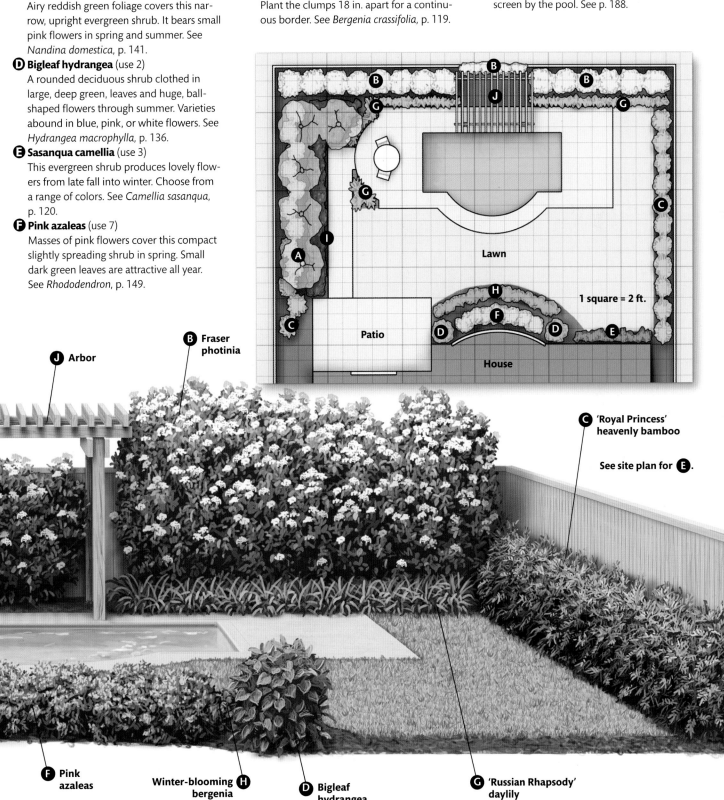

1 square = 2 ft.

Lawn

Patio

House

J Arbor

B Fraser photinia

C 'Royal Princess' heavenly bamboo

See site plan for **E**.

F Pink azaleas

H Winter-blooming bergenia

D Bigleaf hydrangea

G 'Russian Rhapsody' daylily

Private haven

This design has a different look than the previous one, but it accomplishes the same goal: integrating a backyard pool into a larger outdoor living space.

Here, spectacular hedges surround the pool like thick, luxuriant drapes. They create a lush backdrop as well as privacy for pool activities; they can also screen an unsightly building from view.

Once again, evergreen foliage predominates. In summer, there are flowers in cool blues and whites. In winter, red camellias and orange kumquats are lively accents. Gardenia, sweet olive, pittosporum, and Asian jasmine ensure lovely fragrance for many months.

Plants & Projects

A Fraser photinia (use 3)
These small trees wear a dense canopy of glossy oval leaves. Small white flowers bloom for weeks in spring. See *Photinia x fraseri*, p. 145.

B Shrubby yew pine (use 21)
This columnar tree makes a fine-textured, fairly dense hedge that may eventually reach 15 ft. tall. Evergreen foliage is flat and needlelike. It grows right to the ground and is soft to the touch. See *Podocarpus macrophyllus*, p. 146.

C Pittosporum (use 8)
This fast-growing shrub will quickly form a dense screen of large, glossy, evergreen leaves that showcase clusters of sweetly scented white flowers from spring into summer. See *Pittosporum undulatum*, p. 146.

D Sweet olive (use 2)
This evergreen shrub retains its compact, vase-shaped habit as it grows. Leaves are small, glossy, and dark green. Spring flowers are inconspicuous but very fragrant. See *Osmanthus x fortunei*, p. 143.

E 'Yuletide' sasanqua camellia (use 4)

SITE: Sunny

SEASON: Spring

CONCEPT: Colorful, lush, and fragrant plants increase poolside pleasures.

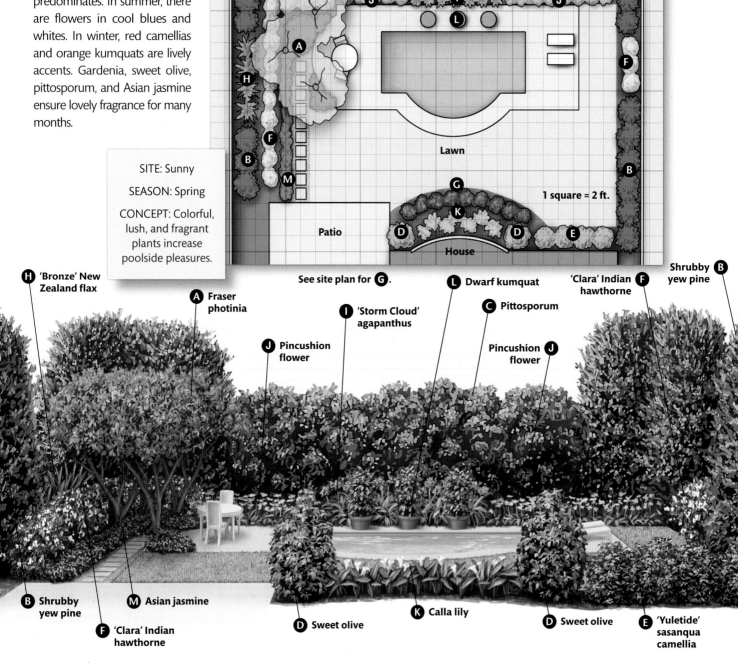

1 square = 2 ft.

This evergreen shrub has single red flowers that bloom abundantly in winter among lustrous small green leaves. See *Camellia sasanqua*, p. 120.

F **'Clara' Indian hawthorne**
(use 16)
A beautiful compact evergreen shrub bearing bright green leaves, red new growth, and clusters of small white flowers in spring, followed by blue berries. See *Rhaphiolepis indica*, 'Clara', p. 147.

G **Gardenia** (use 9)
Sweetly fragrant white flowers open over a long period in spring on this low, spreading, evergreen shrub See *Gardenia jasminoides*, p. 132.

H **'Bronze' New Zealand flax**
(use 4)
This bold perennial forms a clump of spiky, bronzy red, straplike leaves and makes a striking backdrop to the photinia. See *Phormium tenax* 'Bronze', p. 144.

I **'Storm Cloud' agapanthus**
(use 7)
Big clusters of blue flowers top 4 ft. stalks that rise above this evergreen perennial's fountain of dark foliage. See *Agapanthus* 'Storm Cloud', p. 115.

J **Pincushion flower** (use 13)
This perennial has soft-textured gray-green foliage topped with wiry-stemmed blue flowers from spring through fall. Plant 2 ft. apart for a continuous fuzzy carpet. See *Scabiosa caucasia*, p. 150.

K **Calla lily** (use 7)
Large, pure white flowers unfurl from tall stalks above this perennial's dark glossy foliage. The center of each tubular flower is decorated with an erect yellow spike. See *Zantedeschia aethiopica*, p. 155.

L **Dwarf kumquat** (show 3)
A delightful container plant, this evergreen tree produces a heavy crop of orange, sweet and sour fruit from October to May. See *Citrus*, p. 126.

See p. 73 for the following

M **Asian jasmine (as needed)**

VARIATIONS ON A THEME

These three approaches to landscaping around swimming pools have one thing in common: the designs take their cue from the landscapes in which they are set.

A whitewashed wall and gray to deep green foliage plants help to blend this poolside planting with the natural vegetation beyond it.

Plantings and an arbor keep their distance in framing this pool and lawn.

The landscape below can be admired while you're floating in the water.

A Beginning Border

FLOWERS AND A WALL MAKE A TRADITIONAL DESIGN

A perennial border can be one of the most delightful of all gardens. Indeed, that's usually its sole purpose. Unlike many other types of landscape plantings, a traditional border is seldom yoked to any function beyond that of providing as much pleasure as possible.

Using durable plants that are easy to establish and care for, this border is designed for a beginning or busy gardener. Behind the planting, providing a solid backdrop, is a simple wall. The border is meant to be viewed from the front, so taller plants go at the back. Draped over the wall, a trumpet vine adds a swath of dark green leaves to the backdrop, dappled for weeks in late summer with lovely deep pink flowers.

The planting offers a selection of flowers in blues, reds, pinks, and purples. Blooming over many months, there are small flowers borne in spiky clusters as well as bright cheerful daisies.

The garden's foliage is at least as compelling as its flowers. A range of textures and colors contrast with and complement one another. At the back of the planting, the striking spiky purple leaves of New Zealand flax contrast with the bushy green mound of the autumn sage. These plants are in turn framed by lacy masses of silver-gray foliage. Similar juxtapositions of color and texture are repeated on a smaller scale at the front of the planting.

If you want a larger border, just plant more of each plant to fit the space, or repeat parts of the design.

'Atropurpureum' Ⓐ
New Zealand flax

Mexican Ⓑ
bush sage

Sunrose Ⓛ   'Powis Castle' Ⓖ   'Burgundy' Ⓚ
artemisia   gazania

Plants & Projects

Removing spent flowers and seasonal pruning are the main chores here. (To allow for maintenance, leave a space between the plants at the front of the border and those at the back, as shown on the site plan.) In winter, cut the gaura and Russian sage almost to the ground; cut the germander sage back by one-third; and prune the trumpet vine to control its size. Once established, the plants require little supplemental water.

Ⓐ **'Atropurpureum' New Zealand flax** (use 1 plant)
A bold, colorful accent, this

perennial offers long, reddish purple, straplike leaves to create a dramatic effect. From late spring to midsummer, branched stalks of reddish flowers rise above the foliage. See *Phormium tenax*, p. 144.

Ⓑ **Mexican bush sage** (use 1)
This perennial forms a billowy mass of silver-gray foliage. It bears long spikes of velvety purple-and-white flowers from midsummer into fall. See *Salvia leucantha*, p. 150.

Ⓒ **Gaura** (use 1)
Another wispy perennial, its graceful arching stems bear

small leaves and spikes of small pink and white flowers from spring through fall. See *Gaura lindheimeri*, p. 132.

Ⓓ **Autumn sage** (use 5)
This bushy perennial's green foliage bristles with striking spikes of red flowers from spring into fall. See *Salvia greggii*, p. 150.

Ⓔ **Russian sage** (use 1)
From early summer into fall, small lavender-blue flowers float amidst this perennial's airy clump of stiff gray-green stems and sparse silvery foliage. See *Perovskia atriplicifolia*, p. 144.

Ⓕ **'Mme. Galen' trumpet vine** (use 1)
This vigorous deciduous vine bears large compound leaves on thick stems. Showy clusters of salmon flowers bloom in late summer. Stake it the first year; after that its aerial rootlets will cling to the wall. See *Campsis x tagliabuana*, p. 122.

Ⓖ **'Powis Castle' artemisia** (use 3)
This perennial makes a mound of lacy silver foliage that looks good year-round. It is an excellent companion for the colorful gazania and New Zealand flax. See *Artemisia*, p. 118.

F 'Mme. Galen' trumpet vine

SITE: Sunny

SEASON: Early summer

CONCEPT: Easy-care perennials with colorful flowers and foliage make this border ideal for beginning and busy gardeners alike.

E Russian sage

C Gaura

J Blue marguerite

D Autumn sage

I 'Majestic' lilyturf

H Germander sage

H **Germander sage** (use 1)
Forming a low, spreading mass of small silvery leaves, this perennial bears wispy spikes of bright blue flowers from summer into fall. See *Salvia chamaedryoides*, p. 150.

I **'Majestic' lilyturf** (use 3)
This evergreen perennial makes a clump of grassy dark green leaves topped by tall spikes of purple flowers in summer. See *Liriope muscari*, p. 139.

J **Blue marguerite** (use 3)
Cheerful blue daisies nod above the spreading foliage of this perennial throughout the

year (if you deadhead them). See *Felicia amelloides*, p. 130.

K **'Burgundy' gazania** (use 4)
This perennial produces large reddish purple daisies in late spring and early summer. Dark green foliage looks good for months. See *Gazania*, p. 132.

L **Sunrose** (use 3)
Small, bright-colored flowers sparkle in spring and early summer on the evergreen foliage of this small shrub. Choose a cultivar with red flowers and green leaves for this design. See *Helianthemum nummularium*, p. 133.

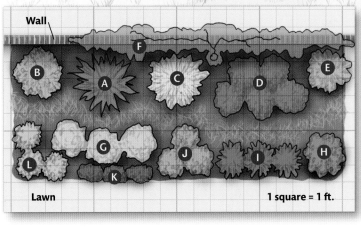

Wall

Lawn

1 square = 1 ft.

Mixing it up

In a mixed border, shrubs join perennials, broadening the plant palette and the border's possibilities. Where winters are cold and perennials die back after hard frosts, shrubs provide interest while the perennials are dormant. However, for gardeners in much of California, mixing shrubs and perennials in a border simply adds interest to borders that are already year-round performers. This planting shares the color scheme of the preceding design. Flowers in pinks, blues, and purples bloom for many months against a backdrop of handsome foliage in shades of silver, gray, and green. The contrasts in form and texture are perhaps less dramatic than those in the previous design. But the result is no less lovely.

Plants & Projects

Ⓐ 'Edward Goucher' abelia (use 1 plant)
An evergreen shrub with abundant rosy purple flowers from early summer to frost. Glossy foliage turns bronze-purple in winter. Flowers attract butterflies and hummingbirds. See *Abelia* x *grandiflora*, p. 114.

Ⓑ Cape mallow (use 1)
Small pink hollyhock-like flowers grace this fast-growing evergreen shrub for many months (year-round where winters are mild). See *Anisodontea* x *hypomandarum*, p. 116.

Ⓒ 'Rubens' clematis (use 1)
A deciduous vine, trained on wires attached to the wall. Fragrant pink flowers bloom in late spring. See *Clematis montana*, p. 126.

Ⓓ 'Autumn Joy' sedum (use 3)
This perennial forms clumps of fleshy gray-green leaves topped with flat flower clusters that turn from light pinkish green

in summer to russet seed heads in fall. See *Sedum*, p. 151.

Ⓔ Siberian iris (use 2)
Prized for its elegant spring flowers, this perennial's graceful narrow leaves look good for many months. A purple-flowered cultivar will look best here. See *Iris sibirica*, p. 137.

Ⓕ Salvia (use 3)
A perennial topped with numerous spikes of tiny flowers from early summer through fall. Flowers range from purple to blue depending on cultivar. See *Salvia* x *superba*, p. 150.

Ⓖ Garden penstemon (use 5)
Prized for leafy spikes of showy tubular flowers, this perennial blooms from late spring to frost if deadheaded. See *Penstemon gloxinioides*, p. 144.

Ⓗ Aster (use 2)
This is a lower-growing long-blooming version of the popular perennial. It bears lilac-blue to purple flowers (depending

SITE: Sunny

SEASON: Fall

CONCEPT: Mixing perennials and shrubs increases possibilities for a border.

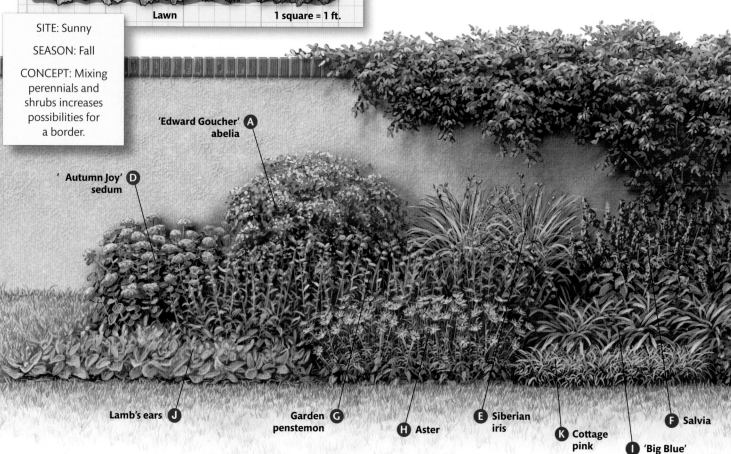

on the cultivar) from spring through fall if deadheaded. See *Aster x frikartii*, p. 118.

① **'Big Blue' lilyturf** (use 4)
This perennial forms a clump of grassy evergreen foliage and bears spikes of small blue flowers in summer. See *Liriope muscari*, p. 139.

① **Lamb's ears** (use 5)
The furry silver-gray leaves of this perennial are favorites of children. Bears stalks of small purple flowers in early summer. See *Stachys byzantina*, p. 152.

⑥ **Cottage pink** (use 2)
From late spring into fall, wonderfully fragrant light pink flowers rise above this perennial's mat of fine-textured, silvery evergreen foliage. See *Dianthus plumarius*, p. 128.

① **Dwarf plumbago** (use 6)
This perennial ground cover is covered with blue flowers in late summer and fall. See *Cerato-stigma plumbaginoides*, p. 124.

C 'Rubens' clematis

B Cape mallow

L Dwarf plumbago

VARIATIONS ON A THEME

Whether your taste runs to native plants or formal English perennial gardens, there are countless ways to create an attractive border.

Tall and short, bold and fine-textured plants mingle in this mixed border. Its glory is traditional—the display of beautiful flowers.

Ornamental grasses are a striking addition to a border and provide interest throughout the year.

An Outdoor "Living" Room

PATIO AND SHADY ARBOR PROVIDE OPEN-AIR OPPORTUNITIES

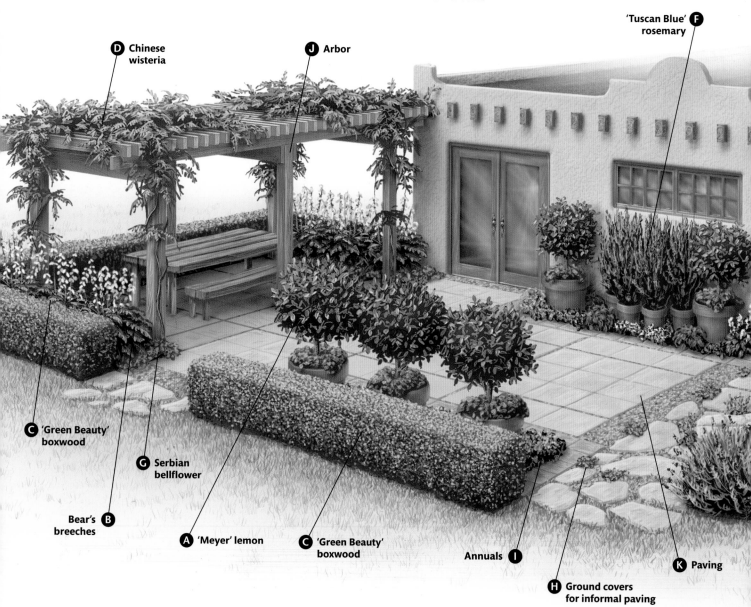

D Chinese wisteria

J Arbor

F 'Tuscan Blue' rosemary

C 'Green Beauty' boxwood

G Serbian bellflower

B Bear's breeches

A 'Meyer' lemon

C 'Green Beauty' boxwood

I Annuals

H Ground covers for informal paving

K Paving

In California, opportunities for year-round outdoor living abound. This design demonstrates how a patio next to the house can become a true extension of your living space with the addition of an arbor and plants that create an attractive setting.

At one end of a formal patio, a vine-covered arbor provides a shady, cool spot for dining or relaxing. At the opposite end, random paving and a seat-height curved wall invite informal gatherings when the heat of the day has passed.

A neatly trimmed boxwood hedge, clipped trees, and shrubs in terra-cotta pots reinforce the formality of the gridwork paving, while annuals and ground covers spilling onto the pavement soften the effect. Backing the curved seating wall, a loose hedge of rosemary is an informal echo of its boxwood counterpart. Easily accessed and viewed from the house, the arbor, patio, and plants nicely mingle the "indoors" with the "outdoors."

Scale is particularly important when you're landscaping near the house. This design can be adapted to suit houses and properties in a range of sizes. The gridwork patio can be altered by adding or removing rows of pavers. And the plantings can be extended or reduced along the edges.

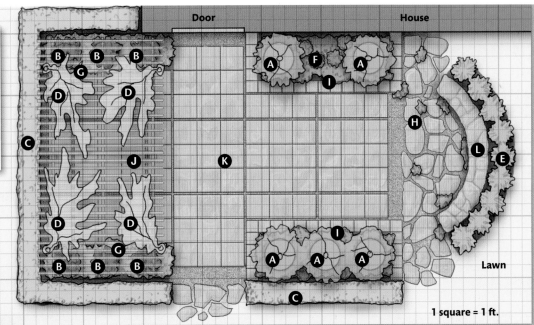

SITE: Sunny

SEASON: Summer

CONCEPT: Arbor, paving, and plants provide shade and a pleasant ambiance for outdoor relaxation and entertaining.

Door   House

Lawn

1 square = 1 ft.

L Seating wall

E 'Goodwin Creek Gray' lavender

Plants & Projects

The patio and arbor are sizable projects, but their rewards are large, too. Grow the lemon trees in 3-ft.-diameter terra-cotta pots, the rosemary in deep pots, 12 in. in diameter. Prune these plants to emphasize their natural shapes: a loose ball for the lemons, a narrow column for the rosemary. Keep the boxwood hedge neatly clipped. Train a single stem of each wisteria to twist up its arbor post.

A **'Meyer' lemon** (use 5 plants)
The evergreen foliage of these small trees showcases fragrant white flowers and tangy yellow fruits borne on and off all year. Bellflowers planted in the pots provide additional interest. See *Citrus*, p. 126.

B **Bear's breeches** (use 6)
As if this perennial's big, bold, deeply divided green leaves aren't striking enough, in late spring, spikes of white or deep pink flowers rise several feet above the foliage. See *Acanthus mollis*, p. 114.

C **'Green Beauty' boxwood** (use 20)
The small leaves and dense, compact habit of this evergreen shrub make it ideal for the formal, neatly clipped hedge edging the arbor. See *Buxus microphylla* var. *japonica*, p. 120.

D **Chinese wisteria** (use 4)
A vigorous deciduous vine with lacy leaves and clusters of fragrant purple, lavender, or white flowers in spring. See *Wisteria sinensis*, p. 155.

E **'Goodwin Creek Gray' lavender** (use 9)
This evergreen shrub's mounding gray foliage makes an attractive informal hedge. Bears spikes of blue flowers in early summer. See *Lavandula*, p. 138.

F **'Tuscan Blue' rosemary** (use 4)
Trim this evergreen shrub to a tall, narrow column. Foliage is aromatic; light blue flowers bloom in winter and spring, sometimes in fall. See *Rosmarinus officinalis*, p. 149.

G **Serbian bellflower** (use 31)
This spreading perennial is used as a ground cover and as an underplanting in the lemon tree pots (3 per pot). In spring and early summer, blue flowers float about a foot above the foliage on slender stalks. See *Campanula poscharskyana*, p. 122.

H **Ground covers for informal paving** (as needed)
Planted in the gaps between the flagstones, these perennials accent the informality of this end of the design. Snow-in-summer (*Cerastium tomentosum*, p. 124) has silver leaves and bears white flowers in early spring. Coralbells (*Heuchera*, p. 134) features neat tufts of round leaves topped from spring to late summer by red flowers. Creeping thyme (*Thymus praecox* ssp. *arcticus*, p. 153) withstands light foot traffic and smells good when you step on it.

I **Annuals** (as needed)
Change the plantings of annuals in the beds around the potted trees and shrubs for seasonal interest. In summer (the season shown here), try phlox, snapdragons, alyssum, and purple basil.

J **Arbor**
This large arbor is designed to serve as a sunscreen for the area beneath even without a foliage canopy. See p. 188.

K **Paving**
Use flagstone pavers, 24 in. square, in the formal area. Press rounded pebbles into the gaps between pavers for added interst. Irregular flagstones pave the informal area. See p. 170.

L **Seating wall**
This low wall provides seating and should be constructed with mortared fieldstone. If your budget doesn't allow hiring a mason, buy commercially made curved wooden or precast concrete benches.

VARIATIONS ON A THEME

Each of these outdoor rooms takes inspiration from our sunny region's distinctive architecture.

Several patio rooms extend along the side of this house. Crushed rock lined with flagstones makes a stunning centerpiece to the design.

Reminiscent of a desert oasis, this free-form pond is a wonderful addition to an extensive naturalistic Southwestern patio.

Cut-stone paving and steps set off mounds of striking plants.

A patio oasis

This design creates an outdoor room with the feel of a lush Southern California oasis. A small "grove" of queen palms is the most striking element. With their long arching fronds, the palms provide dappled shade as well as character. A tall yew hedge screens the patio from neighboring properties and creates a sense of enclosure, aided by a low mortared stone wall that doubles as casual seating. The flagstone paving is roomy enough for several groups of tables, chairs, and shade umbrellas. If you're ambitious, add a small pond and fountain to enhance the oasis theme.

Free-form beds wrap around the patio. Foliage is a year-round attraction here. Swaths of daylilies, with their broad, grassy leaves, complement the palm fronds. Mounding shrubs and perennials and carpet-forming ground covers add softer outlines. Flowers bloom for many months in a range of colors, including white, pale yellow, and blue. The fragrant flowers of the Natal plum are a heady enticement to linger on the patio.

Plants & Projects

Ⓐ Queen palm (use 5 plants)
Glossy green fronds arch from atop this fast-growing South American palm. See Palms: *Syagrus romanzoffianus*, p. 143.

Ⓑ 'Tuttle' Natal plum (use 5)
This evergreen shrub offers shiny dark green leaves, fragrant star-shaped flowers that bloom throughout the year, and bright red edible fruits. See *Carissa macrocarpa*, p. 123.

Ⓒ Irish yew (use 11)
A dense upright evergreen with small needles, it is clipped to form a solid dark green hedge about 6 ft. tall. See *Taxus baccata* 'Stricta', p. 152.

Ⓓ Santa Barbara daisy (use 7)
The airy foliage of this sprawling perennial is covered from late spring to fall with small white flowers. See *Erigeron karvinskianus*, p. 130.

Ⓔ Daylily (use 17)
A popular perennial with grassy foliage and short-lived but plentiful flowers. There are many lovely cultivars; the apricot and pale yellow varieties look good with this design. See *Hemerocallis*, p. 134.

F Alstroemeria (use 8)

This perennial forms a patch of erect leafy stems that bear striking azalealike flowers from spring to mid-summer. Choose from the long-blooming evergreen Meyer hybrids. See *Alstroemeria*, p. 116.

G 'Bronze Beauty' ajuga (use 30)

This durable perennial ground cover forms a bronzy green mat of evergreen leaves covered in spring and early summer with short spikes of tiny deep blue flowers. See *Ajuga reptans*, p. 115.

H Thrift (as needed)

Planted between flagstones at the edges of the paving, this perennial offers grassy evergreen leaves topped with rose, pink, or white flowers. Blooms heaviest in spring, scattered blooms until fall. See *Armeria maritima*, p. 118.

I Paving

Irregular flagstones on a sand-and-gravel base form the patio. See p. 170.

J Mowing strip

Flat, random-size fieldstones make a durable mowing strip around the beds. See p. 194.

See p. 81 for the following:

K Serbian bellflower (use 22)

L Creeping thyme (as needed)

M Seating wall

SITE: Sunny

SEASON: Summer

CONCEPT: Palms set the tone for an outdoor room with a tropical feel.

1 square = 1 ft.

C Irish yew

A Queen palm

B 'Tuttle' Natal plum

G 'Bronze Beauty' ajuga

I Paving

D Santa Barbara daisy

L Creeping thyme

K Serbian bellflower

E Daylily

D Santa Barbara daisy

B 'Tuttle' Natal plum

F Alstroemeria

M Seating wall

J Mowing strip

E Daylily

See site plan for **H** .

An Island Retreat

CREATE A FREESTANDING PATIO GARDEN

Patios and outdoor entertainment areas are often right next to the house. While this proximity has many advantages, it isn't always practical or most effective to graft a patio onto the house. The landscaped freestanding patio shown here offers more flexibility in planning and using your landscape. Place it to take advantage of a view or a particularly private spot on your property. Use it as a retreat from household hubbub. If you already have a deck or patio off the family room or kitchen, a free-standing area can help accommodate large gatherings, perhaps as an area for quiet conversation away from more raucous activities.

In this design, a small multitrunked tree and mid-height shrubs provide a sense of place and enclosure without walling out the surroundings. The wispy foliage of the gaura, artemisia, and rosemary, along with the blue fescue grass and the silvery lamb's ears, gives the planting a Mediterranean look. The design also provides a show of flowers year-round.

A freestanding patio garden like this one looks self-contained on paper, but like all landscape features, it looks and functions best when carefully correlated with other elements on your property. Transitions, both physical and visual, between major landscape features are particularly important. An expanse of lawn, changes of level that separate one area from another, or a planting that screens sight lines can all help different elements in your landscape coexist effectively.

'Marina' **A** arbutus

Japanese **F** anemone

'Palace Purple' **H** heuchera

Paving **L**

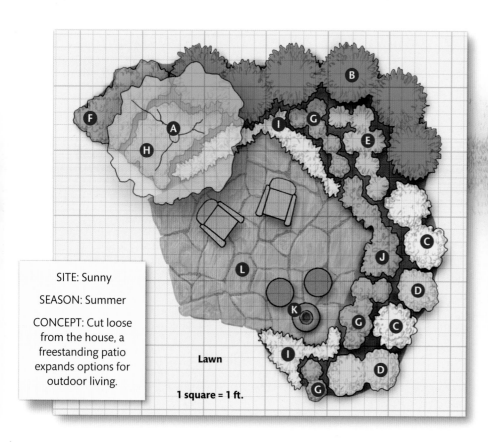

SITE: Sunny

SEASON: Summer

CONCEPT: Cut loose from the house, a freestanding patio expands options for outdoor living.

Lawn

1 square = 1 ft.

Plants & Projects

Installing the patio and preparing the planting beds are strenuous but not difficult work. (Install the patio first.) The plants can be set out in a weekend. Once the plants are established, you'll have very little to do beyond seasonal pruning, division when the perennials get crowded, and cleanup.

A **'Marina' arbutus** (use 1 plant)
This small multitrunked tree offers bell-shaped pink flowers in fall, red berries, and glossy evergreen leaves. Shiny, reddish bark is eyecatching, too. See *Arbutus*, p. 117.

B **'Majorca Pink' rosemary** (use 6)
An evergreen shrub with fragrant deep green foliage, it bears lavender-pink flowers in late winter and early spring. See *Rosmarinus officinalis*, p. 149.

C **'Iceberg' rose** (use 3)
This shrub rose displays fragrant white flowers against attractive green foliage. Blooms nearly all year. See *Rosa*, p. 149.

D **'Powis Castle' artemisia** (use 3)
A billowy mass of silver foliage makes this perennial a striking garden accent. See *Artemisia*, p. 118.

E **Gaura** (use 6)
Another wispy perennial, it forms a loose clump of small lance-shaped green leaves on arching stems. Pale pink-and-white flowers dot the foliage from spring through fall. See *Gaura lindheimeri*, p. 132.

F **Japanese anemone** (use 10)
This perennial forms a low clump of large, dark green leaves. Tall stems carry small daisylike flowers from late summer into fall. See *Anemone* x *hybrida*, p. 116.

G **Pincushion flower** (use 13)
Frilly light blue flowers adorn this perennial's neat mounds of airy foliage from late spring through fall. See *Scabiosa caucasica*, p. 150.

H **'Palace Purple' heuchera** (use 18)
A perennial grown for its distinctive purple foliage, which is shaped like small maple leaves. It bears tiny white flowers on tall thin stalks from spring into summer. See *Heuchera*, p. 134.

I **Blue fescue grass** (use 27)
This perennial forms mounds of thin blue-green leaves at the edge of the flagstones. Narrow flower spikes emerge from the clumps in early summer. See *Festuca ovina* var. *glauca*, p. 142.

J **Lamb's ears** (use 9)
Children can't resist touching this perennial's soft silver foliage. Plants form a low mat topped by purple flowers in early summer. See *Stachys byzantina*, p. 152.

K **Container plantings**
Plants in pots brighten up the patio with seasonal plantings of annuals or, as shown here, perennial scented geraniums. See *Pelargonium*, p. 144.

L **Paving**
Irregular flagstone pavers set on a sand-and-gravel base make a durable, informal patio. See p. 170.

B **'Majorca Pink' rosemary**

E Gaura

C **'Iceberg' rose**

Blue fescue grass **I**

Container plantings **K**

I **Blue fescue grass**

G **Pincushion flower**

J **Lamb's ears**

D **'Powis Castle' artemisia**

Oasis in the shade

This design allows you to make an outdoor living area in a shady spot anywhere on your property. As in the preceding design, this patio is bordered by mid-height shrubs and lower-growing perennials. The plants create a sense of enclosure and provide attractive companions when you're relaxing or entertaining on the patio.

While there are lovely flowers in spring and summer, the enduring attraction of this planting is its foliage. Largely evergreen, the leaves provide a pleasing variety of shapes and textures in a blend of greens that are tinged, at certain times of year, with other hues.

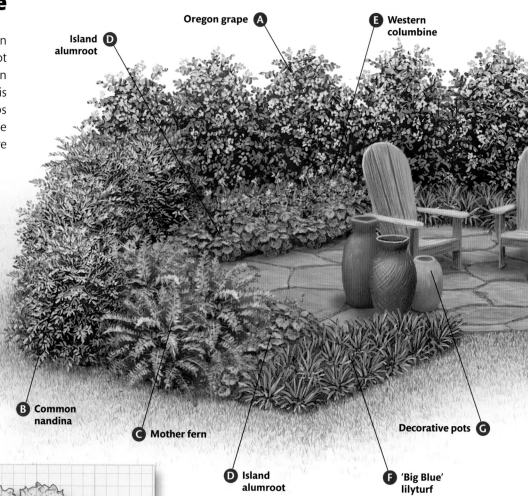

Oregon grape **A**

Island alumroot **D**

E Western columbine

B Common nandina

C Mother fern

D Island alumroot

Decorative pots **G**

F 'Big Blue' lilyturf

Lawn

SITE: Shady

SEASON: Early spring

CONCEPT: This patio garden makes the most of existing shade on your property.

Plants & Projects

A Oregon grape (use 6 plants) This spreading evergreen shrub offers distinctive, spiny foliage year-round. In spring it bears showy clusters of yellow flowers, which are followed by dark blue berries. New foliage is tinged with red. See *Mahonia aquifolium*, p. 140.

B Common nandina (use 7) An evergreen shrub, it has finely cut foliage that changes color with the seasons. Fluffy clusters of white flowers bloom in summer and produce long-lasting red berries. See *Nandina domestica*, p. 141.

C Mother fern (use 8) The light green fronds of this fern form an attractive airy mound. Evergreen where winters are mild. See Ferns: *Asplenium bulbiferum*, p. 131.

D Island alumroot (use 27) The dark, heart-shaped evergreen foliage of this native perennial is its main attraction. Tall stems bearing long clusters of tiny white or pink flowers rise above spreading mounds in early spring. See *Heuchera maxima*, p. 134.

B Common
nandina

C Mother fern

'Big Blue' **F**
lilyturf

H Paving

VARIATIONS ON A THEME

Both of these island retreats owe much of their charm to skillful color coordination between the hardscape and furniture and the plantings.

A cheerful informality pervades this cozy patio setting.

E **Western columbine** (use 8)
This native perennial produces striking red-and-yellow flowers from spring to early summer. The lacy mounds of foliage look good, too. See *Aquilegia formosa*, p. 117.

F **'Big Blue' lilyturf** (use 27)
Grown as a ground cover for its grassy, mounding evergreen foliage, this perennial also bears pretty spikes of small blue flowers in summer. See *Liriope muscari*, p. 139.

G **Decorative pots**
Place interesting pots or other decorative focal points on the patio, as shown here. Or add planted containers as described for the preceding design.

See p. 85 for the following:

H **Paving**

Informal plantings in subdued colors skirt a more formal patio and arbor, a combination that affords a range of entertainment options.

Backyard Makeover

GETTING A LOT OUT OF A SMALL, FROST-FREE LOT

Space is at a premium on many suburban lots, but this needn't cramp your outdoor living style. The design shown here makes use of the entire area in a small backyard to provide opportunities for open-air gatherings as well as family relaxation and play. (The rendering is shown as if viewed from the house, which is indicated on the plan.)

At the center is a large flagstone patio bordered by grassy verges where children can play or adults can kick off their shoes and recline. A continuous garden bed meanders along a privacy fence enclosing the lot. As the shade tree matures, its generous canopy will accommodate a table or recliners. To cater outdoor feasts, there's a barbecue. Across the patio, a small pool and fountain provide a cooling presence and the music of bubbling water.

Curving gently around the perimeter, the plantings comprise a pleasing array of trees, shrubs, and trellised vines. Several "boulders" add to the natural composition and provide a few extra places to sit.

Many of the plants originate in exotic parts of the world and are chosen for their proven performance in frost-free areas of California. South America's native tipu tree is a striking focal point, with long clusters of spring flowers and fine-textured foliage. Equally eyecatching are the diverse and sculptural palms, the extraordinary flowers of the tropical bird of paradise, and the flamboyant blossoms of dwarf ixora.

Plants & Projects

Ambitious do-it-yourselfers can install the entire design. If you're less energetic, have a landscaping service put in the hardscape and do the planting yourself. A layer of small river-washed rocks mulches the beds, complementing the look of the plants and helping to conserve water.

A Tipu tree (use 1)
Long clusters of yellow- to apricot-colored blossoms dangle among this small evergreen tree's fine-textured leaves in spring and early summer. Long seedpods add interest in autumn and winter. See *Tipuana tipu*, p. 153.

B Mediterranean fan palm (use 1)
This compact palm fits nicely under the tree and thrives in its shade. It forms a clump of trunks crowned with coarse blue-gray fronds, each looking

SITE: Sunny

SEASON: Spring

CONCEPT: A large patio and gorgeous plants make the most of a small backyard.

Tipu tree **A**

F Arabian jasmine

C Bottle palm

Bird of Paradise **H**

I 'Flower Carpet Pink' rose

I 'Flower Carpet Pink' rose

M Barbecue

J Annuals

Annuals **J**

'Thai Dwarf' ixora **E**

'Flower Carpet Pink' rose **I**

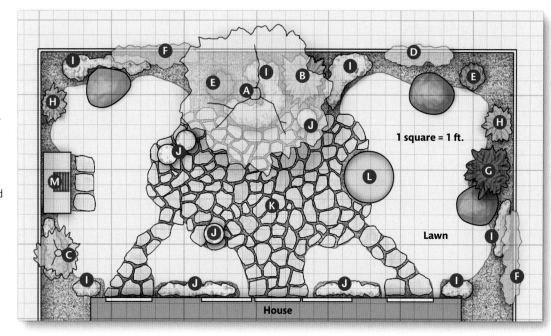

like a giant handheld fan. See
Chamaerops humilis, p. 125.

ⓒ Bottle palm (use 1)
Another palm with great structural appeal. The trunk starts swollen and then narrows before branching into a shaggy bright green crown. See *Nolina recurvata*, p. 141.

ⓓ 'New Gold' Bougainvillea
(use 1)
This vigorous climber is clothed in golden flowers spring and summer. Leaves add texture and color in winter. See *Bougainvillea*, p. 119.

ⓔ 'Thai Dwarf' ixora (use 2)
In a sheltered spot, this beautiful shrub promises a bounty of large colorful flowers. Evergreen foliage. See *Ixora* 'Thai Dwarf', p. 137.

ⓕ Arabian jasmine (use 2)
Two of these white-flowering vines are enough to perfume the entire backyard on summer nights. Evergreen. *Jasminum sambac*, p. 137.

ⓖ Madagascar palm (use 1)
This shrub produces a single thorned trunk topped with straplike dull green leaves. See *Pachypodium lamerei*, p. 143.

ⓗ Bird of Paradise (use 2)
An evergreen perennial that forms a wide clump of long-stemmed bluish green leaves and an abundance of large and unusual orange flowers. See *Strelitzia reginea*, p. 152.

ⓘ 'Flower Carpet Pink' rose
(use 13)
Shear this ground-cover rose once in winter to keep it compact and blooming vigorously. Forms a nearly continuous mass of pink. See *Rosa*, p. 149.

ⓙ Annuals
Grow your favorites in large pots and narrow beds next to the house to enliven the patio. Ivy geranium is shown here.

ⓚ Paving
Choose a flagstone that complements the color of your home. See p. 164.

ⓛ Water feature
A small fiberglass pool and a simple fountain add interest at a modest cost. See p. 172.

ⓜ Barbecue
You can install a custom grill of stone or adobe as shown here or use a moveable gas unit.

Desert vista

If you live in a dry, nearly frost-free climate, here's a small-backyard design that's as natural as your environment. Inspired by desert landscapes, the design uses striking plants that thrive in desert soils and need less water than the exotic plants too often grown in desert and semi-arid gardens.

The plantings are designed to complement an existing patio or deck off the house, as indicated on the plan. (The rendering shows a view from the house.) In place of a water-thirsty lawn, birds-eye gravel covers the entire area, providing a natural-looking setting for the desert plants.

The plants are grouped on two low, wide mounds, indicated by broken lines on the plan. Thorny ocotillos and cacti top the mounds with tropical bougainvilleas below, where they'll receive runoff from rainfall. Little supplemental watering will be needed after the plants are established.

The garden is at its most colorful in springtime, as shown here, when just about everything is in bloom. If the climate doesn't compel you outdoors, the blossoms will. When the summer heat bleaches most things gray, you'll still be able to enjoy splashes of gold bougainvillea and drifts of lavender lantana from your vantage point in the shade. In winter, the evergreen foliage of the palo verde and Mexican tree grass will contribute lush green color to the landscape.

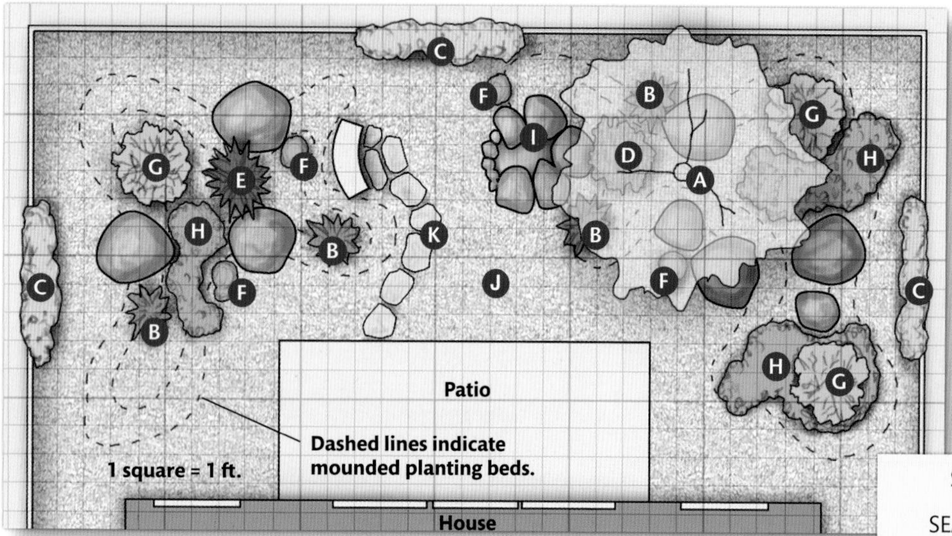

Plants & Projects

Ⓐ Blue palo verde (use 1)
This native desert tree is prized for its spectacular burst of yellow bloom in spring and its bluish branches and foliage. Evergreen in mild winter areas. See *Cercidium floridum*, p. 124.

Ⓑ Twin-flower agave (use 4)
This succulent forms a single rosette of narrow leaves about 3 ft. high. In spring it bears tall spikes of white flowers. See *Agave geminiflora*, p. 115.

Ⓒ 'New Gold' bougainvillea (use 2)
Unfazed by desert heat and aridity, this tropical vine covers the fence in a profusion of gold flowers and evergreen foliage. See *Bougainvillea*, p. 119.

Ⓓ 'Rosenka' bougainvillea (use 1)
Masses of flowers open gold and age to pink on this compact evergreen shrub. See *Bougainvillea*, p. 119.

Ⓔ Mexican grass tree (use 1)
This tropical-looking evergreen shrub forms a large fountain of narrow leaves that are completely unarmed, unlike many desert natives. See *Dasylirion longissima*, p. 128.

Patio

Dashed lines indicate mounded planting beds.

1 square = 1 ft.

House

Blue palo verde Ⓐ

SITE: Sunny

SEASON: Spring

CONCEPT: This desert garden will thrive in an arid climate.

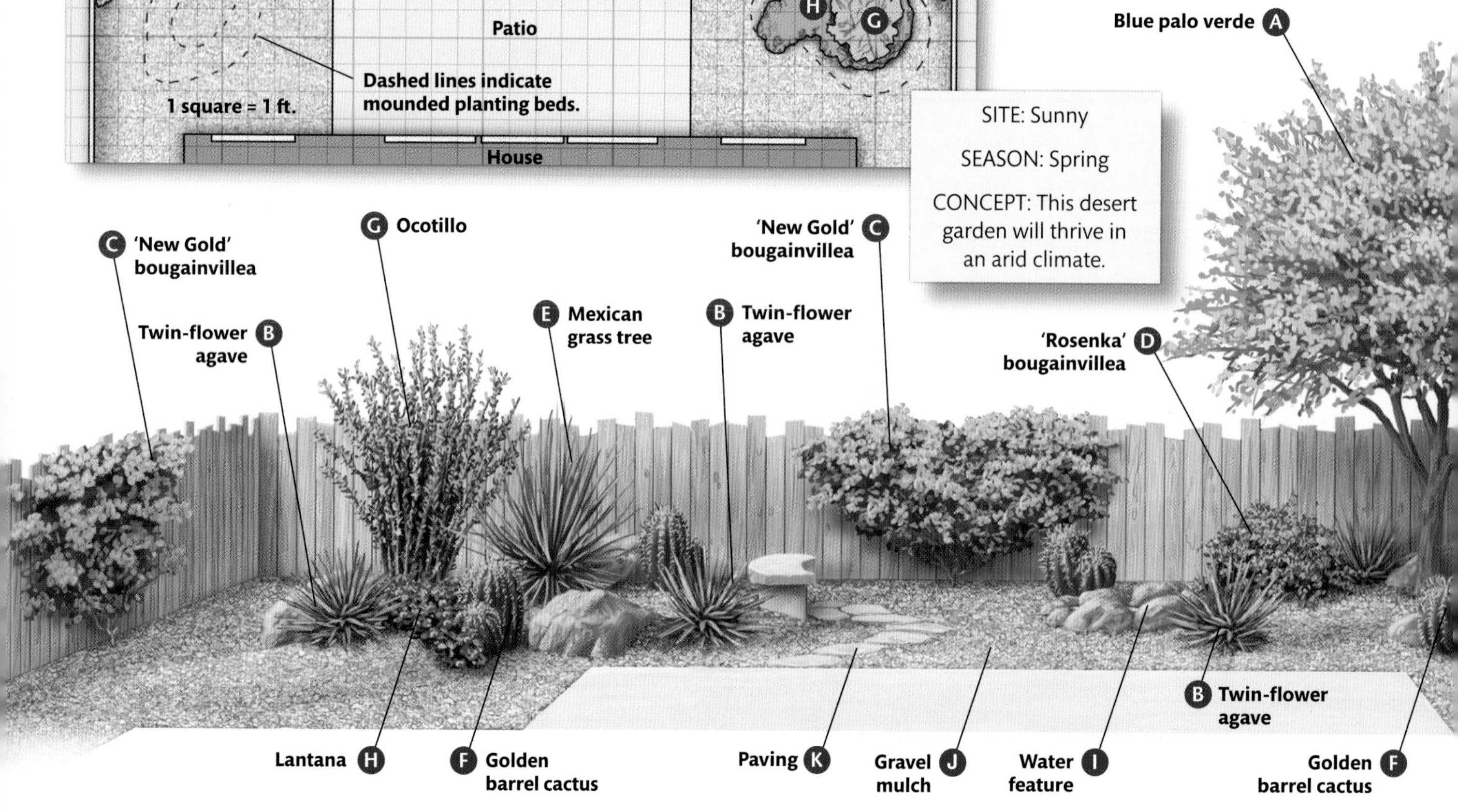

Ⓒ 'New Gold' bougainvillea

Ⓖ Ocotillo

'New Gold' Ⓒ bougainvillea

Twin-flower Ⓑ agave

Ⓔ Mexican grass tree

Ⓑ Twin-flower agave

'Rosenka' Ⓓ bougainvillea

Ⓑ Twin-flower agave

Lantana Ⓗ

Ⓕ Golden barrel cactus

Paving Ⓚ

Gravel mulch Ⓙ

Water feature Ⓘ

Golden Ⓕ barrel cactus

F **Golden barrel cactus** (use 4)
Shaped like a barrel and adorned with golden thorns, this small cactus wears a crown of small yellow flowers in summer. See *Echinocactus grusonii*, p. 129.

G **Ocotillo** (use 3)
Bright orange-red flower clusters bloom from the tips of this shrub's thorny branches from early spring to summer. See *Fouquieria splendens*, p. 130.

H **Lantana** (use 3)
This low-spreading shrub forms a solid mat of crinkly green leaves and plentiful lavender flowers all year. See *Lantana montevidensis*, p. 138.

I **Water feature**
A small fiberglass shell or even a barrel surrounded by large stones makes a pleasant little pool. See p. 172.

J **Gravel mulch**
Shape the planting mounds with soil and then cover the entire area with small-diameter stones such as bird's-eye gravel. See p. 202.

See p. 89 for the following:

K **Paving**

It's not quite an instant garden, but containers of tree roses and tulips added character and interest to this patio in short order.

VARIATIONS ON A THEME

These designs run the gamut from a weekend makeover to makeovers requiring weeks of work.

G Ocotillo

C 'New Gold' bougainvillea

H Lantana   **J** Gravel mulch

On a steeply sloped backyard, a hillside garden is a lot more fun than a lawn. This one includes a little patio retreat created by a low retaining wall.

Vibrant tropical plants give this lush patio garden some pizzazz.

A Shady Hideaway

BUILD A COZY RETREAT IN A CORNER OF YOUR YARD

One of life's little pleasures is sitting in a shady spot reading a book or newspaper or just looking out onto your garden, relishing the fruits of your labors. If your property is long on lawn and short on shade, a chair under a leafy arbor can provide a cool respite from the heat or the cares of the day. Tucked into a corner of the yard and set among attractive trees, shrubs, vines, and perennials, the arbor shown here is a desirable destination even when the day isn't sizzling.

Picturesque redbuds help create a cozy enclosure, affording privacy as well as shade. Plantings in front of the arbor and extending along the property lines integrate the hideaway with the lawn and make a handsome scene when viewed from the house. The design is equally effective in an open corner or backed by a property-line fence. The arbor is small; if you'd like more company beneath it, it's easy to make it wider and longer.

Flowers and foliage contribute color and fragrance around the arbor throughout the year. The redbuds, clematis, roses, and columbines bloom in spring. The roses carry on blooming through the summer, joined by lavender and plumbago. Camellias grace the fall and winter. Leaves in a range of greens, purple, maroon, and silver-gray provide background and balance to the floral display and are eye-catching in their own right.

Plants & Projects

The arbor and plants can be installed in a few weekends. Plant dwarf plumbago between the new shrubs. It will be shaded out as the shrubs mature, but you'll enjoy its summerlong blue carpet of flowers in the meantime. Once the plants are established, seasonal pruning and cleanup should keep this durable planting looking good for years.

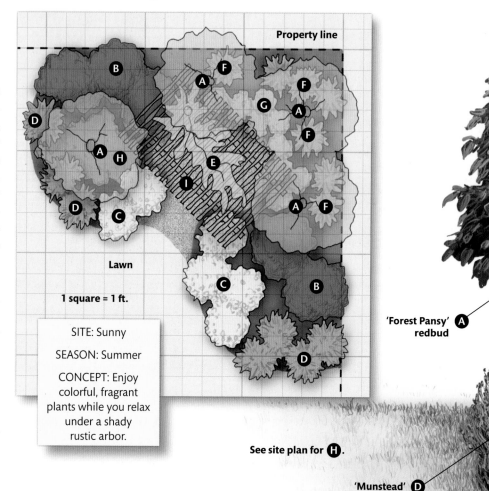

Property line

Lawn

1 square = 1 ft.

SITE: Sunny

SEASON: Summer

CONCEPT: Enjoy colorful, fragrant plants while you relax under a shady rustic arbor.

'Forest Pansy' **A** redbud

See site plan for **H**.

'Munstead' **D** lavender

A **'Forest Pansy' redbud** (use 4 plants)
The heart-shaped purple leaves of this small deciduous tree shade the arbor in summer and early fall. Eye-catching tiny red flowers line bare branches in spring. See *Cercis canadensis*, p. 124.

B **'Setsugekka' camellia** (use 5)
A compact low-growing form of this popular evergreen shrub. White flowers are showcased against the glossy green foliage in late fall and winter. See *Camellia sasanqua*, p. 120.

C **'Margaret Merril' rose** (use 6)
Fragrant white roses welcome visitors to the arbor from spring to fall. This floribunda rose has attractive dark green leaves and a bushy habit. See *Rosa*, p. 149.

D **'Munstead' lavender** (use 7)
The silver-gray foliage of this evergreen shrub contrasts handsomely with its neighbors. Bears spikes of blue flowers in summer. See *Lavandula angustifolia*, p. 138.

E **Anemone clematis** (use 1)
This vigorous deciduous vine covers the arbor. Choose from cultivars offering generous displays of white or pink flowers in early spring. Some are strongly scented. See *Clematis montana*, p. 126.

F **Leatherleaf fern** (use 7)
The finely cut, glossy foliage of this evergreen fern makes a lush patch beneath the redbuds. See Ferns: *Rumohra adiantiformis*, p. 131.

G **Rocky Mountain columbine** (use 9)
Elegant blue-and-white flowers sway on thin stalks in late spring and early summer. This perennial's delicate lacy foliage complements nearby ferns. See *Aquilegia caerulea*, p. 117.

F Leatherleaf fern

B 'Setsugekka' camellia

C 'Margaret Merril' rose

E Anemone clematis

H **Dwarf plumbago** (use 20)
A sprawling perennial ground cover, its foliage turns maroon after a frost. It is sprinkled with indigo blue flowers from midsummer to frost. See *Ceratostigma plumbaginoides*, p. 124.

I **Arbor**
This simple structure can be built in a week-end or two. Use cedar or redwood and let the wood weather for a rustic look. (See p. 187.) Crushed rock or decomposed gran-ite makes a durable surface beneath the arbor. (See p. 164.)

C 'Margaret Merril' rose

Rocky Mountain columbine **G**

I Arbor

D 'Munstead' lavender

B 'Setsugekka' camellia

VARIATIONS ON A THEME

What a treat to steal a quiet moment in a shady spot surrounded by lovely plants.

An arched arbor frames a cozy hideaway just large enough for a bench. The canopy of a tree provides a screen behind and shade overhead.

This "hideaway" is located on an island bed in the center of a shady garden. Though in plain view, its trellised walls and leafy surround give the impression of a hidden retreat. A bench swing hangs from the covered roof.

The fieldstone patio beneath this vine-covered rustic arbor has ample room for a gathering of friends and family.

A cozy corner

Small fruit trees and midsize shrubs provide a sense of enclosure and privacy in this shady retreat. The pomegranate and tangerine may reach 10 ft. or so but without the grovelike feel of the previous design because of fewer specimens.

There are flowers for many months. In spring, the back of the planting blooms in red, pink, blue, and white, complementing the fragrant yellow blossoms of the jasmine. The front of the planting comes on from summer through fall with flowering perennials and shrubs in red, yellow, and purple. And much of it is evergreen for year-round good looks.

The design works equally well in the open or against a fence. If your site is fenced, you might omit the small clumps of blue fescue along the back edge.

Plants & Projects

A **'Wonderful' pomegranate**
(use 1 plant)
A small multi-trunked deciduous tree with orange-red flowers in spring and bright yellow leaves and edible fruit in fall. See *Punica granatum*, p. 146.

B **'Clementine' dwarf tangerine**
(use 1)
This small tree has evergreen foliage, fragrant flowers in spring, and tasty fruit in late fall and winter. See *Citrus*, p. 126.

C **'Julia Phelps' ceanothus** (use 3)
This native shrub provides deep blue flowers in spring and dark evergreen foliage year-round. See *Ceanothus*, p. 123.

D **Shrub marigold** (use 3)
Small yellow flowers are scattered on this shrubby perennial throughout the year. The fine-textured leaves are fragrant. See *Tagetes lemmonii*, p. 152.

E **Carolina jasmine** (use 1)
The evergreen foliage of this vine is dark green in summer and maroon in winter. Bears fragrant yel-

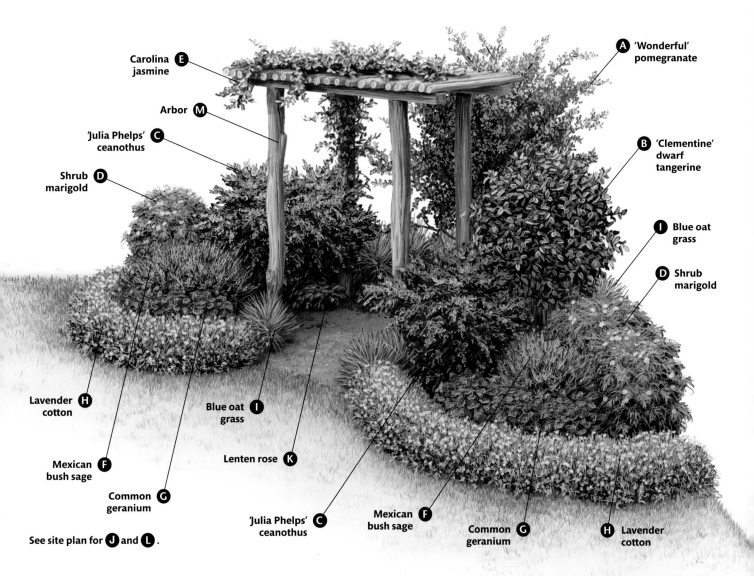

Carolina jasmine **E**

Arbor **M**

'Julia Phelps' **C**
ceanothus

Shrub **D**
marigold

A 'Wonderful'
pomegranate

B 'Clementine'
dwarf
tangerine

I Blue oat
grass

D Shrub
marigold

Lavender **H**
cotton

Blue oat **I**
grass

Mexican **F**
bush sage

Lenten rose **K**

Common **G**
geranium

'Julia Phelps' **C**
ceanothus

Mexican **F**
bush sage

Common **G**
geranium

H Lavender
cotton

See site plan for **J** and **L** .

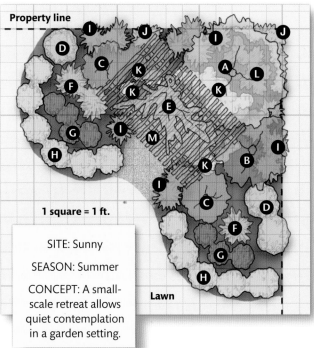

Property line

1 square = 1 ft.

SITE: Sunny

SEASON: Summer

CONCEPT: A small-scale retreat allows quiet contemplation in a garden setting.

Lawn

low flowers in late winter to early spring. See *Gelsemium sempervirens*, p. 132.

F **Mexican bush sage** (use 3)
This perennial forms mounds of gray-green foliage that bristle with spikes of deep purple flowers from late spring into fall. See *Salvia leucantha*, p. 150.

G **Common geranium** (use 7)
Pick a red-flowered cultivar of this popular perennial to complement nearby foliage and flowers. Blooms from spring through fall. See *Pelargonium* x *hortorum*, p. 144.

H **Lavender cotton** (use 11)
A small evergreen shrub with silver-gray foliage and yellow flowers in midsummer. See *Santolina chamaecyparissus*, p. 150.

I **Blue oat grass** (use 13)
Clumps of this evergreen peren-

nial's bluish foliage add texture and color to the planting. See *Helictotrichon sempervirens*, p. 142.

J **Blue fescue grass** (use 16)
Choose a dwarf cultivar (such as 'Blausilber') of this evergreen perennial to form little pincushions of blue-gray foliage. See *Festuca ovina* var. *glauca*, p. 142.

K **Lenten rose** (use 17)
A perennial with distinctive pink, rose, or white flowers and evergreen leaves. See *Helleborus orientalis*, p. 133.

L **Bearded iris** (use 8)
Choose your favorites among these popular perennials with elegant spring-blooming flowers and swordlike leaves. See *Iris*, p. 136.

See p. 93 for the following:

M Arbor

Back to Nature

CREATE A WOODED RETREAT

IN YOUR BACKYARD

The open spaces and squared-up property lines in many new developments (and some old neighborhoods as well) can make a homeowner long for a more natural landscape. It may come as a surprise that you can create just such a retreat on even a small property. By combining a relatively small number of carefully placed trees and shrubs with a healthy selection of perennials, grasses, and ferns, you can have your own backyard nature park.

Trees and shrubs take time to reach the height and spread we associate with a woodland. The plants in this design were chosen in part because they make an attractive setting in their early years, too. Here we show the young planting several years after installation. On the following pages you'll see the planting as it appears at maturity.

This planting is designed to attract wildlife as well as human visitors. With a pond to provide water, a variety of plants, including California natives, it offers cover and food for birds, butterflies, and a range of furry creatures. Stroll through the planting or sit on a bench and enjoy nature's rich tapestry.

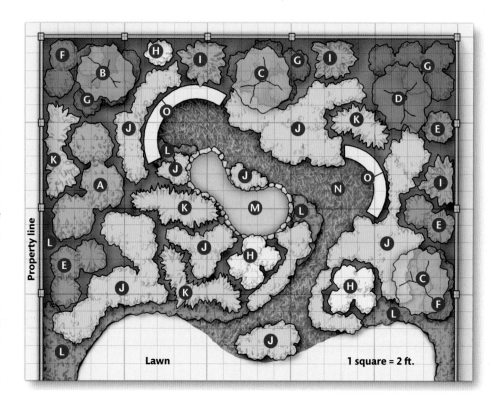

Property line

Lawn

1 square = 2 ft.

SITE: Sunny

SEASON: Summer

CONCEPT: A mixed planting across the back of a lot attracts birds and wildlife. It is shown here just a few years after installation.

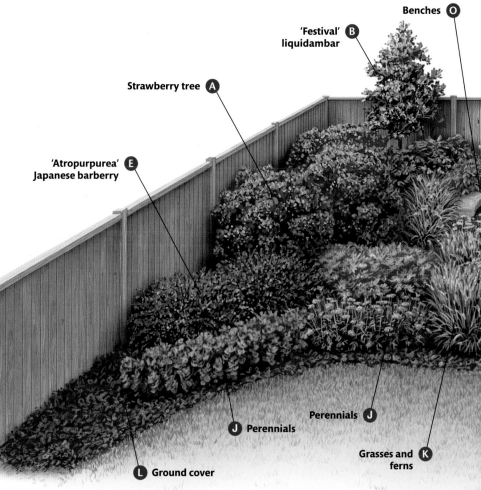

Benches **O**

'Festival' **B**
liquidambar

Strawberry tree **A**

'Atropurpurea' **E**
Japanese barberry

Perennials **J**

J Perennials

Grasses and **K**
ferns

L Ground cover

Plants & Projects

Install the pond, path, and irrigation system. Next, prepare the soil in the planting areas with a rototiller. Then plant, mulching the entire area immediately to control weeds and to keep the soil moist. Add more mulch every year or two in spring.

Ⓐ Strawberry tree (use 3 plants)
This small tree is interesting year-round, with shiny evergreen leaves, white fall flowers, red berries, colorful bark, gnarly branches, and handsome multi-trunk form. See *Arbutus unedo*, p. 117.

Ⓑ 'Festival' liquidambar (use 1)
This upright deciduous tree is prized for its spectacular fall display of yellow, orange, and red foliage. See *Liquidambar styraciflua*, p. 139.

Ⓒ 'Pink Spires' crab apple (use 2)
A small deciduous tree, it features lavender-pink spring flowers followed by long-lasting and colorful fruit. See *Malus*, p. 140.

Ⓓ Washington hawthorn (use 1)
This deciduous tree offers white flowers in early summer, red foliage in fall, and small red fruits that last into winter. See *Crataegus phaenopyrum*, p. 128.

Ⓔ 'Atropurpurea' Japanese barberry (use 6)
The arching branches of this deciduous shrub bear purple-bronze leaves all summer. See *Berberis thunbergii*, p. 118.

Ⓕ 'Spring Bouquet' viburnum (use 6)
This evergreen shrub displays clusters of fragrant white flowers from late fall to spring. See *Viburnum tinus*, p. 154.

Ⓖ Compact Oregon grape (use 12)
A spreading evergreen shrub with spiny leaves and yellow late-spring flowers. See *Mahonia aquifolium* 'Compacta', p. 140.

Ⓗ 'Iceberg' rose (use 9)
Clusters of fragrant white flowers grace this deciduous shrub all year. See *Rosa*, p. 149.

Ⓘ 'Black Knight' butterfly bush (use 3)
This deciduous shrub forms vase-shaped clumps of arching stems. Bears long spikes of butterfly-attracting purple flowers from midsummer through fall. See *Buddleia davidii*, p. 120.

Ⓙ Perennials
Framed by the trees and shrubs, a "meadow" of sun-loving and durable perennials adds a range of colors and textures to the planting. An assortment are shown here: 'Appleblossom' and 'Moonshine' yarrow have silver foliage and colorful flat-topped flower clusters (see *Achillea*, p. 115). 'Powis

Castle' artemisia forms billowing silvery mounds (see *Artemisia*, p. 118). Purple coneflower has tall pinkish purple flowers (see *Echinacea purpurea*, p. 129). Gloriosa daisy bears cheerful orange-yellow flowers (see *Rudbeckia hirta*, p. 150). 'Autumn Joy' sedum offers fleshy leaves and distinctive clustered flowers and seeds (see *Sedum*, p. 151). Finally, plant daylilies to brighten the garden with fresh flowers from summer to fall (see *Hemerocallis*, p. 134).

Ⓚ Grasses and ferns
With their distinctive foliage, these plants enhance the "natural" feel of the planting. Feather reed grass makes an arching clump of leaves that turn golden yellow in fall (see *Calamagrotis* x *acutiflora* 'Stricta', p. 142). Sword fern makes a neat mound of shiny dark green fronds behind the strawberry trees (see Ferns: *Polystichum munitum*, p. 131).

Ⓛ Ground cover
Fill in along the path and in other open spaces with tough, low-growing plants. 'Burgundy Glow' ajuga, an evergreen perennial, is shown here. See *Ajuga reptans*, p. 115.

Ⓜ Pond
You can make a small pond with a plastic liner and a lot of elbow grease (see p. 172). Add fish and water-loving plants (see Water plants, p. 154).

Ⓝ Path
Wood chips make an excellent path as well as a mulch for the planting. See p. 164.

Ⓞ Benches
Simple, curved benches of stone or cast concrete are available at garden centers.

Ⓒ 'Pink Spires' crab apple

Ⓘ 'Black Knight' butterfly bush

Ⓓ Washington hawthorn

Ⓖ Compact Oregon grape

Ⓕ 'Spring Bouquet' viburnum

Ⓛ Ground cover

Ⓜ Pond

Ⓙ Perennials

Ⓝ Path

Ⓙ Perennials

Ⓗ 'Iceberg' rose

Ⓙ Perennials

Ⓛ Ground cover

At maturity: a woodland meadow

Change and growth are the rule among living things, but when plants are small, it's not easy to imagine what they'll look like in 12 or 15 years. So we've done it for you here.

The small plants shown on the preceding pages have matured to make a lovely woodland meadow. The pond is edged, as in nature, by trees and shrubs. The trees screen out surrounding properties and provide privacy. Their dappled shade now makes the nearby benches even more inviting.

Because the planting was designed with growth in mind, trees and shrubs now fill their spaces comfortably, maintained by seasonal pruning. Perennials, ferns, and grasses form robust clumps, kept in bounds by judicious division. Transplanted divisions have helped the sword ferns spread beneath the low-growing strawberry trees. And, in the light shade at the back of the planting, daylilies gathered from divisions elsewhere in the garden have slowly replaced plants that require more sun.

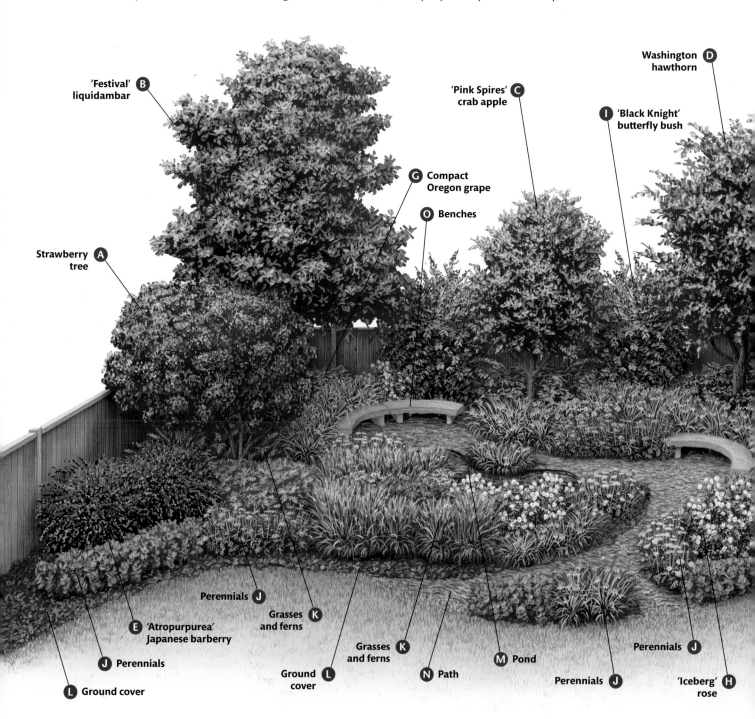

'Festival' liquidambar **B**

Washington hawthorn **D**

'Pink Spires' crab apple **C**

I 'Black Knight' butterfly bush

G Compact Oregon grape

O Benches

Strawberry tree **A**

Perennials **J**

Grasses and ferns **K**

E 'Atropurpurea' Japanese barberry

J Perennials

Perennials **J**

L Ground cover

Grasses and ferns **K**

Ground cover **L**

N Path

M Pond

Perennials **J**

Perennials **J**

H 'Iceberg' rose

VARIATIONS ON A THEME

On an acreage or a sub-urban lot, you can create a garden that welcomes wildlife and offers you a little slice of nature.

A narrow, crushed-rock path lined with spiky bear's breeches and other perennials entices you into this woodland garden.

This lovely garden plays effectively off the woodland beyond the rose-covered bower.

Roses line the stone path lead-ing into this "nature park."

SITE: Sunny

SEASON: Summer

CONCEPT: After 12 to 15 years, the planting is a private shady woodland retreat.

I 'Black Knight' butterfly bush

C 'Pink Spires' crab apple

'Spring Bouquet' **F** virburnum

Ground cover **L**

Splash Out

MAKE A WATER GARDEN THE FOCUS

OF OUTDOOR ACTIVITIES

A water garden adds a new dimension to a home landscape. It can be the eye-catching focal point of the entire property, a center of outdoor entertainment, or a quiet out-of-the-way retreat. A pond can be a hub of activity—a place to garden, watch birds and wildlife, raise ornamental fish, or stage an impromptu paper-boat race. It just as easily affords an opportunity for some therapeutic in-

A Queen palm

B Pittosporum

D 'Yellow Wave' New Zealand flax

J Water plants

L Patio area

C 'Moon Bay' nandina

F Purple fountain grass

M Mowing strip

C 'Moon Bay' nandina

E Bird-of-paradise

K Pond

G Blue oat grass

H Siberian iris

D 'Yellow Wave' New Zealand flax

L Patio area

See site plan for **I**.

J Water plants

activity; a few minutes contemplating the ripples on the water's surface provide a welcome break in a busy day.

This design places a pond at the center of all the activities mentioned above. At one end, a "public" patio of brick accommodates gatherings of family and friends. At the other is a semicircular retreat, a "private" patio of crushed rock, where a simple bench is sheltered by a chest-high hedge. A flagstone walkway links the two areas and defines two sides of the pond. Completing the perimeter, the surface of the crushed-rock patio slopes down gently into the pond, the smaller stones blending in with larger river rock placed above and below the water level. Moving away from the water, the gravel extends, as mulch, back into the beds.

The planting is dramatic and can be enjoyed from both patios. Two palms stand like sentinels at the center of the composition and announce its tropical theme. Exotic flowers and spiky foliage in various forms display spectacular colors and shapes throughout the year.

Plants & Projects

Installing a pond is arduous but simple work, requiring several weekends of energetic digging. Lay out and install the patios at the same time as the pond. Once established, the plants require only seasonal maintenance. The pond will need regular attention to keep a healthy balance of water plants and fish (if you have them) in order to maintain oxygen levels and to keep algae in check. Consult local or mail-order suppliers to help you get the right mix.

Ⓐ Queen palm (use 2 plants)
With long, glossy green fronds and straight trunks, a pair of these palms establish the planting's character. See Palms: *Syagrus romanzoffianus*, p. 143.

Ⓑ Pittosporum (use 9)
An excellent hedge plant, this evergreen shrub makes a dense growth of small green leaves. Bears small purple flowers in spring if buds aren't sheared off. See *Pittosporum tenuifolium*, p. 146.

Ⓒ 'Moon Bay' nandina (use 12)
This compact, dwarf evergreen shrub forms a low natural hedge edging the planting bed.

It doesn't flower, but its leaves are a striking red in winter. See *Nandina domestica*, p. 141.

Ⓓ 'Yellow Wave' New Zealand flax (use 8)
This evergreen perennial's colorful spray of swordlike leaves is topped in summer by tall stalks bearing tubular red flowers. See *Phormium tenax*, p. 144.

Ⓔ Bird-of-paradise (use 3)
Spectacular, long-lasting flowers bloom year-round above this evergreen perennial's long blue-green leaves. The flowers are best in spring. See *Strelitzia reginae*, p. 152.

Ⓕ Purple fountain grass (use 5)
The reddish brown leaves of this perennial turn gold or tan in autumn. Purple-red summer flowers become fluffy bronze seed heads in fall. See *Pennisetum setaceum* 'Rubrum', p. 142.

Ⓖ Blue oat grass (use 11)
This small ornamental grass forms tight spiky blue clumps of evergreen leaves. The wispy flowers turn tan in fall. See *Helictotrichon sempervirens*, p. 142.

Ⓗ Siberian iris (use 3)
Elegant flowers and handsome clumps of erect, grasslike foliage distinguish this popular perennial. Blooms in spring. See *Iris sibirica*, p. 137.

Ⓘ 'Silvery Sunproof' liriope (use 5)
This perennial ground cover forms clumps of grassy green leaves with gold stripes. Bears lilac flowers in early summer. See *Liriope muscari*, p. 139.

Ⓙ Water plants
There are many fascinating plants for water gardens. At one end of the pond we've shown the colorful foliage and flowers of canna 'Tropicanna', (*Canna*) grown in pots placed in shallow water. At the other end, the grassy foliage of acorus (*Acorus gramineus*) echoes the iris foliage nearby. See Water plants, p. 154.

Ⓚ Pond
You can make this pond with a commercially available liner. The flagstone walk and edging are supported on concrete blocks. See p. 172.

Ⓛ Patio areas
Both the formal brick and informal crushed-rock patio areas can be laid on bases of sand and gravel. See p. 170.

Ⓜ Mowing strip
A brick mowing strip frames the plantings, helps keep the planting beds tidy, and makes lawn mowing easier. See p. 194.

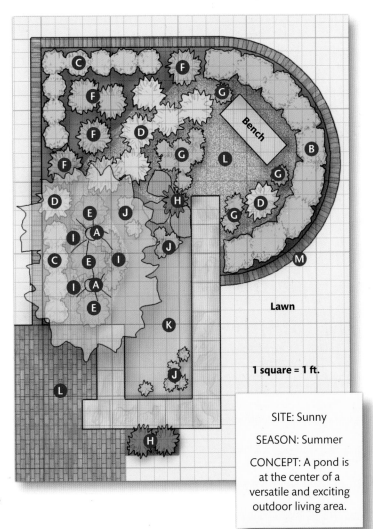

Bench

Lawn

1 square = 1 ft.

SITE: Sunny

SEASON: Summer

CONCEPT: A pond is at the center of a versatile and exciting outdoor living area.

Mini-pond

This little pond provides the pleasures of water gardening for those without the space or energy required to install and maintain a larger pond. Within its smaller confines you can enjoy one or more water plants as well as a few fish. Or you might install a small fountain, as shown here. Pond and plantings can stand alone in an expanse of lawn, but they will look their best integrated into a larger scheme. The scale is just right for use as the focal point of a small patio or as part of a larger patio planting.

The pond is simple and inexpensive. Use a wide terra-cotta pot (plug the drainage hole with modeling clay), a half barrel, or a fiberglass pond shell.

The planting displays a delightful collection of foliage textures and colors chosen to complement or contrast with those of their neighbors. A smattering of flowers accent the foliage throughout the year.

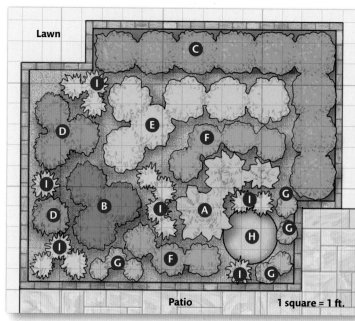

Lawn

Patio   1 square = 1 ft.

SITE: Sunny

SEASON: Summer

CONCEPT: A miniature pond is the focal point of a small-scale but varied planting.

B 'Spring Bouquet' viburnum

D Mugo pine

E 'Powis Castle' artemisia

A Sago palm

C 'Crimson Pygmy' Japanese barberry

D Mugo pine

I 'Silvery Sunproof' liriope

G Peach-leafed bellflower

F Lantana

I 'Silvery Sunproof' liriope

H Pond

G Peach-leafed bellflower

Plants & Projects

A **Sago palm** (use 3 plants)
This slow-growing relative of conifers produces fine, fernlike foliage atop a thick trunk. Pick three plants graduated in size. See *Cycas revoluta*, p. 128.

B **'Spring Bouquet' viburnum** (use 3)
A compact evergreen shrub, it bears lightly scented white flowers against dark foliage from late fall to spring and blue fruit through the summer. See *Viburnum tinus*, p. 154.

C **'Crimson Pygmy' Japanese barberry** (use 9)
This dwarf deciduous shrub makes a colorful informal hedge. Its foliage is purplish red

in summer and turns a striking red in fall. See *Berberis thunbergii*, p. 118.

D **Mugo pine** (use 4)
This shrubby tree forms a low compact mound of evergreen needles, contrasting nicely with the nearby viburnums. See *Pinus mugo*, p. 145.

E **'Powis Castle' artemisia** (use 6)
A woody perennial, it forms a loose hedge of lacy, deeply divided silver foliage that echoes the pine and contrasts with the barberry. See *Artemisia*, p. 118.

F **Lantana** (use 7)
This evergreen perennial produces cheerful clusters of small flowers from spring

through fall (year-round in mild-winter areas). A lavender-flowered cultivar suits this planting. See *Lantana montevidensis*, p. 138.

G **Peach-leafed bellflower** (use 7)
Tall spikes of blue flowers rise above this perennial's low foliage in summer. See *Campanula persicifolia*, p. 122.

H **Pond**
Bury a watertight container about 30 in. in diameter, and add water plants or a fountain, as you wish. See p. 172.

See p. 101 for the following:

I **'Silvery Sunproof' liriope** (use 14)

VARIATIONS ON A THEME

Well-chosen plants can make a pond, large or small, the centerpiece of a natural environment as well as a part of your landscaping.

With its natural contours, native plants, and fieldstone edging, this pond blends beautifully into its setting.

Sheltered from the lawn, this small pond makes a secret garden. A ribbon of rounded stones ties the pond to the larger landscape.

Set in a beautiful and extensive garden, this pond and its flagstone surround are perfect for entertaining guests.

Under the Old Shade Tree

CREATE A COZY GARDEN IN A COOL SPOT

This planting is designed to help homeowners blessed with a shade tree make the most of their good fortune. The bench is essential—what better spot to rest on a hot summer day? But why stop there? The tree's canopy affords an ideal setting for a planting of understory shrubs and perennials. The result is an oasis of dappled shade, colorful flowers, and handsome foliage that warrants a visit any day of the year.

With its bright colors and drought-tolerant plants, the planting has a Southwestern feel. The mature Mexican palo verde tree at its center and the stucco wall are characteristic of the Southwest. Extending beyond the tree's canopy, the plants used in this design are equally at home in the sun or under any tree that casts light, dappled shade.

Summer is the most colorful season. Flowers in shades of red, yellow, and purple stand out against a backdrop of blue, gray, and dark green leaves. Much of the foliage is evergreen and attractive from fall through spring, when cooler temperatures make relaxing on the bench particularly enticing.

> SITE: Shady
>
> SEASON: Summer
>
> CONCEPT: A colorful garden beneath a mature tree makes a lovely spot for sitting or strolling.

Plants & Projects

To provide headroom, remove limbs of the shade tree to a height of 7 ft. or more. The tree's roots compete for moisture with anything planted nearby. The plants in this design do well in these conditions and, after they're established, need infrequent supplemental watering. A generous mulch helps to conserve water. (For more on planting under a shade tree, see p. 160.)

A **'Howard McMinn' manzanita** (use 4 plants)
This native evergreen shrub bears shiny dark green leaves on stems with eye-catching red bark. In spring, there are small white to pink flowers. See *Arctostaphylos densiflora*, p. 117.

B **'Point Reyes' bearberry** (use 3)
Related to manzanita, this low, wide-spreading evergreen shrub also bears bright green leaves, small spring flowers, and red berries. Leaves turn red in winter. It is an excellent ground cover. See *Arctostaphylos uva-ursi*, p. 117.

C **Autumn sage** (use 8)
This bushy shrub offers long-lasting green leaves and spikes of small fragrant flowers from late spring to fall. A red-flowered cultivar will look good in this design. See *Salvia greggii*, p. 150.

D **Sageleaf rockrose** (use 2)
This evergreen shrub forms a spreading mound of crinkled gray-green leaves covered from late spring into summer with white flowers. See *Cistus salviifolius*, p. 126.

E **Blue oat grass** (use 20)
An evergreen perennial, it forms spiky but graceful clumps of thin blue-gray leaves. Wispy flower stalks turn tan or beige in fall. See *Helictotrichon sempervirens*, p. 142.

F **'Moonshine' yarrow** (use 27)
This perennial makes a patch of narrow, finely divided, gray foliage. In summer, stiff stalks topped by tight clusters of small lemon yellow flowers rise above the leaves. See *Achillea*, p. 115.

G **Purple coneflower** (use 13)
Purple daisylike flowers with dark centers rise on sturdy stalks above this perennial's mound of dark green foliage. See *Echinacea purpurea*, p. 129.

H **Path**
A shredded-bark surface is just right for this casual setting. (Use it as a mulch for the beds, too.) Spread bark directly on the ground or on a prepared base. See p. 164.

I **Bench**
Select a comfortable bench for relaxing in the shade and enjoying the plantings.

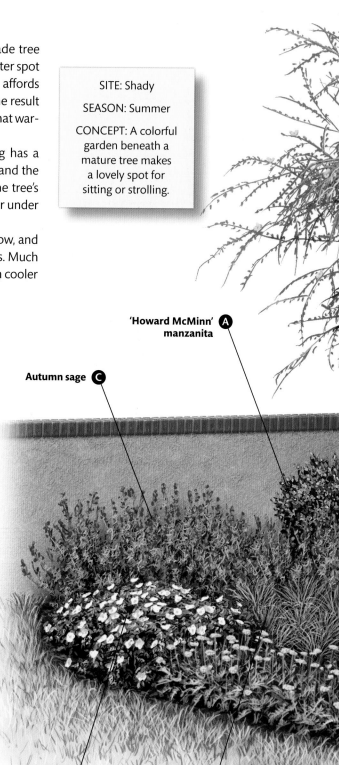

'Howard McMinn' manzanita **A**

Autumn sage **C**

Sageleaf rockrose **D**

Blue oat grass **E**

1 square = 1 ft.

Lawn

Existing
tree

Fence

Existing palo verde

A 'Howard McMinn'
manzanita

B 'Point Reyes'
bearberry

C Autumn sage

F 'Moonshine'
yarrow

E Blue oat grass

F 'Moonshine'
yarrow

I Bench

G Purple
coneflower

H Path

Cool spot, cool look

Nestled in the cool shade of a stately sycamore, this design offers a more subdued, woodsy atmosphere. Filling in the shady area are evergreen shrubs and massed plantings of mostly evergreen perennials, including grasses and ferns. We've shown a perimeter fence, as is common on many properties, but the large shrubs will also provide privacy if the planting is in an open area.

Flowers in purple and white grace the planting for most of the year, with the biggest display coming in spring. Foliage in a range of greens and a variety of textures is attractive throughout the year. A mature tree like the sycamore shown here casts welcome shade in summer, but for best results with the plants below, thin the tree canopy if necessary to produce shade that is dappled rather than deep.

SITE: Shady

SEASON: Fall

CONCEPT: A venerable shade tree and an evergreen underplanting give this garden a cool, quiet atmosphere.

Existing sycamore

B 'Royal Robe' Paraguay nightshade

Feather reed grass **D**

Mother fern **C**

G Bench

Island alumroot **E**

Plants & Projects

A Red cestrum (use 4 plants)
The arching branches of this evergreen shrub bear dark green leaves, a handsome backdrop to its spring display of purple-red flowers and the bright red berries that follow. Birds like the flowers and fruit. See *Cestrum elegans*, p. 125.

B 'Royal Robe' Paraguay nightshade (use 6)
This shrub's bright green leaves are evergreen in mild-winter areas. Striking dark

purple flowers with star-shaped yellow centers bloom as long as the weather is warm. See *Lycianthes rantonnetii*, p. 139.

C Mother fern (use 17)
This fern's delicate light green fronds make an airy mound that heightens the woodland feel and contrasts nicely with nearby plants. Evergreen where winters are mild. See Ferns: *Asplenium bulbiferum*, p. 131.

D Feather reed grass (use 18)
A perennial grass, it forms an erect clump of bright green leaves. Flowering stems rise above the foliage in spring, turning tan in fall and winter. Foliage is evergreen where winters are mild. See *Calamagrostis x acutifolia* 'Stricta', p. 142.

E Island alumroot (use 42)
This California native perennial forms spreading mounds of dark, heart-shaped

Fence

C
A
B
E
D
C
Existing
tree
D
C
C
G
D
A
C
Lawn
D
C
E
D
E
F

1 square = 1 ft.

VARIATIONS ON A THEME

A large shade tree is enticing all on its own. Add a bench and some well-chosen plants and you'll have an irresistible garden destination.

A curved wall and shade-loving plants embrace weathered benches under an old redbud tree.

D **Feather reed grass**

A **Red cestrum**

Path F

E **Island alumroot**

Mother C
fern

evergreen foliage. In early spring, tall stems bear long clusters of tiny white or pink flowers. See *Heuchera maxima*, p. 134.

See p. 104 for the following:

F **Path**

G **Bench**

This spectacular native oak extends its reach over a large brick patio and an amphitheater-like shade garden of drought-tolerant plants to produce an exceptional space for socializing.

Planting in the Pines

SURROUND YOUR WOODLAND DECK WITH FLOWERING SHRUBS

This simple patio planting is located on the wooded slopes of a mountain range.

Many desirable ornamental plants thrive in the dry mid-elevations of California's mountains. This design features drought-tolerant and fire-resistant trees and shrubs that look beautiful and natural in a setting of mature conifers.

Native western redbuds planted around the deck create a leafy canopy among the bare trunks of taller pines. Beneath and around them are a variety of lower-growing shrubs displaying contrasting bold and fine-textured foliage and springtime flowers. The entire planting is edged in a foot-high swath of bright green foliage.

Like the surrounding hillsides, the planting will be in full bloom in spring, with masses of white, yellow, and pink flowers. The evergreen foliage looks fresh throughout the rest of the year.

Wildfires are always a concern in the foothills of California. To protect your home, keep areas near the house well irrigated and keep vegetation 15 to 20 feet from the house. For other tips on how to keep your home safe from wildfires, contact your local fire department or state Department of Forestry.

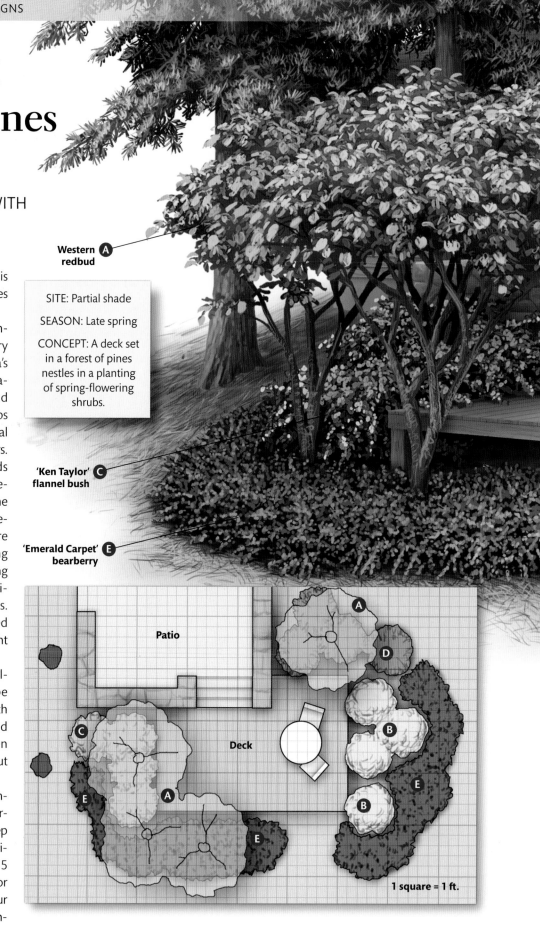

Western redbud **A**

SITE: Partial shade

SEASON: Late spring

CONCEPT: A deck set in a forest of pines nestles in a planting of spring-flowering shrubs.

'Ken Taylor' flannel bush **C**

'Emerald Carpet' bearberry **E**

Patio

Deck

A **B** **C** **D** **E**

1 square = 1 ft.

'Majorca Pink' **D**
rosemary

'Emerald Carpet' **E**
bearberry

B Bush anemone

Plants & Projects

Preparing the planting beds and installing the shrubs can be done in a few weekends. Then sit back and enjoy the display. Once established, these plants require little care beyond seasonal pruning.

A **Western redbud** (use 4)
   Native to the foothills, this small tree is so vivid in bloom it stops drivers along the roads in spring. The purplish pink flowers give way to bright green deciduous leaves that turn yellow in fall. Purplish seedpods

decorate the bare branches in winter. See *Cercis occidentalis*, p. 124.

B **Bush anemone** (use 4)
   One of California's loveliest chaparral shrubs. Dark glossy leaves with whitish undersides create a beautiful backdrop in spring for masses of showy white flowers sporting bright yellow centers. See *Carpenteria californica*, p. 123.

C **'Ken Taylor' flannel bush** (use 4)
   Cup-shaped golden yellow-to-orange flowers stand out brightly against this evergreen

shrub's felty, dark green leaves. See *Fremontodendron* 'Ken Taylor', p. 131.

D **'Majorca Pink' rosemary** (use 4)
   Lavender-pink flowers adorn this tough, upright evergreen shrub in late winter and early spring. See *Rosemarinus* 'Majorca Pink', p. 149.

E **'Emerald Carpet' bearberry** (use 12)
   Exceptional as a ground cover, this low-spreading shrub forms a dense, slightly mounding carpet of small oval leaves that are bright green throughout the year. See *Arctostaphylos* 'Emerald Carpet', p. 117.

VARIATIONS ON A THEME

You don't have to live in the foothills or mountains to appreciate these handsome designs.

This playful pattern of paths and planting beds edged in native rock is ideal for a rustic setting in the sun.

This stacked platform deck and plantings would be striking even without the huge boulder that anchors the design.

Pink geraniums and pink-tinged stones make an attractive combination in this hillside patio.

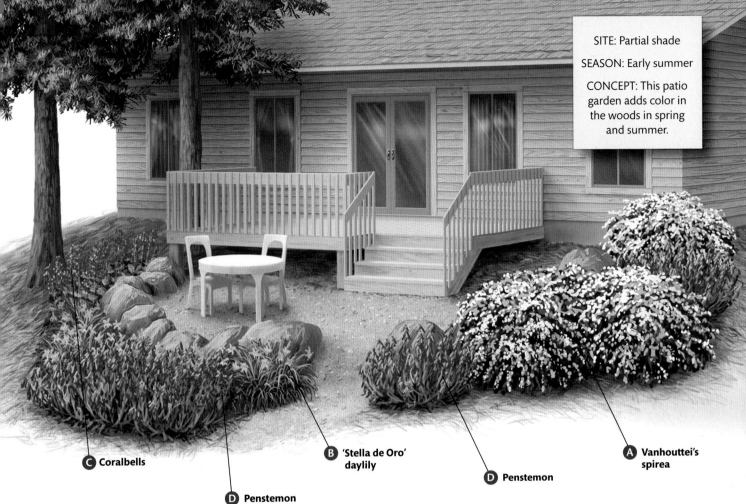

SITE: Partial shade

SEASON: Early summer

CONCEPT: This patio garden adds color in the woods in spring and summer.

C Coralbells

B 'Stella de Oro' daylily

D Penstemon

D Penstemon

A Vanhouttei's spirea

D Penstemon

Rustic charm

In this design, a simple ground-level patio augments an existing deck for outdoor entertaining. This design requires only a small initial investment in materials and time and promises years of enjoyment.

The patio is created by an artless (if not effortless) arrangement of large rocks, shrubs, and perennials in a clearing near the deck. Pine needles make a servicable surface and are in abundant supply.

Chosen for a location at a higher elevation than the previous design, the carefree perennials and shrubs that loosely border the patio are right at home in the shade of tall pines. Relax on a comfortable chair to enjoy the flowers and watch the acrobatics of hummingbirds drawn to penstemon.

Plants & Projects

A **Vanhouttei's spirea** (use 3)
This deciduous shrub forms a large bushy mound of arching branches lined with small dark green leaves. They disappear in spring under a heavy bloom of small white flowers. See *Spiraea x vanhouttei*, p. 151.

B **'Stella de Oro' daylily** (use 11)
Golden yellow flower shaped like trumpets bloom just above this perennial's grassy foliage through the summer. See *Hemerocallis*, p. 134.

C **Coralbells** (use 7)
This perennial's beautifully scalloped leaves form neat almost evergreen mounds. In spring and early summer, the plants send up countless thin flower stalks nodding with clusters of tiny, bright red, bell-shaped flowers. See *Heuchera sanguinea*, p. 134.

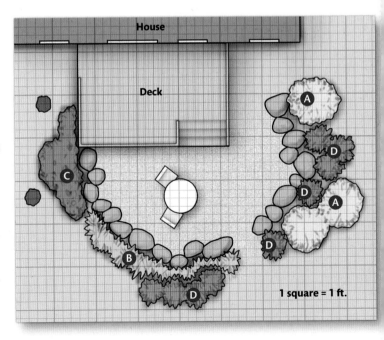

D **Penstemon** (use 9)
This popular perennial produces a tall clump of wiry flower spikes that open into sprays of tubular red flowers above a low mat of dark green foliage. Attracts hummingbirds. See *Penstemon*, p. 144.

House

Deck

A

D

C

D

A

B

D

1 square = 1 ft.

Plant Profiles

Plants are the heart of the designs in this book. In this section you'll find descriptions of all the plants used in the designs, along with information on planting and maintaining them. These trees, shrubs, perennials, grasses, bulbs, and vines have all proven themselves as dependable performers in California. They offer a wide spectrum of lovely flowers and fruits, handsome foliage, and striking forms. Most contribute something of note in at least two seasons. You can use this section as an aid when installing the designs in this book and as a reference guide to desirable plants for other home landscaping projects.

Using the plant profiles

All of these plants are proven performers in many of the soils, climates, and other conditions commonly found in California. But they will perform best if planted and cared for as described in the Guide to Installation, beginning on p. 156. In the following descriptions and recommendations, the term "regular water" means plants need to be watered on a regular basis throughout the growing season. Plants described as needing "occasional water" need less water once established but still look their best if given thorough watering several times throughout the growing season. Here also, "full sun" means a site that gets at least eight hours a day of direct sun throughout the growing season. "Partial sun" and "partial shade" both refer to sites that get direct sun for part of the day but are shaded the rest of the time by a building, fence, or tree. "Full shade" means sites that don't receive direct sunlight.

The plants are organized here alphabetically by their scientific name. While many plants are sold by common name, scientific names help ensure that you get what you want. If you're browsing, page references direct you to the designs in which the plants appear.

Abelia x grandiflora 'Edward Goucher'

'EDWARD GOUCHER' ABELIA. A dependable evergreen shrub that bears countless small rosy purple flowers from early summer until frost and attracts many butterflies. Lustrous pointed leaves are bronzy green in spring, dark green in summer, purple-bronze in winter. This cultivar grows 3 to 5 ft. tall. It needs full or partial sun and regular water. Prune annually in late winter to early spring to keep the plants compact and neat. Page: 78.

Acanthus mollis

BEAR'S BREECHES. A perennial with bold, deeply lobed, dark green leaves that grow up to 2 ft. long. Tall spikes of white to pinkish purple flowers bloom in late spring, reaching 2 to 3 ft. above the foliage. Grows best in moist shade but can take some sun.

Abelia x grandiflora
'EDWARD GOUCHER' ABELIA

Acanthus mollis
BEAR'S BREECHES

Cut back flowers after bloom. Divide crowded plants in spring. A vigorous plant, it can be invasive. Pages: 27, 81.

Acer palmatum

JAPANESE MAPLE. A neat, small deciduous tree with delicate-looking leaves that have jagged edges. There are many kinds, with leaves that are green, bronze, or red in summer. You can buy seed-grown plants (p. 28) or named cultivars. Most turn red or scarlet in fall. 'Oshio-Beni' (p. 48) stays dark red all season. Coralbark maple, A. p. 'Sango Kaku' (pp. 30, 48, 62), is an upright tree with foliage that is reddish in spring, light green in summer, and yellow in fall. Bark is bright red. All grow best in partial shade and rich, moist soil covered with a layer of mulch. In cooler climates they can take more sun. Leaf burn is common in hot-summer areas, especially Southern California. Water deeply at least once a week during dry weather. Japanese maples grow slowly, so buy the biggest tree you can afford to start with. Plants are sold in containers or balled-and-burlapped. Prune trees to open and highlight branching. Plants grow 10 to 20 ft. tall and wide.

Acer palmatum
JAPANESE MAPLE

Achillea

YARROW. A long-blooming perennial with flat clusters of small flowers on stiff stalks and finely divided gray-green leaves that have a pungent aroma. Spreads to form an irregular patch. 'Moonshine' (pp. 38, 97, 104) grows about 2 ft. tall and has lemon yellow flowers. *A. millefolium* 'Appleblossom' (p. 97) reaches up to 3 ft. tall and bears clear pink flowers. Yarrow needs full sun and well-drained soil. Thrives with little water. Cut off old flower stalks when the blossoms fade; they're often used in dried-flower arrangements. Divide clumps every few years in spring or fall.

Achillea millefolium 'Moonshine'
YARROW

Agapanthus

AGAPANTHUS, LILY-OF-THE-NILE. Very useful flowering perennials with arching, straplike leaves and ball-shaped clusters of blue or white flowers in late spring and summer. A. orientalis (pp. 31, 71) grows 2 to 3 ft. tall and bears flower clusters on stalks up to 5 ft. tall. A. 'Storm Cloud' (p. 75) grows 3 to 4 ft. tall and is topped with blue-violet flowers. A. 'Midnight Blue' has captivating, deep blue flowers. A. 'Peter Pan' (pp. 24, 45, 61) is a dwarf variety with leaves reaching only 12 in. tall and blue flowers on stalks up to 18 in. tall. Plant in full sun or light shade and well-drained soil. All grow best with regular water but can take dry periods. Evergreen in mild-winter climates, they go dormant in cold winters. Divide only when very crowded—every 5 to 7 years. Excellent in pots or near pools.

Achillea millefolium 'Appleblossom'
YARROW

Agapanthus 'Midnight Blue'
LILY-OF-THE-NILE

Agave geminiflora

TWIN-FLOWER AGAVE. This succulent desert perennial forms a tight rosette 2 to 3 ft. round of stiff, narrow, bright green leaves. Tall spikes of pale yellow bell-shaped flowers rise from the center in spring or summer. Foliage dies back after bloom, followed by new growth at the base. Plant in full sun. Needs well-drained soil and only an occasional watering in summer. Pages: 33, 90.

Ajuga reptans

AJUGA, BUGLEWEED. A low-growing, mat-forming perennial, used as a ground cover. The glossy leaves are evergreen. Erect, 6-in. spikes densely packed with small flowers are very showy for a few weeks in spring and early summer. 'Bronze Beauty' (pp. 31, 48, 83) has dark purplish bronze foliage and blue flowers. 'Burgundy Glow' (p. 97) has glossy leaves marked purple, green,

Ajuga reptans 'Bronze Beauty'

and white. Both grow best in full sun or partial shade and rich, moist soil. After flowers fade, cut them off with a string trimmer, lawn mower, or hedge shears. Plants spread quickly and will invade a lawn unless you keep cutting along the edge or install a mowing strip.

Ajuga reptans 'Burgundy Glow'

Alstroemeria, Meyer hybrid

Alstroemeria aurantiaca

Alstroemeria

ALSTROEMERIA. Colorful perennials with tall stalks bearing azalealike flowers in a rainbow of speckled and striped shades. White, pink, red, yellow, orange, or purple flowers open from late spring to midsummer and make great cut flowers. Plants grow 2 to 5 ft. tall and eventually form large clumps. Evergreen types such as the Cordu and Meyer hybrids (pp. 45, 83) bloom for the longest period. Plant in full sun or partial shade and rich, well-drained soil. Water regularly. Pull out flower stalks after blooming. Divide infrequently.

Alyogyne huegelii

BLUE HIBISCUS. Evergreen shrub with large, bright blue to purple flowers borne on and off throughout the year. Grows 5 to 8 ft. tall and has dark green, coarse, deeply cut leaves. Best adapted to coastal areas. Plant in full sun. Gets by with little water, but grows better with more. Prune to maintain attractive shape. Page: 24.

Anemone x hybrida

JAPANESE ANEMONE. A perennial with small daisy-like flowers on branching stalks held well above a bushy clump of large, soft-textured, dark green leaves. Blooms for several weeks in late summer into fall. Most varieties have white flowers, some pink. All need partial shade and rich, moist soil. Cut down old stalks in fall. Divide every few years, in fall or early spring. Plants grow 3 to 4 ft. tall and spread at least as wide. Pages: 31, 85.

Anisodontea x hypomandarum

CAPE MALLOW. Fast-growing evergreen shrub with a long season of bloom. Small pink hollyhocklike flowers with dark veins appear almost year-round in mild-winter areas. (Bloom time is shorter in inland and foothill areas.) Grows 6 ft. tall. Full sun. Needs little water once established. Pages: 24, 78.

Alyogyne huegelii
BLUE HIBISCUS

Anemone x hybrida
JAPANESE ANEMONE

Anisodontea x hypomandarum
CAPE MALLOW

Aquilegia

COLUMBINE. A large group of wonderfully delicate flowering perennials with lovely spurred flowers in many single and multicolored shades. They bloom in spring and early summer and form neat mounds of blue-green, scalloped leaves that range from 12 to 48 in. high. There are many hybrids and species to choose from. The western columbine, *A. formosa* (p. 87), is native to California. It grows 18 to 36 in. tall and bears lovely red-and-yellow flowers. Rocky Mountain columbine, *A. caerulea* (p. 92), grows to a similar height but has blue-and-white blooms. Columbines grow best in light shade but can also take full sun where summers are cool. Water regularly. Carefree. Individual plants live only a few years, but replacements will pop up here and there if you let the seeds mature and scatter naturally.

Arbutus

ARBUTUS. Striking evergreen trees with shiny red to orange bark and small, bell-shaped flowers followed by red fruits. Leaves are shiny green. Usually grown with multiple trunks. Strawberry tree, *A. unedo* (pp. 69, 97), grows 10 to 25 ft. tall and has distinctive, gnarly branches and white flowers in fall and winter. A great small-garden tree throughout most of the state. *A.* 'Marina' (pp. 28, 85) can grow to 40 ft. but is usually smaller, with larger leaves and pinkish flowers in fall. It is a perfect substitute for the California native madrone, *A. menziesii*, which is hard to grow in garden situations. Plant in full sun or partial shade and well-drained soil. Arbutus gets by on little water. Prune to expose branches.

Arctostaphyllos

MANZANITA. Native evergreen shrubs with shiny red bark, lustrous deep green foliage, and small white to pink flowers in spring followed by red berries. *A. densiflora* 'Howard McMinn' (pp. 52, 104) grows 5 to 6 ft. tall and spreads a little wider. *A. uva-ursi* 'Point Reyes' (p. 104) is an excellent ground cover less than a foot high but spreading up to 15 ft. wide. *A.* 'Emerald Carpet' (bearberry, p. 109) grows 8 to 14 in. high by 5 ft. wide and has brilliant green leaves. Best used in dry areas and on slopes where there is infrequent watering. Plant in fall in full sun to partial shade.

Aquilegia caerulea
ROCKY MOUNTAIN COLUMBINE

Arbutus 'Marina'

Arbutus

Arctostaphyllos densiflora 'Howard McMinn'
MANZANITA

Arctostaphylos 'Emerald Carpet'
BEARBERRY

Armeria maritima THRIFT

Artemisia 'Powis Castle'

Aster x frikartii ASTER

Baccharis pilularis 'Twin Peaks'
DWARF COYOTE BRUSH

Armeria maritima

THRIFT. A perennial that forms a neat tuft of grassy evergreen leaves and bears spherical flower heads on stiff stalks about 1 ft. tall. Blooms generously in spring, with scattered blossoms throughout the summer and fall, in shades of rose, pink, or white. Needs full sun and well-drained soil. Looks best with occasional water. Remove flowers as they fade, and shear off old foliage in early spring. Pages: 56, 61, 69, 83.

Artemisia

ARTEMISIA. Shrubby perennials, woody at the base, with fragrant, gray-green, finely divided leaves. Beautiful accent plants. Rarely flower. *A.* 'Powis Castle' (pp. 76, 85, 97, 102) grows 3 to 4 ft. tall and spreads up to 6 ft. wide. Lovely lacy, silver foliage. *A. schmidtiana* 'Silver Mound' grows only 1 to 2 ft. high and wide and has feathery silver leaves. It is a good alternative where space is limited. Plant artemisia in full sun. Will tolerate dry soil but grows faster with water. Cut back hard in winter or spring to keep compact.

Aster x frikartii

ASTER. A carefree perennial that blooms over a long season from late spring to fall, bearing thousands of light purple flowers. 'Wonder of Stafa' and 'Mönch' are popular varieties. This hybrid species makes a good cut flower. Thrives in full sun and well-drained soil with regular water. Cut stems back by a third in late fall if the plant has gotten floppy. Divide every year or two in fall or early spring. Grows 2 to 3 ft. tall and wide. Page: 78.

Baccharis pilularis 'Twin Peaks'

'TWIN PEAKS' DWARF COYOTE BRUSH. California native evergreen shrub valuable as a ground cover for sunny, dry, low-maintenance areas. Grows 10 to 24 in. high and spreads about 6 ft. wide, forming a dense cover of small bright green leaves. 'Twin Peaks' is a male selection that doesn't produce messy seeds. Shear back and fertilize in early spring. Needs little water near the coast, once a month in warmer areas. Page: 52.

Berberis thunbergii

JAPANESE BARBERRY. A deciduous shrub with stiff, spiny stems and small leaves. Small red berries hang on most of the fall and winter. Can grow into a broad mound 6 ft. tall and 8 ft. wide but is typically kept smaller by shearing. 'Atropurpurea' (p. 97) has purple-red foliage through the summer and fall. 'Crimson Pygmy' (pp. 36, 69, 102) is a dwarf form grown for its colorful foliage and compact, spreading habit. The small leaves are showy purplish red all summer, bright crimson in fall. Can grow into a broad mound 2 ft. tall and 3 to 5 ft. wide. It makes an excellent ground cover. Barberries need full sun, well-drained soil, and occasional water. Shear anytime, as desired.

Bergenia crassifolia

WINTER-BLOOMING BERGENIA. A low-growing perennial with large, dark green, wavy-edged leaves that are evergreen except in cold-winter areas. In January and February, tall stems bear clusters of pink flowers. Plant in partial shade (or full sun where summers are cool). Will withstand poor conditions but looks best grown in good soil and with regular watering. Pages: 63, 73.

Bougainvillea

BOUGAINVILLEA. One of the most spectacular flowering plants, it blooms in striking shades of white, pink, red, orange, yellow, or purple in late spring and summer. Foliage is evergreen. Habit varies by variety, of which there are many. Most are sprawling vinelike plants that can spread over 20 ft. wide and need lots of room. Others are smaller and more shrublike. 'Barbara Karst' (pp. 56, 59) is one of many vigorous types that need the support of a strong fence or trellis but can be used as ground covers on banks. It has red to crimson flowers. 'New Gold' (pp. 33, 89, 90) has bronzy yellow flowers and grows 5 to 6 ft. tall with the support of a trellis. The shrublike 'Rosenka' (pp. 33, 90) forms an arching mound 4 ft. tall and 5 ft. wide and bears gold flowers aging to pink. Bougainvilleas are reliably hardy only in mild climates of Southern California. Widely grown elsewhere, they may lose leaves or die back partially in colder areas. Can also be grown in pots or treated as summer annuals in cold climates. Plant in spring in full sun, or light shade in hot areas. Be careful not to damage roots when planting. Plants get by with little water once established but bloom better with summer irrigation. In spring, fertilize and prune as necessary to keep within bounds. Page: 66.

Brunfelsia pauciflora 'Floribunda Compacta'

YESTERDAY-TODAY-AND-TOMORROW. A very floriferous evergreen shrub, named for its changing flower colors, from purple (yesterday) to lavender (today) to white (tomorrow). Blooms spring to summer. Large, attractive oblong leaves are dark green above and light green below. Grows best in partial shade and with regular water. Reaches a compact, bushy 3 to 4 ft. tall. Page: 35.

Berberis thunbergii 'Crimson Pygmy'
JAPANESE BARBERRY

Bergenia crassifolia
WINTER-BLOOMING BERGENIA

Bougainvillea 'Barbara Karst'
BOUGAINVILLEA

Brunfelsia pauciflora 'Floribunda Compacta'
YESTERDAY-TODAY-AND-TOMORROW

Buddleia davidii

BUTTERFLY BUSH. A fast-growing shrub that blooms from midsummer through fall and is sometimes evergreen where winters are mild. Arching shoots make a vase-shaped clump. Spikes of small white, pink, lilac, blue, or purple flowers form at the end of each stem. The flowers have a sweet fragrance and really do attract butterflies. 'Black Knight' (pp. 19, 52, 97) has purple flowers. 'Nanho Blue' (pp. 24, 71) reaches 4 to 5 ft. tall and is a better choice for small spaces. Both need full sun and well-drained soil. Cut old stems down to 1-ft. stubs in late winter to early spring to promote vigorous growth and maximum flowering. Plants will grow 5 to 8 ft. tall and wide by the end of the summer. Require regular watering.

Buddleia davidii
'Black Knight'
BUTTERFLY BUSH

Bulbs

The bulbs recommended in this book are all perennials that come up year after year and bloom in late winter, spring, or early summer. After they flower, their leaves continue growing until sometime in summer, when they gradually turn yellow and die down to the ground. To get started, you must buy bulbs from a garden center or catalog in late summer or fall (they usually aren't available until after Labor Day). Plant them promptly in a sunny or partly sunny bed with well-prepared, well-drained soil, burying them to a depth two to three times the bulb's height. In subsequent years, all you have to do is pick off the flowers after they fade and remove (or ignore, if you choose) the old leaves after they turn yellow in summer. Most bulbs can be divided every few years if you want to spread them to other parts of your property. Dig them up as the foliage is turning yellow, shake or pull them apart, and replant them right away. For more information on specific bulbs, see the box on the facing page.

Buxus microphylla var. japonica

JAPANESE BOXWOOD. This shrub forms a dense mass of neat, small, glossy evergreen leaves that make it ideal for shearing. The leaves, and also the small

Buxus microphylla var. *japonica* 'Winter Gem'
JAPANESE BOXWOOD

flowers in spring, have a distinct fragrance. Japanese boxwood forms soft 4- to 6-ft.-high mounds if left alone. It can be sheared into formal globes, cones, hedges, or topiary. Leaves turn brownish in cold winters. 'Green Beauty' (pp. 44, 81) has small leaves that stay bright green in winter. It forms a compact globe up to 4 ft. tall. 'Winter Gem' (pp. 17, 28, 31) is similar. Boxwoods grow slowly, so buy the largest plants you can afford. They need well-drained soil and grow best in full or partial sun. Use mulch to protect their shallow roots. Water regularly. Shear in late spring.

Camellia

CAMELLIA. Evergreen shrubs with glossy foliage and large, lovely white, pink, or rose flowers. There are hundreds of cultivars, differing mostly in flower color, size, and form (single or double) as well as in overall plant habit, mature size, and hardiness. Japanese camellia (*C. japonica*, p. 64) is the most popular, usually ranging in height from 6 to 12 ft. and blooming in late winter to early spring. Reliable California varieties include 'Debutante', a vigorous plant with pink, peonylike flowers; 'Eleanor McCown', with white flowers streaked red and pink; 'Kramer's Supreme', with deep red, lightly fragrant blooms; and 'Tom Knudson', sporting deep red flowers marked with deeper red veins. Sasanqua camellias (*C. sasanqua*, pp. 22, 73, 75) are smaller plants that generally range from 2 to 3 ft. upward to 10 ft. and are useful as ground covers. They bloom in late fall and winter and can take more sun than Japanese camellias. Favorite varieties include 'Setsugekka' (p. 92), with white flowers borne on an upright plant; 'White Doves', producing white flowers on a low, spreading plant; and 'Yuletide' (pp. 27, 75), with single red flowers on an upright plant. Camellias need moist, well-drained, acid soil with a layer of mulch, and shade from midday sun. Prune and fertilize immediately after flowering, if desired.

Camellia sasanqua 'Setsugekka'
CAMELLIA

Camellia sasanqua 'Yuletide'

Camellia japonica
CAMELLIA

Recommended bulbs

Allium, Ornamental onion
Dependable onion relatives with grassy or straplike foliage and eye-catching, ball-shaped flower clusters in late spring to early summer. Blue allium (*A. caeruleum*, p. 37) produces 2-in.-wide bright blue flowers on 12-in. stems. Star of Persia (*A. christophii*, p. 67) bears large clusters of glistening lilac-colored, star-shaped blooms on 12- to 15-in. stems. Leaves are hairy white underneath. Golden garlic (*A. moly*, p. 38) has bright clusters of yellow flowers on 9- to 18-in. stems. Round-headed garlic (*A. sphaerocephalum*, p. 67) has reddish purple flowers on 24-in. stems. Alliums grow best in full sun or partial shade and well-drained soil. Plant the bulbs at a depth 2 to 3 times their width. Water while bulbs are growing. Flowers are great for bouquets and look good on the plant even after they dry.

Muscari armeniacum, Grape hyacinth
Grapelike clusters of sweet-scented purple flowers last for several weeks in April and May. Plant bulbs 3 in. deep, 3 in. apart. Don't be surprised to see the grassy foliage appear in fall; it lasts through winter. Blooms best in full sun. Naturalizes and blooms on forever. Page: 37.

Narcissus, Daffodil
The most popular spring bulb. There are hundreds of cultivars, with flowers in shades of yellow or white on stalks 6 to 24 in. tall, blooming in sequence from early to late spring. Some kinds have a lovely fragrance. 'February Gold' and 'Tête-à-Tête' are two of the first to bloom. Both have yellow flowers on stalks under 12 in. tall and are good for interplanting in flower beds because their flowers are large enough to be showy but their leaves are short enough to be inconspicuous after the flowers bloom. Plant the bulbs 4 to 6 in. deep, 6 in. apart. Page: 37.

Allium christophii
STAR OF PERSIA

Allium sphaerocephalum
ROUND-HEADED GARLIC

Allium moly
GOLDEN GARLIC

Muscari armeniacum
GRAPE HYACINTH

Narcissus 'Tête-à-Tête'
DWARF DAFFODIL

Campanula isophylla
ITALIAN BELLFLOWER

Campanula persicifolia
PEACH-LEAFED BELLFLOWER

Campanula poscharskyana
SERBIAN BELLFLOWER

Campsis x *tagliabuana* 'Mme. Galen'
TRUMPET VINE

Campanula

BELLFLOWER. A large group of useful flowering perennials (a few are annuals) that vary in plant habit and flower form. Plant them in flower beds, rock gardens, or containers. Spreading types are useful as small-scale ground covers. Italian bellflower (*C. isophylla*, p. 27) is a low-growing, sprawling plant that reaches 6 in. tall but can spread up to 2 ft. wide. Small white or blue flowers appear in late summer to fall. Peach-leafed bellflower (*C. persicifolia*, p. 102) is upright to 2 to 3 ft. tall and bears white, pink, or blue flowers on slender stalks in summer. Serbian bellflower (*C. poscharskyana*, pp. 48, 63, 81) is spreading and has flower stalks about 1 ft. tall. Blooms in spring to early summer in shades of blue to lavender. All grow best in partial shade but can take full sun near the coast. Water regularly. Cut back after bloom. Divide as necessary in fall.

Campsis x tagliabuana 'Mme. Galen'

'MME. GALEN' TRUMPET VINE. A vigorous deciduous vine with a stout woody trunk and thick stems, large compound leaves, and very showy clusters of salmon flowers in late summer. Needs full sun, room to grow, and regular water. Once started, it can climb and cover a trellis, wall, or fence with no further assistance or care. Can reach 30 to 40 ft. Prune in winter to control size, if desired. Page: 76.

Carissa macrocarpa 'Tuttle'

'TUTTLE' NATAL PLUM. A colorful evergreen shrub best adapted to coastal areas of southern California. Rich, shiny green leaves on spiny stems. Wonderfully fragrant, star-shaped white flowers appear throughout the year and are followed by bright red, edible fruits. Grows 2 to 3 ft. tall, spreading up to 5 ft. Useful as a ground cover or short hedge. Full sun or partial shade. Needs little water near the coast; more inland. Prune at any time. Page: 82.

Carpenteria californica

BUSH ANEMONE. Native to California's foothills, this evergreen shrub is grown for its lovely, lightly fragrant white flowers with yellow centers, which are displayed in late spring and early summer against handsome, glossy, dark green leaves. Grows upright 4 to 6 ft. high and equally as wide. Plant in full sun except in the hottest areas, where partial shade is best. Needs little water once established. Prune to shape after flowering. Sometimes gets aphids or mites. Page: 109.

Cassia

FEATHERY CASSIA. An airy, light-textured evergreen shrub well adapted to hot, dry conditions. Small yellow flowers bloom in winter and spring, sometimes longer. Leaves are gray-green and needle-like. Requires full sun and well-drained soil. Water occasionally during summer for best appearance. Will be damaged by a hard freeze. Spreads 3 to 5 ft. tall and wide. Prune after bloom if necessary. Page: 36.

Ceanothus

CEANOTHUS, WILD LILAC. California native evergreen shrubs useful in dry landscapes, especially on slopes. Blue or (rarely) white flowers appear in early spring. Leaves are deep green. 'Julia Phelps' (pp. 52, 94) reaches 4 to 7 ft. tall and up to 9 ft. wide and has deep blue flowers. Carmel creeper (C. griseus var. horizontalis) is low-growing to 2 to 3 ft. tall and 5 to 10 ft. wide. The cultivar 'Yankee Point' (p. 54) has dense, darker green foliage and slightly darker blue flowers than the species. Plant ceanothus in full sun in fall. Do not water once established.

Carissa macrocarpa 'Tuttle'
NATAL PLUM

Carpenteria californica
BUSH ANEMONE

Cassia artemisioides
FEATHERY CASSIA

Ceanothus griseus var. *horizontalis* 'Yankee Point'
CARMEL CREEPER

Ceanothus 'Julia Phelps'

Cerastium tomentosum
SNOW-IN-SUMMER

Ceratostigma plumbaginoides
DWARF PLUMBAGO

Cercidium floridum
BLUE PALO VERDE

Cercis occidentalis
WESTERN REDBUD

Cercis canadensis 'Forest Pansy'
EASTERN REDBUD

Cerastium tomentosum

SNOW-IN-SUMMER. A perennial often used as a ground cover, with silvery evergreen foliage and masses of white flowers in early summer. Forms a low mat 6 to 8 in. high, with stems that trail 2 to 3 ft. wide. Requires full sun or partial shade and well-drained soil. Water regularly. Shear off the top of the plant, cutting it back by about one-half, right after it blooms. Pages: 36, 51, 67, 81.

Ceratostigma plumbaginoides

DWARF PLUMBAGO. A perennial ground cover with indigo blue flowers in summer and fall and dark green foliage that turns maroon or crimson after a frost. Deciduous in cold winters and late to emerge in spring, it looks good with early-spring bulbs. Adapts to full or partial sun. Looks best with regular water. Cut old stems to the ground in early spring. Stays under 1 ft. high, spreads 2 to 3 ft. wide or more. Pages: 56, 69, 79, 93.

Cercidium floridum

BLUE PALO VERDE. A fast-growing deciduous desert tree prized for its toughness, its blue-tinged foliage and branches, and its stunning display of small yellow flowers in spring. Useful as a shade tree, it grows 30 to 35 ft. tall and almost as wide at the crown. Needs little water once established. Prune in winter to enhance form. Page: 90.

Cercis

REDBUD. Small, early-spring-flowering, deciduous trees. Eastern redbud (C. canadensis, p. 19) is native to the Mid-Atlantic region but does well in all of California except the mild-winter, coastal areas of the south. Clusters of bright pink-purple flowers line the twigs in mid-spring, before the leaves unfold. Heart-shaped leaves are medium green all summer, turning gold in fall. Available with single or multiple trunks. May reach 20 to 25 ft. tall and wide. 'Forest Pansy' (p. 92) has purple foliage. Eastern redbuds grow best in partial shade in most areas and require well-drained soil with regular water. Western redbud (C. occidentalis, pp. 52, 54, 71 109) is native to California and is a good choice for dry or natural landscapes. Less refined than its eastern relative, it is often grown as a large multitrunked shrub. Magenta flowers are followed by seedpods some people find unsightly. Leaves turn yellow in fall. Grows 10 to 20 ft. tall. Thrives in poor, dry soils. In hot-summer climates, it looks best if given some water. Prune to maintain shape and to open canopy.

Cestrum elegans

RED CESTRUM. Fast-growing, arching, evergreen shrub best adapted to mild climates of Southern California. Purple-red flowers in spring and summer are followed by bright red berries. Both fruit and flowers attract birds. Can grow over 10 ft. tall. Prune regularly to maintain shape and size. Best in partial shade, rich soil, and with regular water. Page: 106.

Chamaerops humilis

MEDITERRANEAN FAN PALM. A bushy palm with coarse, blue-green, palm-shaped leaves arising from the tops of multiple stalks. Yellow flowers are borne in long panicles in spring but are mostly hidden

Cercis canadensis
EASTERN REDBUD

Cestrum elegans
RED CESTRUM

Chilopsis linearis
DESERT WILLOW

in the dense foliage. Grows 6 to 10 ft. tall and half as wide. This adaptable palm does well in full sun to partial shade and in moderately fertile to poor soils. Page: 88.

Chilopsis linearis

DESERT WILLOW. Native to desert areas, this small deciduous tree has an open, twisting, multitrunked habit and willowy green-gray leaves. From spring to fall, fragrant clusters of trumpetlike flowers bloom in shades of red, purple, pink, and white, sometimes with yellow and purple throat streaks. Flowers are followed by many long thin seedpods. Desert willow may reach 15 to 30 ft. tall and about half as wide at the crown. It survives on little water once established. Prune to keep it open and to expose its attractive branching habit. Extremely drought tolerant and has few pests. Page: 32.

x Chitalpa tashkentensis

CHITALPA. A deciduous tree with narrow leaves that quickly grows 20 to 30 ft. tall. Large clusters of ruffled, trumpet-shaped flowers bloom in early summer. 'Pink Dawn' (pp. 24, 60) has pink blooms. 'Morning Cloud' has white flowers. Grows best with occasional water in hot-summer climates. Plant in full sun. Prune in winter to maintain shape. Page: 52.

Chrysactinia mexicana

DAMIANITA. This tough little evergreen shrub stands up well to desert heat and is useful for lining walkways and borders. It forms a densely branched 2 ft. mound of highly aromatic, dark green, needle-like leaves. Small, fragrant, golden yellow "daisies" are borne in spring and fall, and sometimes through the summer where temperatures are mild. Grows in full sun. Needs little water but will bloom more with occasional irrigation. Shear lightly in early spring to promote dense new growth. Page: 33.

x *Chitalpa tashkentensis*
'Pink Dawn'

Chrysactinia mexicana
DAMIANITA

Cistus salviifolius

SAGELEAF ROCKROSE. Evergreen flowering shrub particularly valuable in low-water-use landscapes, on dry hillsides, and near the coast. Makes a fine ground cover. Crisp-looking, gray-green, crinkled foliage. White flowers with yellow spots bloom heavily in late spring. Grows about 2 ft. tall and 6 ft. wide. Plant in full sun and well-drained soil. Needs little water once established. Shear lightly to keep compact. Page: 104.

Citrus

CITRUS. Probably the most useful ornamental-edible plants for California landscapes, these evergreen trees offer handsome dark green leaves, fragrant spring flowers, and colorful, edible fruits in winter. The many varieties vary in adaptation, tree height, and form. One type or another can be grown almost anywhere in the state except higher-elevation areas. Check with local nurseries for the best varieties for your area. Good landscape varieties include 'Meyer' lemon (pp. 47, 81), which forms a compact tree seldom over 8 ft. tall; 'Washington' navel orange, which grows 12 to 16 ft. tall; 'Satsuma' and 'Clementine' mandarins (p. 94; also sold as 'Algerian' tangerine), neat-looking trees 8 to 12 ft. tall; and 'Bearss' lime, a productive plant 8 to 10 ft. tall. 'Nagami' kumquat (dwarf kumquat, p. 75) makes a fine container plant. It grows slowly to 10 ft. tall and 5 ft. wide and bears fragrant white flowers in spring, miniature orangelike fruits in fall, and small, leathery, bright green leaves year-round. Citrus trees will be at least 50 percent smaller if grown on

'Flying Dragon' rootstock. Plant in full sun and well-drained soil. Water and fertilize frequently for quality fruit. Prune to keep the center of the tree open or to maintain size. Protect trees if temperatures drop below 30°F for prolonged periods.

Clematis

CLEMATIS. Deciduous or evergreen vines that climb or sprawl, forming a tangle of leafy stems adorned with masses of flowers, which can be tiny or large. Evergreen clematis (*C. armandii*, p. 51) produces large clusters of fragrant white flowers in spring. Anemone clematis (*C. montana*, p. 92) bears numerous spring flowers that turn from white to pink. The cultivar 'Rubens' (p. 78) has reddish bronze foliage and fragrant pink to rosy red flowers. Large-flowered hybrids, of which there are many, produce flowers up to 10 in. across in single and multicolored shades of white, pink, red, purple, and blue. 'Mme. Le Coultre' (p. 51) bears large white flowers in midsummer and fall. Clematis need partial or full sun, consistent moisture, and soil rich in organic matter. Plant where the branches can reach sunlight but the roots are shaded and cool. Mulch heavily. Unlike most plants, clematis needs a hole deep enough to cover the root ball and base of the stem with about 2 in. of soil. Cut the stem back to the lowest set of healthy leaves to encourage the plant to branch out near the base. Guide the new stems into position and use twist-ties or other fasteners to secure them as soon as they reach the trellis, wire, or other support. Prune

Cistus salviifolius
SAGELEAF ROCKROSE

Citrus 'Meyer'
LEMON

Citrus 'Clementine'
DWARF TANGERINE

Citrus 'Nagami'
DWARF KUMQUAT

Clematis
LARGE-FLOWERED HYBRID

Clematis montana 'Rubens'
CLEMATIS

Clematis armandii
EVERGREEN CLEMATIS

annually. It takes most clematis a few years to cover a fence or trellis 6 to 8 ft. tall, but many can eventually climb 15 to 20 ft.

Coleonema pulchrum 'Sunset Gold'

'Sunset Gold' pink breath of heaven. Wispy evergreen shrub with small, fragrant yellow leaves and pink flowers over a long period in winter and spring. Grows 2 ft. tall but spreads 4 ft. Plant in full sun and well-drained soil. Needs regular water but suffers if overwatered or planted in poorly drained soil. Shear after bloom. Page: 28.

Convolvulus mauritanicus

Ground morning glory. An evergreen, creeping perennial 1 to 2 ft. high but spreading up to 3 ft. Soft, gray-green leaves are a backdrop for lavender-blue flowers summer to fall. Makes a good small-scale ground cover. Plant in full sun or light shade and well-drained soil. Can take periods of drought but does best with occasional water. Shear after bloom to keep plants compact. Pages: 36, 41.

Coreopsis verticillata 'Moonbeam'

'Moonbeam' coreopsis. Long-blooming perennial that bears hundreds of small, lemon yellow, daisylike blossoms from summer to fall. The dark green leaves are short and threadlike. Spreads to form a patch 2 to 3 ft. tall and wide. Needs full sun. Gets by with little water once established. Remove spent flowers to extend bloom. Cut back to a few inches aboveground in fall. Page: 67.

Coleonema pulchrum 'Sunset Gold'
PINK BREATH OF HEAVEN

Convolvulus mauritanicus
GROUND MORNING GLORY

Coreopsis verticillata 'Moonbeam'

Cotoneaster horizontalis

ROCK COTONEASTER. One of a varied group of useful evergreen and deciduous shrubs. This is a wiry deciduous shrub with dark green leaves that turn orange and red in fall. Clusters of small white or pinkish flowers in spring are followed by colorful berries. Grows 2 to 3 ft. tall, 10 to 15 ft. wide, and is an excellent, low-maintenance ground cover. Plant in full sun or light shade. Requires little care once established. Prune as necessary to maintain size and shape. Page: 71.

Cotoneaster horizontalis
ROCK COTONEASTER

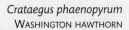

Crataegus phaenopyrum
WASHINGTON HAWTHORN

Crataegus phaenopyrum

WASHINGTON HAWTHORN. A small, well-behaved tree that grows upright with a rounded crown, reaching about 25 ft. tall and 15 to 20 ft. wide. It has very thorny twigs, deciduous leaves that are glossy green all summer and turn red in fall, clusters of white flowers in June, and small bright red fruits that ripen in early fall and last into the winter. Needs full or partial sun. Requires only minimal pruning. A trouble-free, adaptable tree best kept on the dry side. Page: 97.

Cycas revoluta

SAGO PALM. Though not a true palm (it is a relative of conifers), this distinctive evergreen plant has the overall appearance of a small palm. Its long, arching leaves are shiny dark green. The slow-growing plants are usually sold 1 to 2 ft. tall but take years to reach a maximum height of 10 ft. Plant in partial shade and water regularly. A great container subject and perfect for a tropical touch near pools or water features. Separate "pups" (small new plants that grow at the base of the old plant) whenever they appear. Page: 102.

Dasylirion longissima

MEXICAN GRASS TREE. An evergreen shrub forming a grassy fountain of narrow, olive green, succulent leaves. With age it bears spikes of tiny white flowers in early summer and develops a tree-like trunk. Usually reaches 4 to 5 ft., but may get as tall as 10 ft. Grows best in full sun or light shade and needs good drainage. Its smooth tropical appearance is especially attractive in desert areas, where it survives on little water. Pages: 33, 90.

Dianthus plumarius

COTTAGE PINK. Low-growing perennial with very fragrant flowers that look like small carnations. They bloom in shades of pink and white from late spring into fall. The grassy, blue-green, evergreen foliage forms a dense mat about 4 to 6 in. high and 1 to 3 ft. wide. Flower stalks are about 1 ft. tall. Needs full sun, well-drained soil, and regular water. After they bloom, shear off the flower stalks and cut the leaves back halfway. Fresh new foliage will soon develop. Divide every few years in early spring. Pages: 21, 79.

Cycas revoluta
SAGO PALM

Dasylirion longissima
MEXICAN GRASS TREE

Dietes vegeta

FORTNIGHT LILY. Grassy, evergreen perennial with lovely white flowers marked with orange, brown, and purple. Blooms appear every two weeks or so atop airy stalks 3 to 4 ft. tall from spring to fall. Plant in full sun or light shade. Can take dry periods but blooms best with regular water. Snap off individual seed heads to prolong bloom. Divide large clumps in fall or winter. Pages: 66, 69.

Dodonaea viscosa 'Purpurea'

PURPLE HOP BUSH. A tough evergreen shrub valuable for its ability to withstand difficult conditions, including poor soil, heat, wind, and drought. Narrow leaves are bronzy green, picking up a stronger purplish tone in winter. Flowers are inconspicuous, but seedpods are interesting late in summer. Grows 10 to 15 ft. tall, about 8 ft. wide. Ideal hedge or screen. Prune as necessary to maintain size. Best foliage color when planted in full sun. Page: 52.

Echinacea purpurea

PURPLE CONEFLOWER. A flowering perennial with large purplish daisylike blossoms held on stiff branching stalks above a basal mound of dark green foliage. Blooms over a long period in summer. Flower stalks reach 4 to 5 ft.; foliage spreads 3 ft. wide. Needs full sun and well-drained soil. Grows best with regular water but will tolerate dry periods. Cut back flower stalks if you choose, or let the seed heads ripen for winter interest. May self-sow but isn't weedy. Older plants can be divided in spring or fall. Pages: 61, 69, 97, 104.

Echinocactus grusonii

GOLDEN BARREL CACTUS. Popular in Southwestern gardens, this barrel-shaped cactus grows slowly to about 4 ft. tall and half as wide. Its pale green body sports neat rows of showy yellow thorns 3 in. long. In summer, small yellow flowers bloom in a circle near the top of the dome. Offshoots at the base eventually form clumps of new plants. This cactus needs well-drained soil, partial shade in the hottest areas, protection from hard frosts, and occasional water in summer. Page: 91.

Dianthus plumarius   COTTAGE PINK

Dietes vegeta
FORTNIGHT LILY

Dodonaea viscosa 'Purpurea'
PURPLE HOP BUSH

Echinacea purpurea
PURPLE CONEFLOWER

Echinocactus grusonii
GOLDEN BARREL CACTUS

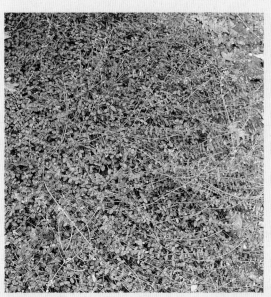

Erigeron karvinskianus
Santa Barbara daisy

Euonymus japonicus 'Microphyllus'
Boxleaf euonymus

Euphorbia 'Jerry's Choice'

Felicia amelloides
Blue marguerite

Erigeron karvinskianus

Santa Barbara daisy. Attractive, sprawling perennial well suited for low-water-use gardens and as a ground cover. Bears small, white to pinkish, daisylike flowers from late spring to fall. Pink buds are pretty, too. Grows 1 to 2 ft. high, spreading 2 to 3 ft. or more. Plant in full sun and well-drained soil. Naturalizes easily but can spread into unwanted areas if given too much water. Shear off faded flowers. Pages: 38, 82.

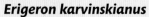

Euonymus japonicus 'Microphyllus'

Boxleaf euonymus. Tough, dependable evergreen shrub with a compact habit and small shiny leaves. Has a refined look as a clipped hedge or planted closely as a ground cover. Grows 1 to 2 ft. tall and roughly a foot wide. You can shear or prune plants at any time to control size or shape. Plant in full sun. Best with some water. Not well adapted to southern California, where mildew is a serious problem. Trim off damaged shoots in spring, and new growth will follow. Pages: 19, 47, 71.

Euphorbia hybrids

Euphorbias are evergreen shrubs that come in a wide variety of sizes, shapes, and colors; some have the appearance of thorny palm trees; others are bushy and thornless. Crown of thorns (*E. milii*) is a compact shrub growing 18 in. tall and wide. Evergreen leaves cluster at ends of thorny stems and are topped with bright red flower bracts all year. Carefree. Page: 33.

Felicia amelloides

Blue marguerite. Dependable perennial covered with small, blue, daisylike flowers for a long season, usually starting in late winter and spring. Some bloom year-round in warm-winter areas. Grows about 18 in. tall and 3 to 4 ft. wide. Plant in full sun and water regularly. Often grown as an annual. Great in pots. Remove spent flowers to promote more bloom. Cut back by half in late summer. Page: 77.

Ferns

Ferns provide distinctive, lush foliage for shady sites. Despite the delicate appearance of their lacy leaves, they are among the most durable and trouble-free plants you can grow. Most perform best in soil that has been amended with extra organic matter and is kept moist. However, some ferns adapt to dry conditions. Divide them every few years if you want more plants, or leave them alone for years. See the box on the facing page for specific ferns.

Fouquieria splendens

Ocotillo. This distinctive desert shrub forms a wiry clump of upright, gray-green, thorned and furrowed branches. Very showy clusters of tubular orange-red flowers form quickly at branch tips after spring rains and attract hummingbirds. The deciduous gray-green leaves are small and fleshy, and drop during dry spells. Ocotillo can reach 20 to 25 ft. tall. It makes an attractive silhouette in desert gardens or an impenetrable barrier. Grows in full sun and well-drained soil. Pages: 33, 91.

Fouquieria splendens   OCOTILLO

Fremontodendron 'Ken Taylor'

KEN TAYLOR FLANNEL BUSH. A smaller cultivar of a large showy evergreen shrub found in California's dry woodlands and mountain slopes. Golden yellow cup-shaped flowers bloom continuously from spring to fall among dark green, lobed leaves, leathery above and downy below. Flowers are followed by bristly seedpods. Grows 4 to 6 ft. tall and about twice as wide. Requires full sun and excellent drainage, making it ideal for a hillside location. Page: 109.

Gaillardia x grandiflora

BLANKETFLOWER. A perennial wildflower with cheerful red-and-yellow flowers all summer long. Forms a clump 2 to 4 ft. tall. 'Goblin' grows about 1 ft. high. Plants need full sun and well-drained soil but can get by on little water. Remove old flowers as they fade. Divide every year or two in fall or early spring. Page: 43.

Gaillardia x grandiflora   BLANKETFLOWER

Recommended ferns

Asplenium bulbiferum, Mother fern

Delicate fern with lacy, light green fronds up to 4 ft. tall. Small plantlets on fronds can be planted. Likes water and shade. Where temperatures regularly drop below 26°F, use sword fern (see below). Pages: 48, 86, 106.

Asplenium bulbiferum   Mother fern

Dicksonia antarctica, Tasmanian tree fern

Spectacular, almost prehistoric-looking fern with arching, 3- to 6-ft.-long fronds emerging from a thick, fuzzy trunk. Grows slowly but can eventually reach 15 ft. tall. Keep moist. Can take some sun near the coast, otherwise plant in shade. Page: 30.

Dicksonia antarctica   Tasmanian tree fern

Polystichum munitum, Sword fern

California native fern with shiny, 2- to 4-ft.-long fronds. One of the most dependable ferns for shady areas. Needs little water once established but looks better if watered occasionally. Pages: 48, 54, 64, 97.

Polystichum munitum   Sword fern

Rumohra adiantiformis, Leatherleaf fern

Coarse-textured, finely cut, glossy deep green fronds grow up to 3 ft. long. Best in light or partial shade. Water regularly. (Often sold as *Aspidium capense.*) Where temperatures drop below 24°F, use sword fern. Pages: 27, 62, 92.

Rumohra adiantiformis   Leatherleaf fern

Gardenia jasminoides 'Veitchii'
GARDENIA

Gaura lindheimeri
GAURA

Gelsemium sempervirens
CAROLINA JASMINE

Gardenia jasminoides

GARDENIA. An evergreen shrub with intensely fragrant white flowers in summer. 'August Beauty' (p. 64) is a popular cultivar with double flowers up to 4 in. wide and an upright or rounded habit, reaching 5 ft. or taller and 3 to 5 ft. wide. Variegated gardenia ('Radicans Variegata', p. 62) has 1-in. flowers and white-tinged gray-green leaves. It grows about 1 ft. tall and 2 to 3 ft. wide. 'Veitchii' (pp. 17, 22, 60) is 3 to 4 ft. tall and wide and blooms in summer or from late spring through fall where winters are mild. All need full or partial sun, acid soil, and regular water. They bloom best in warmer areas. Great in pots. Feed with acid-type fertilizer and apply iron to improve yellowed foliage. Prune in winter to control size and shape. Page: 75.

Gaura lindheimeri

GAURA. A perennial wildflower that forms a loose clump of graceful arching stems and bears pale pink-and-white flowers from spring through fall. Needs full sun, well-drained soil, and just a little water. Too much shade or moisture makes the stems floppy. Cut to the ground in winter. Grows 2 to 4 ft. tall and wide. Pages: 76, 85.

Gazania 'Burgundy'

'BURGUNDY' GAZANIA. Clumping evergreen perennial with showy daisylike flowers. 'Burgundy', with wine-colored flowers, is just one of many varieties that bloom in festive shades of yellow, orange, red, and purple. They make excellent small-scale ground covers. Upright blooms reaching 6 to 10 in. high appear mostly in spring and early summer. Can bloom year-round in mild-winter areas. Dark green leaves have hairy, gray-green undersides. Tough plants that adapt to most soils but look best with occasional water in summer. Plant in full sun. Divide every three to four years. Page: 77.

Gelsemium sempervirens

CAROLINA JASMINE. An evergreen vine beloved for its showy display of bell-shaped, fragrant yellow flowers in late winter to early spring. The neat small leaves are dark green all summer and turn maroon in winter. Can climb trees but is usually trained against a fence, trellis, or post and pruned annually (right after it blooms) to keep it under 10 ft. tall. Can also be used as a ground cover; prune annually to keep it within bounds and about 3 ft. tall. Needs full or partial sun. Looks best with regular water. Pages: 41, 94.

Geranium sanguineum var. *striatum*

BLOODY CRANESBILL. A perennial that forms a low mound or mat of small, very finely cut leaves, topped with pale pink flowers in spring and early summer. Can spread several feet wide. Plant in full sun or partial shade in well-drained garden soil. Water regularly. Cut off flower stalks when the blossoms fade. If plants look tattered or get floppy in midsummer, cut them back partway and they will bush out again. Otherwise wait until late fall to cut them to the ground. Page: 31.

Hardenbergia violacea 'Happy Wanderer'

'HAPPY WANDERER' HARDENBERGIA. A useful evergreen that can be grown as a vine or a shrub. It produces clusters of pretty pinkish purple flowers in late winter and early spring. Grown as a vine, it will twine around a trellis or up a fence, reaching about 10 ft. high. As a shrubby ground cover, it forms a mound 1 to 2 ft. high and spreads about 10 ft. wide. Plant in full sun or, in hot climates, partial shade. Needs well-drained soil and occasional water (but don't overdo it). Prune to keep within bounds. Pages: 43, 48, 51, 52.

Helianthemum nummularium

SUNROSE. Cheerful flowering evergreen shrublets with small, bright-colored spring flowers in shades of white, yellow, orange, pink, and red. Grows 6 to 8 in. high, 2 to 3 ft. wide. Plant in full sun and well-drained soil. Needs little water. Good on dry banks. Cut back after bloom. Page: 77.

Helleborus orientalis

LENTEN ROSE. A clump-forming perennial with dark leathery leaves and pink, rosy, white, or greenish flowers 2 to 3 in. wide in early spring. Plant in partial shade and rich, well-drained soil. Water regularly. Slow-growing, it self-sows and spreads gradually to form a patch. Once established, it is carefree and long-lived. Groom once a year by cutting off any dead leaves when the flower buds appear. Established clumps are typically about 18 in. tall, 18 to 24 in. wide. Pages: 22, 48, 64, 95.

Geranium sanguineum var. *striatum*
BLOODY CRANESBILL

Hardenbergia violacea 'Happy Wanderer'
HARDENBERGIA

Helianthemum nummularium   SUNROSE

Helleborus orientalis   LENTEN ROSE

Hemerocallis DAYLILY

Hemerocallis 'Stella d'Oro'
DAYLILY

Hemerocallis

DAYLILY. Among the most popular of perennials, daylilies display large lilylike flowers above dense clumps of narrow, arching leaves. Almost all daylilies today are hybrids (pp. 26, 97) sold as named cultivars. There are many thousands to choose from. Some are evergreen; others die back in winter. Some are low growing, while others have flower stalks reaching 3 ft. tall. Flowers last only a day but are replaced daily. They come in many shades of white, yellow, orange, red, and purple, and bloom from a few weeks to several months. Mix early-blooming, midseason, and late-blooming varieties to ensure months of color. 'Stella d'Oro' has golden yellow flowers (pp. 21, 56, 61, 69, 82, 111) on compact plants 1½ ft. tall and wide. 'Black-Eyed Stella' has gold flowers with a dark reddish eye and grows 1½ ft. tall and wide. Both Stellas bloom for months. 'Lavender Bonanza' has paste-colored flowers. 'Texas Sunlight' (p. 85) has larger gold flowers and grows 2 ft. tall and wide. 'Russian Rhapsody' (p. 73) has large purple flowers. All daylilies prefer full sun and well-drained soil. Water regularly during bloom. Pinch off spent flowers and then cut off flower stalks after blooming is finished. Divide in fall or late winter if you wish to propagate more plants. When planting, space shorter daylilies about 1 ft. apart and taller kinds 2 ft. apart. They will gradually fill in. Daylilies can occasionally be plagued with aphids in the spring and rust disease during humid summers.

Heteromeles arbutifolia

TOYON. A dependable California native evergreen shrub with shiny dark green leaves, clusters of white flowers in early summer, and bright red berries in fall and winter. Birds love the berries. Withstands dry periods but looks best with occasional water. Usually grown as a dense shrub 6 to 12 ft. tall but can also be trained as a multi- or single-trunked tree to almost twice that height. Page: 54.

Heuchera

ALUMROOT, CORALBELLS, HEUCHERA. Perennials that form low clumps of almost evergreen foliage and bloom spring into summer, bearing clouds of tiny red, coral, pink, or white flowers on slender stalks about 18 in. tall. They're fine accent plants or small-scale ground covers. Often sold as *H.* x *brizoides* or *H. sanguinea;* there are a number of other species and a variety of hybrids. 'Palace Purple' (pp. 27, 48, 85) has large purplish brown leaves and tiny white flowers. Island alumroot (*H. maxima*, pp. 86, 106), a Southern California native, has hairy leaves and white to pink flowers. 'Wendy' (p. 54) has bright pink flowers. All heucheras prefer full to partial sun, well-drained soil, and some summer water. Remove flower stalks as the blossoms fade. Divide

Heteromeles arbutifolia
TOYON

Heuchera sanguinea CORALBELLS

Heuchera 'Palace Purple'

every few years, replanting the divisions an inch or two deeper than they were growing before. Pages: 22, 63, 81, 111.

Hibiscus rosa-sinensis

TROPICAL HIBISCUS. Evergreen shrub with shiny dark green leaves and huge single or double flowers in stunning shades of white, pink, red, yellow, and orange. Blooms in summer. Can be trained as a small tree or grown in containers. Many named varieties to choose from; the largest reach 10 to 15 ft. tall in California. 'Santa Ana', with coral-salmon flowers, is one of a number of compact varieties that reach 4 to 8 ft. Tropical hibiscus are best in warm-summer, mild-winter areas where hard frosts are uncommon. Ideal for Southern California. In colder areas, grow in pots and protect in winter. Or substitute rose-of-Sharon (*H. syriacus*), a hardy deciduous but similar long-blooming shrub. Plant in full sun. Well-drained soil is a must. Water regularly and fertilize monthly. Prune out about a third of the old growth each year after bloom. Use insecticidal soap if aphids are a problem. Page: 56.

Heuchera maxima
ISLAND ALUMROOT

Heuchera maxima 'Wendy'
ISLAND ALUMROOT

Hosta

HOSTA. A long-lived, carefree, shade-tolerant perennial with beautiful leaves in a wide variety of colors and sizes. Plants form dome-shaped clumps or spreading patches of foliage that look good from spring to fall and die down in winter. Lavender, purple, or white flowers appear on slender stalks in mid- to late summer. Hostas grow best in partial or full shade. Can take more sun in coastal areas. All need fertile, moist, well-drained garden soil. Cut off flower stalks before seedpods ripen. Clumps can be divided in late summer or early spring if you want to make more plants; otherwise leave them alone. Snails can ravage hostas. Page: 64.

Hosta

Hydrangea macrophylla
'Nikko Blue'
HYDRANGEA

Hydrangea macrophylla
BIGLEAF HYDRANGEA

Hypericum calycinum
AARON'S BEARD

Iberis sempervirens
'Little Gem'
CANDYTUFT

Hydrangea macrophylla

BIGLEAF HYDRANGEA. A medium-size deciduous shrub with large round leaves and very showy clusters of papery-textured blue, pink, or white flowers in summer. Grows 6 to 10 ft. tall and equally wide. There are many varieties. 'Tricolor' (sometimes sold as 'Variegata') and 'Mariesii Variegata' have light- green-and-white leaves. 'Nikko Blue' (p. 48) is a popular cultivar with blue flowers. It grows only 4 to 6 ft. wide. Hydrangeas are usually grown in partial shade but can be planted in full sun near the coast. Need fertile, moist, well-drained soil. Stalks grow one year, bloom the next year. In fall, cut to the ground stalks that have bloomed. Head

back others if you need to control size. Plants may require application of aluminum sulfate to produce blue flowers. Pages: 27, 62, 73.

Hypericum calycinum

AARON'S BEARD, CREEPING ST.-JOHNSWORT. A tough, creeping ground cover that adapts to poor soils and can help control erosion on slopes. Evergreen where winters are mild. Grows about 1 ft. high and bears sunny yellow flowers in summer. Easily planted from rooted stems. Prune or mow close to the ground every year or two in early winter or spring; it regrows quickly. Hypericum adapts to most soils, in full sun or partial shade. Looks best with occasional summer water. Page: 71.

Iberis sempervirens 'Little Gem'

'LITTLE GEM' EVERGREEN CANDYTUFT. A bushy perennial that forms a sprawling mound of glossy evergreen foliage topped for several weeks in spring with white flowers. 'Little Gem' is a compact plant growing 6 to 8 in. tall. Can be used as a ground cover. Needs full sun, well-drained soil, and regular water. Shear off the top half of the plants after they bloom. Needs no other care. Don't try to divide it; buy new plants if you want more. Pages: 19, 21.

Iris

BEARDED IRIS. A popular perennial with stiff, bladelike, gray-green leaves about 1 ft. tall. Elegant flowers in shades of white, blue, lavender, purple, pink, and yellow are borne on stalks 1 to 3 ft. tall. Plant the thick fingerlike rhizomes in fall or early spring, in full sun or partial shade. Bury the roots, but expose the rhizome on the soil surface. Irises need good drainage and regular water during periods of growth. Fertilize in spring. Divide when the clumps become crowded. Page: 95.

Iris sibirica

SIBERIAN IRIS. A perennial that forms a large arching clump of tall slender leaves. Stalks 2 to 3 ft. tall bear elegant flowers in shades of white, blue, lavender, purple, and pink. Plant in full sun or partial shade, burying the rhizomes 1 to 2 in. deep in well-drained soil. Water regularly and fertilize in spring. Divide when clumps become crowded. Pages: 78, 101.

Ixora 'Thai Dwarf'

'THAI DWARF' IXORA. Ixoras are frost-tender evergreen shrubs grown for their showy clusters of brightly colored and highly perfumed flowers atop lustrous rounded leaves. Cultivars come in many sizes. 'Thai Dwarf' reaches 4 ft. tall and wide and bears multicolored flower clusters in shades of red, orange, gold, pink, and yellow. Ixoras require full sun, acid soil, and regular watering. They respond well to pruning but don't require it. Pages: 35, 89.

Jasminum sambac

ARABIAN JASMINE. This tropical evergreen vining shrub bears deep green, glossy leaves and intensely fragrant small white flowers in summer. Grown as a vine, it will reach 10 ft. tall and at least as wide if tied to a trellis for support. Grows well in full sun. Water regularly. Does best where winters are mild. Pages: 35, 89.

Lagerstroemia indica

CRAPE MYRTLE. A deciduous small tree or large shrub, usually grown with multiple trunks. Blooms for many weeks in the heat of summer, with large clusters of papery-textured pink, rose, or white flowers at the end of each stem. Leaves typically turn red, orange, or purplish in fall. Flaking bark is attractive in winter. Many varieties to choose from. In coastal areas, select mildew-resistant members of the Indian Tribe Series. They include 'Cherokee', with red flowers; 'Seminole', with pink blooms; and 'Catawba', with purple flowers. 'Zuni' (p. 28) is a hybrid variety reaching 10 ft. tall that bears large, dark lavender blooms. All crape myrtles need full sun, well-drained soil, and only occasional water. Prune in winter, removing weak, broken, and crowded shoots. Page: 17.

Iris   BEARDED IRIS

Iris sibirica   SIBERIAN IRIS

Jasminum sambac
ARABIAN JASMIN

Lagerstroemia indica 'Zuni'
CRAPE MYRTLE

Lagerstroemia indica   CRAPE MYRTLE

Lamium maculatum 'White Nancy'   *Lamium maculatum* 'Roseum'

Lantana montevidensis   *Lavandula* 'Goodwin Creek Gray'
LAVENDER

Lavandula angustifolia 'Munstead'
LAVENDER

Lamium maculatum

LAMIUM. A creeping perennial that makes an excellent ground cover for shady areas. Gray-green heart-shaped leaves are marked with silver and topped with clusters of pink flowers in early summer. Plants form low mats less than 6 in. high and spreading 2 ft. or wider. Foliage is evergreen in mild-winter areas. 'White Nancy' (p. 64) has white flowers and silvery leaves edged with green. 'Roseum' (p. 64) is similar but has pink flowers continuously all year and less white on the foliage. Lamiums grow best in shade but can take more sun in coastal areas. Water regularly. Cut back halfway with hedge shears after bloom and again in late summer if plants look shabby. Divide every few years in spring or fall. Page: 22.

Lantana montevidensis

LANTANA. A colorful, spreading, evergreen shrub widely grown as a ground cover. Clusters of small flowers top plants in spring, summer, and fall; year-round in mild-winter areas. Varieties available in many shades of white, yellow, pink, orange, red, and purple. 'Confetti' has multicolored flowers of yellow, pink, and purple. Generally about 2 to 4 ft. tall but can be taller. Spreads 3 to 6 ft. Excellent ground cover for slopes or poor soils. Will spill over walls. Plant in full sun; mildews otherwise. Needs little water. Shear after bloom to keep compact and to encourage more flowers. Pages: 33, 91, 102.

Lavandula

LAVENDER. Choice evergreen shrubs ideal for dry-summer climates. They form bushy mounds of fragrant gray-green foliage topped in early summer with countless long-stalked spikes of very fragrant flowers. English lavender, *L. angustifolia*, generally grows 3 to 4 ft. tall, with 1- to 2-ft. flower spikes. 'Munstead' (pp. 19, 38, 92) reaches about 18 in. and has pale lavender flowers. 'Hidcote' (p. 51) grows about 1 ft. tall and wide, with gray foliage and rich purple flowers. L. 'Goodwin Creek Gray' (pp. 24, 41, 47, 51, 81) has gray foliage and deep blue blooms from early summer into fall, or longer where summers are mild. Grows 2 to 3 ft. tall and wide. 'Otto Quast' (pp. 28, 38), a cultivar of Spanish lavender (*L. stoechas*), has showy, tufted, dark lavender flowers on a 1- to 3-ft. plant. All lavenders need full sun, well-drained soil, and little water. Shear flower stalks to foliage height when the petals fade.

Ligustrum japonicum 'Texanum'

TEXAS PRIVET. A fast-growing evergreen shrub or small tree with very glossy bright green leaves, clusters of heavy-scented white flowers in early summer, and dark blue-black berries in fall and winter. Usually grown as a hedge or screen. Grows 6 to 9 ft. tall but can be clipped lower. Needs full or partial sun and occasional water. Grows in almost any soil. Prune in spring and summer. Pages: 17, 47.

Liquidambar styraciflua

LIQUIDAMBAR. Widely popular (some feel too popular), narrow, upright deciduous tree loved for its reliable fall color. Lobed leaves turn bright shades of purple, red, orange, and yellow in fall. Good for narrow areas; it can reach over 50 ft. tall but takes many years to get there. Spiked seedpods are attractive in winter but messy when they drop. 'Festival' (p. 97) turns a kaleidoscope of yellows, oranges, and reds in fall. Liquidambar prefers acid soils and occasional deep waterings in summer. Surface roots can be a problem near sidewalks and patios and in lawns. Prune to shape.

Liriope muscari

LILYTURF. A perennial that forms clumps of grass-like evergreen leaves and bears spikes of small flowers in summer. It is a fine small-scale ground cover, especially near walks and patios. 'Big Blue' (pp. 27, 48, 79, 87) has blue flowers and dark green foliage. 'Majestic' (p. 77) is similar but bears purple flowers. 'Silver Dragon' (p. 31) has lilac flowers and leaves edged with narrow yellow stripes that fade to creamy white. 'Silvery Sunproof' (p. 101) is similar but takes more sun and has showier flowers. Lilyturf prefers partial shade inland. Can take more sun near the coast. Mow or shear off old foliage in early spring. Divide every few years if you want to make more plants. Can be invasive.

Lycianthes rantonnetii 'Royal Robe'

'ROYAL ROBE' PARAGUAY NIGHTSHADE. A shrub with bright green leaves that are evergreen in mild-winter areas. Purple flowers with star-shaped yellow centers bloom throughout warm weather. Grows 4 to 6 ft. tall. Plant in full sun. Tolerates dry conditions but does best with occasional water. Prune to control size. Page: 106.

Ligustrum japonicum 'Texanum'
TEXAS PRIVET

Liquidambar styraciflua 'Festival'
LIQUIDAMBAR

Liriope muscari 'Majestic'
LILYTURF

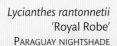

Lycianthes rantonnetii 'Royal Robe'
PARAGUAY NIGHTSHADE

Liriope muscari 'Silvery Sunproof'
LIRIOPE

Magnolia x *soulangiana*
SAUCER MAGNOLIA

Mahonia aquifolium
OREGON GRAPE

Malus 'Pink Spires'
CRAB APPLE

Magnolia x *soulangiana*

SAUCER MAGNOLIA. Deciduous tree with large bold leaves and huge flowers in shades of white, pink, and purple borne on leafless stems. Many varieties to choose from. Often the inside and the outside of the flower differ in color. Grows 15 to 25 ft. tall and spreads as wide, usually with multiple trunks. Saucer magnolias need full sun, well-drained soil, and regular water. Prune in early summer, removing only weak or crossing limbs. Page: 17.

Mahonia

MAHONIA. Spreading evergreen shrubs with handsome deeply divided leaves. Showy yellow flower clusters in spring produce blackish blue berries later in the year. Oregon grape (*M. aquifolium*, pp. 54, 86) grows about 6 ft. tall and has glossy green leaves that are tinged red when new, purplish in cold winters. 'Compacta' (p. 97) grows only 2 to 3 ft. tall but spreads to form a mid-height ground cover. M. lomariifolia grows 6 to 10 ft. tall and has large, spiny, shiny green leaves. It is the best choice for southern California. Mahonias can be grown in sun or shade but usually look their best with some shelter. They grow well among tree roots. Water occasionally. Prune to open the center and expose the stems.

Malus 'Pink Spires'

'PINK SPIRES' CRAB APPLE. Small deciduous tree with showy pink flowers in early spring and bright purple-red fruits that ripen in early fall and last all winter. Grows about 25 ft. tall and has foliage tinged with red. There are many other fine crab apples that could be used as substitutes. 'Hopa' also reaches about 25 ft. and has lovely red-rose flowers and orange-red fruits that make excellent jelly. It is one of the better choices for Southern California. 'Snowdrift' grows 20 to 25 ft. tall and bears white flowers that start out red in the bud and become orange-red fruits. M. x zumi var. calocarpa grows to 25 ft. but has a narrow crown only 15 ft. wide. White flowers are followed by bright red fruits. All crab apples need full sun and regular water. They are not well adapted to the mild-winter climates of coastal Southern California. Train young trees by spreading narrow crotches and removing lower limbs to form a crown you can walk underneath. Prune off any suckers that sprout from the base of the tree, and any water sprouts (shoots that grow straight up). Page: 97.

Mandevilla 'Alice du Pont'

'ALICE DU PONT' MANDEVILLA. Sprawling evergreen vine with twining stems and shiny dark green leaves. Glorious clusters of pink flowers bloom from spring to

Mandevilla 'Alice du Pont'

Nandina domestica 'Harbour Dwarf'
HEAVENLY BAMBOO

fall. With support it will grow 20 to 30 ft. high. Provide a wire trellis to train along eaves. Will also climb over an arbor or fence. Plant in full sun near the coast and in partial shade in warmer inland areas. Water regularly during summer. Prune anytime to control size. Hardy only in coastal Southern California and warmer inland areas. Substitute wisteria in colder areas. Pages: 27, 44.

Nandina domestica
HEAVENLY BAMBOO, NANDINA. An evergreen shrub that forms a clump of slender, erect stems. Fine-textured compound leaves change color with the seasons, from gold to green to red. Fluffy clusters of white flowers in summer are followed by red berries that last for months. Common nandina (p. 86) grows 4 to 6 ft. tall, 2 to 3 ft. wide; 'Royal Princess' (p. 73) and 'Compacta' (p. 21) are somewhat smaller, growing 3 to 4 ft. tall and 2 to 3 ft. wide. 'Moon Bay' (p. 101) is one of several new nonflowering dwarf forms, only 2 ft. tall and wide. It turns a beautiful red in winter. 'Harbour Dwarf' (pp. 41, 56), 'Gulf Stream' (pp. 30, 54), and 'Nana' (pp. 38, 60) are dwarf varieties that bloom. Nandina adapts well to most soils, in sun or shade. Looks best with regular water. Prune old, weak, or damaged stems at ground level.

Nandina domestica 'Gulf Stream'
HEAVENLY BAMBOO

Nolina recurvata
BOTTLE PALM. A curious-looking small evergreen tree with a large swollen base, one or more tapering trunks, and drooping clusters of bright green, straplike leaves. Bottle palm grows slowly and may eventually reach 12 to 15 ft. high. It needs full sun and well-drained soil. Does best where frosts are light or nonexistent. Page: 89.

Recommended ornamental grasses

Calamagrostis x acutiflora 'Stricta', Feather reed grass

A perennial grass that forms narrow, erect clumps about 2 ft. wide. Slender stalks 5 to 6 ft. tall are topped in late spring to summer with flower spikes that resemble pipe cleaners. In cold-winter areas, the whole plant gradually turns beige or tan by fall. Stays ever-green in mild-winter areas. Full sun or partial shade. Pages: 54, 97, 106.

Calamagrostis x *acutiflora* 'Stricta'
FEATHER REED GRASS

Helictotrichon sempervirens
BLUE OAT GRASS

Festuca ovina var. glauca, Blue fescue grass

A neat, compact grass that forms a dense tuft about 1 ft. tall and wide of very slender, blue-green leaves. Narrow flower spikes appear in early summer and soon turn tan. (There is considerable confusion over the Latin name, and plants are often sold as *F. cinerea* or *F. glauca*.) 'Blausilber' is one of several cultivars with especially

Festuca ovina var. *glauca*
BLUE FESCUE GRASS

Pennisetum setaceum 'Rubrum'
PURPLE FOUNTAIN GRASS

blue-colored foliage. All make fine-textured ground covers for small areas. Full sun or partial shade; can take some drought. Must be cut to the ground at least once a year. If cut in late summer, fresh new foliage appears in the fall and lasts all winter. Pages: 59, 85, 95.

Helictotrichon sempervirens, Blue oat grass

A clump-forming grass with thin, wiry, pale blue, evergreen leaves. Blooms sparsely, with thin flower spikes that turn beige or tan. Do not cut back. Simply comb your fingers through the clump to pull out any loose, dead leaves. Old clumps may die out in the middle; if so, divide them in fall or early spring. Plant in full sun. Grows 2 to 3 ft. tall and wide. Pages: 28, 36, 95, 101, 104.

Miscanthus sinensis 'Variegatus', Varigated eulalia grass

A showy grass that forms vase-shaped or rounded clumps of long arching leaves striped white from top to bottom. Blooms in late summer or fall on stalks up to 6 ft. tall; fluffy seed heads last through the winter. Best in full sun; tol-erates some shade. Needs frequent wa-tering and well-drained soil. Page: 30.

Pennisetum setaceum 'Rubrum', Purple fountain grass

A perennial grass that forms a hassock-like clump, about 4 ft. tall and 3 ft. wide, of arching leaves that are reddish brown in summer, gold or tan in fall. Blooms over a long season from mid-summer to fall, with fluffy purple spikes on arching stalks. Grow in full sun. Needs little water. Can go many years without being divided. Pages: 28, 38, 59, 101.

Osmanthus fragrans SWEET OLIVE

Ornamental grasses

A group of perennial plants that are becoming very popular in California gardens. Their narrow leaves provide a soft texture that contrasts beautifully with the foliage of other plants. Leaves come in shades of red, yellow, blue, and green, and striped combinations. In fall and winter, some turn mingled shades of gold, brown, silver, or red. The flowers, often wispy plumes on tall stalks, last long into winter and sway with the slightest breeze. Most ornamental grasses grow best in full sun and with regular water, although some can take partial shade. Divide in fall or spring when the clumps become crowded. Cut back almost to the ground in winter or whenever the plant becomes floppy or unruly. For information on specific ornamental grasses, see the box on the facing page.

Osmanthus x *fortunei*

SWEET OLIVE. A desirable shrub for screening patios and decks, sweet olive has a compact, vase-shaped growth habit, polished evergreen leaves, and intoxicatingly fragrant, though not showy, white flowers in late spring and early summer, and occasionally throughout the year. Flowers are followed by blue-black berries. Grows 8 to 10 ft. tall and about half as wide. Does best in full sun, except in hot summer climates, where partial shade is preferable. Needs well-drained soil and regular watering. Can be lightly sheared to keep compact. Page: 74.

Pachypodium lamerei

MADAGASCAR PALM. This palmlike succulent shrub makes an exotic specimen in a pot or planted in the ground in frost-free areas. The plump spiny trunk is topped with long, strap-shaped, dull green leaves. In summer, mature plants bear fragrant, white crepe-papery flowers with yellow centers, followed by seedpods that resemble long gourds. Grows slowly up to 8 ft. tall. Adapted to full sun or partial shade. A carefree exotic. Pages: 33, 89.

Recommended palms

Archontophoenix cunninghamiana, King palm

Bold, shiny trunks and huge, arching, dark green leaves that are 8 to 10 ft. long. Quickly grows to 20 to 40 ft. and sometimes taller. Full sun or partial shade. Likes lots of water and protection from wind. Hardy to 28°F. Page: 56.

Phoenix roebelinii, Pygmy date palm

A uniquely soft-textured palm that grows only about 6 ft. tall. Usually grown with several trunks, it has fairly dense dark green foliage. Frost-sensitive and grown only where winters are very mild. Elsewhere it can be grown in pots and protected in winter. Best in partial shade. Pages: 35, 56.

Syagrus romanzoffianus, Queen palm

A bold, single-trunk palm that can grow up to 50 ft. tall. Arching, feathery leaves can reach 15 ft. Full sun. Likes lots of water and fertilizer. Leaves damaged below 25°F, but plant will survive 5° to 10° colder. Pages: 82, 101.

Archontophoenix cunninghamiana KING PALM

Syagrus romanzoffianus QUEEN PALM

Phoenix roebelinii PYGMY DATE PALM

Palms

Few plants impart the feeling of mild-winter, tropical climates like palms. In the landscape, their bold presence and sturdy appearance evoke California's warm beaches and cool breezes. Among the many available palms, tolerance to winter cold is the most significant limiting factor. Be sure to check with your local nursery to ensure that you get a palm hardy enough for your climate. Large palms survive transplanting as well as small ones do, so if you want instant results, start with large, boxed specimens. However, planting bigger palms requires professional help and heavy equipment. When planting your own palm, work lots of organic matter into the soil in and around the planting hole. Most palms need little more care than regular watering, fertilizing, and the occasional removal of old leaves. For information on specific palms, see the box on page 143.

Pelargonium

Pelargonium x *hortorum*
COMMON GERANIUM

GERANIUM. Flowering perennials loved for their round flower clusters and long season of bloom from spring into fall. (For hardy geraniums, see Geranium.) Flowers come in many single and bicolored shades of white, pink, red, and purple. Lady Washington pelargonium, P. x domesticum, is a shrubby plant about 3 ft. tall and wide bearing ball-shaped flowers above dark green leaves. Common geranium, P. x hortorum, reaches a similar size and has soft leaves, often with dark markings. Ivy geranium, P. peltatum, is a sprawling plant about 1 ft. tall and 2 to 3 ft. wide. With glossy green leaves, it makes a colorful ground cover. All geraniums grow best in full or partial sun. Water regularly. Remove spent flowers. Cut back in fall or early spring if necessary. Geraniums are ideal container plants and are often grown as annuals. Watch for geranium bud worm, which causes plants to stop blooming. Ask at your nursery about controls. Pages: 85, 95.

Penstemon gloxinioides

Penstemon gloxinioides
GARDEN PENSTEMON

GARDEN OR BORDER PENSTEMON. Late-spring- and summer-flowering perennial with showy tubular flower spikes in shades of white, pink, red, and purple. Grown as an annual in cold-winter areas. Forms erect clumps about 3 ft. tall. Many varieties available. Needs full or partial sun. Looks best with regular water, but plants must have excellent drainage or they die quickly. Cut down spent flower stalks to encourage second bloom.

Perovskia atriplicifolia
RUSSIAN SAGE

In colder, high elevations P. barbatus (p. 111) is a good substitute. It bears red flowers from spring into summer. Also check nurseries for locally native species. Pages: 24, 66, 78.

Perovskia atriplicifolia

RUSSIAN SAGE. A shrubby perennial that forms an open, vase-shaped clump of straight, fairly stiff stems with sparse silver-gray foliage and tiny but abundant lavender-blue flowers. Blooms for weeks in summer and into fall. Grow in full sun and well-drained soil. Needs little water. Cut old stems down to 6-in. stubs in spring. Grows 3 to 5 ft. tall and wide by fall. To control size, cut stems back by one- third in early summer. Pages: 36, 76.

Phormium tenax

NEW ZEALAND FLAX. A perennial prized for its bold evergreen foliage. Stiff, straplike leaves form a fanlike clump about 5 ft. tall and at least as wide. Stalks bearing red or yellow flowers rise high above the leaves. Many varieties with colorful foliage are available. 'Atropurpureum' (p. 76) has reddish purple leaves, and 'Bronze' (pp. 59, 75) has red-brown leaves. Smaller varieties, better suited to small gardens, include 'Yellow Wave' (pp. 52,

Phormium tenax 'Atropurpureum'
New Zealand flax

Phormium tenax 'Yellow Wave'
New Zealand flax

Phormium tenax 'Sundowner'
New Zealand flax

101), with yellow leaves, and 'Sundowner' (p. 28), with foliage that is a blazing mix of red, yellow, cream, green, and bronze. Plant New Zealand flax in full sun. Needs little water. Excellent accent plant, but large types need lots of room. In cold foothill areas, substitute an ornamental grass.

Photinia x *fraseri*

Fraser photinia. Evergreen shrub with dark green leaves and white spring flowers. New leaves are bronzy red and appear all summer (shearing encourages new growth). Grows 10 to 15 ft. tall and wide. Plant in full sun. Needs to be watered regularly. Pages: 59, 73, 74.

Pinus mugo

Mugo pine. A slow-growing pine that forms an irregular shrubby mound, not a conical tree. Needles are dark green. Needs full sun and well-drained soil. Occasional water. Doesn't require pruning, but you can shear it in early summer if you want to, cutting new growth back by less than one-half. Typically grows just a few inches a year, but some plants are faster than others. Usually stays under 3 to 6 ft. tall and 5 to 10 ft. wide for many years. Page: 102.

Photinia x *fraseri*
Fraser photinia

Pinus mugo
Mugo pine

Pittosporum tobira 'Cream de Mint'
TOBIRA

Podocarpus macrophyllus 'Maki'
SHRUBBY YEW PINE

Polygala x *dalmaisiana*
SWEET-PEA SHRUB

Prunus caroliniana 'Compacta'
COMPACT CAROLINA LAUREL CHERRY

Pittosporum

PITTOSPORUM. Dependable evergreen shrubs and small trees with tufts of glossy leaves and fragrant, usually white flowers in early summer. *P. tobira* 'Cream de Mint' (p. 64) has gray-green leaves with white edging and grows about 1 to 2 ft. tall and wide. Its compact, mounded shape makes it useful for a small hedge or as a ground cover. *P. tenuifolium* (p. 101) grows into a 25- to 40-ft. tall round-headed tree if left alone, but it is more often clipped as a hedge. It has wavy, clean-looking, shiny light green leaves. *P. undulatum* (p. 74) is another treelike form with a dense, rounded shape and creamy white flowers. All adapt to sun or shade and look best with regular water. Prune anytime.

Podocarpus macrophyllus

SHRUBBY YEW PINE. A fine-textured columnar shrub or tree covered to the ground in bright green, flat, needle-thin leaves. It makes a fine specimen or a fairly dense screen. Grows slowly to 50 ft. tall and 20 ft. wide. Prefers full sun, well-drained soil, and regular watering. Page: 74.

Podocarpus macrophyllus 'Maki'

SHRUBBY YEW PINE. This is a useful, full-foliaged, evergreen shrub or small tree with attractive needlelike leaves. Well behaved and easy to train or prune to any shape or size. Grows 6 to 12 ft. tall if left unpruned. Good as a background plant, screen, or hedge and also does well in containers. Plant in full sun or partial shade and well-drained soil. Water regularly. Prune anytime. Page: 30.

Polygala x dalmaisiana

SWEET-PEA SHRUB. Evergreen shrub with small narrow leaves and a long season of purplish pink, pea-shaped flowers. Grows 5 ft. tall, with a spreading habit, often bare near the ground. Plant in full sun or partial shade. Water regularly. Shear to keep full-foliaged. Page: 24.

Prunus caroliniana 'Compacta'

COMPACT CAROLINA LAUREL CHERRY. Very useful evergreen hedge or screen plant with glossy green leaves and small spikes of scented white flowers in spring. Flowers are followed by black berries that are messy if the plant is in the wrong spot. 'Bright 'n Tight' is similar and a good substitute. Both reach about 8 to 10 ft. tall and 6 to 8 ft. wide, taller if left unpruned. Can be sheared anytime. Best in full sun but can take partial shade. Plants prefer moist, well-drained soil; tolerate dry sites. Page: 44.

Punica granatum

POMEGRANATE. Very ornamental deciduous fruit tree. 'Wonderful' (pp. 41, 94) is widely grown. Its

Punica granatum 'Wonderful'
POMEGRANATE

Punica granatum 'Nana'
DWARF POMEGRANATE

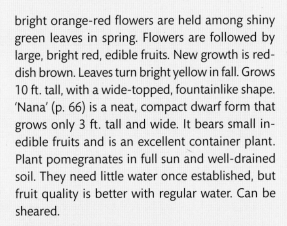

Rhaphiolepis indica 'Clara'
INDIAN HAWTHORN

bright orange-red flowers are held among shiny green leaves in spring. Flowers are followed by large, bright red, edible fruits. New growth is reddish brown. Leaves turn bright yellow in fall. Grows 10 ft. tall, with a wide-topped, fountainlike shape. 'Nana' (p. 66) is a neat, compact dwarf form that grows only 3 ft. tall and wide. It bears small inedible fruits and is an excellent container plant. Plant pomegranates in full sun and well-drained soil. They need little water once established, but fruit quality is better with regular water. Can be sheared.

Rhaphiolepis indica

INDIAN HAWTHORN. An evergreen shrub with thick-textured green leaves, small pink or white flowers in spring, and blue berries that last through the summer and fall. Grows 2 to 3 ft. tall, 3 to 6 ft. wide. Some larger forms can be trained into small trees. There are many fine cultivars. 'Clara' (pp. 44, 75) reaches 3 to 5 ft. tall and wide and has white flowers and red new growth. 'Ballerina' (p. 17) grows only 2 ft. tall and 4 ft. wide and has pink flowers. 'Indian Princess' grows to 3 ft. and bears pink flowers. 'Majestic Beauty' (p. 72) is a large cultivar, growing 20 to 25 ft. tall and bearing light pink flowers in clusters up to 10 in. wide. Indian hawthorn needs full sun and, once established, little water. Requires minimal pruning or care. Pages: 28, 69.

Rhaphiolepis indica 'Ballerina'
INDIAN HAWTHORN

Recommended roses

Rosa 'America'

Rosa 'China Doll'

'America' rose
A vigorous climbing rose with very fragrant orange-red flowers. Easily climbs to 10 to 15 ft. high. Must be tied to a trellis or fence for support. Page: 47.

'China Doll' rose
A favorite polyantha rose bearing large clusters of fluffy pink flowers. Blooms on and on. A compact plant 1½ to 2 ft. tall and about as wide. Good in containers or as a low hedge. Page: 60.

'Double Delight' rose
A hybrid tea rose with very fragrant white flowers edged with red. Exceptional cut flower. Grows 4 to 6 ft. tall. Page: 47.

'Flower Carpet Pink'
A low, spreading rose that forms a mat of dark green leaves topped with pink flowers. Grows 2 ft. high by 3 ft. wide. Pages: 34, 89.

'Iceberg'
One of the best white floribunda roses for California. Blooms off and on all year where where winters are warm. Upright, 3- to 5-ft. plant with excellent disease resistance. Pages: 17, 43, 44, 51, 85, 97.

'Margaret Merril'
Lovely, fragrant white floribunda rose with a compact habit. Grows about 3 ft. tall and wide. Generous bloom. Excellent low hedge. Page: 92.

'Mister Lincoln'
A hybrid tea rose with enchantingly fragrant, deep red flowers. Great cut flower. Grows 4 to 6 ft. tall. Page: 47.

'Papa Meilland'
A hybrid tea rose with very fragrant double crimson flowers. Page: 47.

'Red Meidiland'
Spreading ground-cover rose. Flowers are red with white centers. Blooms over a long season. Grows 2 to 3 ft. high and about 5 ft. wide. Page: 41.

'Tiffany'
Long-stemmed, fragrant pink hybrid tea rose. Grows 4 to 6 ft. tall. Easy to grow. Page: 47.

Rosa 'Iceberg'

Rosa 'Tiffany'

Rhododendron

RHODODENDRON AND AZALEA. An especially diverse and popular group of shrubs with very showy flowers between early spring and early summer. The leaves can be small or large, deciduous or evergreen. The plants can be short, medium, or tall, with spreading, mounded, or erect habits. Northern Californians can grow a great many rhododendrons and azaleas, including a number of native species.

Evergreen azaleas are widely grown in the state and do well in southern California's hot summers. They produce masses of flowers in mid- to late spring on compact shrubs, usually 2 to 4 ft. tall, with small evergreen leaves. They can be sheared to produce a neat, massed effect. Unsheared, they form irregular billowing mounds. 'Gumpo White' (p. 30) and 'Alaska' (pp. 27, 54, 62) are among the best white-flowered azaleas for California. For a pink azalea select 'Gumpo Pink' (p. 73).

Rhododendrons and azaleas have similar cultural requirements. All do best with partial shade, and they need fertile, moist, well-drained soil. Mix a 3-in. layer of peat moss into the soil when you prepare a bed for these shrubs. Plant rhododendrons and azaleas in spring or early fall. Be sure not to plant them too deep—the top of the root ball should be level with, or a little higher than, the surrounding soil. Azaleas are usually sold in containers. When planting them, it's very important that you make a few deep cuts down the outside of the root ball and tease apart some of the roots; otherwise azaleas do not root well into the surrounding soil.

Use a layer of mulch to keep the soil cool and damp around your azaleas and rhododendrons, and water the plants regularly. Prune or shear off the flower stalks as soon as the petals fade to prevent seeds from forming and to neaten the plants. Prune or shear to control the size and shape of the plant at the same time (usually in early summer).

Rosa

ROSE. Fast-growing deciduous shrubs with glossy compound leaves, thorny stems or canes, and very showy, often fragrant flowers. See the box on the facing page for descriptions of specific roses. In winter and early spring, many garden centers stock bare-root roses, with the roots packed in moist wood shavings wrapped in a plastic bag. These are a good investment if you buy them right after they arrive in the stores and plant them promptly, but

Rhododendron
'Alaska'
AZALEA

their quality deteriorates as the weather warms and they begin to grow in the bag. Nurseries may sell bare-root roses in the spring, but they usually grow the plants in containers. If you buy a potted rose, you can plant it anytime.

All roses grow best in full sun and fertile, well-drained soil topped with a few inches of mulch. Once established, the roses recommended in this book require no more care than many other shrubs. Prune them once a year in spring, before new growth starts. (See p. 206 for more on pruning.) The roses recommended here have good resistance to various fungal diseases but may have problems during years when the weather is especially moist. To control fungus, mix 2 tsp. baking soda and 2 tsp. summer oil (available at nurseries) in 1 gal. of water and spray the rose foliage until it's dripping wet. Repeat every 10 days. Aphids—soft-bodied insects the size of a pinhead—may attack the new growth on roses but do no serious damage. You can wash them away with plain or soapy water.

Rosmarinus officinalis
'Tuscan Blue'
ROSEMARY

Rosmarinus officinalis

ROSEMARY. Classic Mediterranean evergreen shrub with gray-green needlelike leaves that combine a lovely fragrance with a tasty flavor. Small blue, lilac, or white flowers bloom in late winter and early spring. Grows upright or spreading, 2 to 6 ft. tall. 'Tuscan Blue' (pp. 19, 36, 52, 71, 81) is upright to 6 ft., has deep blue flowers, and can be grown as a low hedge. 'Majorca Pink' (pp. 85, 109) is upright to 2 to 4 ft. but has lavender-pink blooms. Tough plants. Rosemary is best in full sun and well-drained soil. Needs little water once established. Prune or shear in spring or summer.

Rosmarinus officinalis
'Majorca Pink'
ROSEMARY

Rudbeckia hirta   GLORIOSA DAISY

Salvia chamaedryoides
GERMANDER SAGE

Salvia leucantha
MEXICAN BUSH SAGE

Salvia greggii
AUTUMN SAGE

Salvia x superba
SALVIA

Rudbeckia hirta

GLORIOSA DAISY, BLACK-EYED SUSAN. A summer-flowering perennial with large, daisylike, orange-yellow flowers that have a black center. Grows 3 to 4 ft. tall, with upright stems. Some varieties, such as 'Goldilocks', are much smaller. Plant in full sun and well-drained soil. Looks best with regular water. Remove spent flowers. Cut back in fall. Can be grown as an annual. Page: 97.

Salvia

SAGE, SALVIA. These shrubby perennials are grown for their long bloom season (from late spring into fall) and tough constitution. Germander sage (*S. chamaedryoides*, p. 77) forms a spreading mound of silvery leaves about 2 ft. tall covered with short spikes of beautiful light blue flowers. Autumn sage (*S. greggii*, pp. 52, 76, 104) grows about 2 to 3 ft. tall and wide. Flowers are typically bright red, but they can be pink, salmon, or white. Mexican bush sage (*S. leucantha*, pp. 24, 52, 76, 95) has gray-green leaves and produces long spikes of velvety purple-and-white flowers. It grows 3 to 4 ft. tall and usually wider. *S. x superba* (pp. 43, 78) forms a patch of dark green foliage that is topped with countless flower spikes. It grows 18 to 24 in. tall and spreads 2 ft. wide. A number of fine cultivars are available. Sages prefer full sun but can take a little shade in inland areas. They must have well-drained soil, and most like to be on the dry side. Shear or trim off the old flower stalks from time to time to keep the plant blooming. Mexican bush sage should be cut back to the ground in late fall. Others should be lightly sheared back. Divide spreading types every few years in spring or fall.

Santolina chamaecyparissus

LAVENDER COTTON. A bushy little shrub with soft, fragrant, fine-textured, silver-gray foliage. It is often sheared to make an edging or a formal specimen. Can also be used as a ground cover. If unsheared, it bears round yellow blossoms in midsummer. Needs full sun and well-drained, dry soil. Prune every year in early spring, before new growth starts, cutting the old stems back halfway to the ground. Grows 1 to 2 ft. tall, 2 to 3 ft. wide. Page: 95.

Scabiosa caucasica

PINCUSHION FLOWER. A perennial that forms a clump of gray-green leaves. Thin stalks about 2 ft. tall bear clusters of usually blue but sometimes white flowers from late spring through fall. Plant in full sun and water regularly. Remove spent flowers. Cut back in fall to promote additional bloom. Pages: 19, 24, 75, 85.

Sedum 'Autumn Joy'

'AUTUMN JOY' SEDUM. A perennial that forms a vase-shaped clump of thick stems lined with large, fleshy, gray-green leaves. Grows about 2 ft. tall and 2 to 3 ft. wide. Broad flat clusters of buds form at the top of each stem in late summer and gradually change from creamy white to pink to rust as the flowers open and mature. Needs full sun and little water. Cut stems back partway in early summer to keep them from flopping over and to make the clump bushier. In late fall or spring, cut old stems to the ground. Divide clump every few years in fall or early spring. Pages: 78, 97.

Sedum rubrotinctum

PORK-AND-BEANS SEDUM. Low-growing, spreading perennial succulent with small green and reddish brown leaves resembling beans, particularly when full sun intensifies the reddish tint. Bears reddish yellow flowers in late winter. Can be grown in full sun or partial shade. Needs little water. Can be used as a small-scale ground cover or planted in pots. Divide in spring if you need more plants. You can also pull off and plant individual leaves, which will root easily. Page: 59.

Spiraea x vanhouttei

VANHOUTTEI'S SPIREA. An old-fashioned favorite, this deciduous shrub forms a dense clump of arching branches hidden in spring under thick veils of tiny white flowers. Small leaves are dark green in summer, often purple in fall. Grows 5 to 6 ft. high and about 8 ft. wide. Best in full sun but can take some shade. Water regularly. Prune after flowering. Page: 111.

Santolina chamaecyparissus
LAVENDER COTTON

Scabiosa caucasica
PINCUSHION FLOWER

Sedum 'Autumn Joy'

Sedum rubrotinctum
PORK-AND-BEANS SEDUM

Stachys byzantina
LAMB'S EARS

Strelitzia reginae
BIRD-OF-PARADISE

Syringa vulgaris
COMMON LILAC

Tagetes lemmonii
SHRUB MARIGOLD

Stachys byzantina

LAMB'S EARS. A mat-forming perennial whose large oval leaves are densely covered with soft white fuzz. Typically the leaves are 3 to 4 in. long, and the plant spreads about 18 in. wide. Blooms in early summer, with small purple flowers on thick stalks about 1 ft. tall. Needs full or partial sun, well-drained soil, and occasional water. Cut off the bloom stalks when the flowers fade, or as soon as they appear if you don't like their looks. Use a soft rake to clean away the old leaves in early spring. Divide clumps every few years. Pages: 79, 85.

Strelitzia reginae

BIRD-OF-PARADISE. Beloved, tropical-looking evergreen plant with large, eye-catching flowers that look like the head of a bird. Flowers, mostly orange but touched with blue and white, are concentrated in early spring, but some bloom year-round. Large leathery leaves form a dense clump about 5 ft. tall. Best adapted to frost-free areas of Southern California and the San Francisco area. Needs protection elsewhere. Or plant in pots and move to a covered spot in winter. Best in full sun. Water and fertilize regularly. Remove spent flowers. Pages: 59, 89, 101.

Syringa vulgaris

COMMON LILAC. A large deciduous shrub valued for its sweet-scented flowers in spring. There are dozens of cultivars, with single or double flowers in shades of lilac, purple, pink, and white. Most grow 10 to 20 ft. tall, with many erect stems. Most varieties need winter chilling to bloom well. In Southern California and other mild-winter areas, grow Descanso hybrids such as 'Blue Boy', 'Lavender Lady', and 'White Angel'. Plant in full sun. Water regularly. Remove spent flowers. Prune as needed. Pages: 17, 69.

Tagetes lemmonii

SHRUB MARIGOLD. Shrublike perennial with small aromatic leaves and bright orange, marigoldlike flowers in winter and spring (some year-round). Grows 5 to 6 ft. tall, spreads about as wide. Somewhat rangy in appearance, best used in dry gardens or as a background plant. Plant in full sun. Needs little water. Damaged by hard frost. Prune to mantain size and shape. Page: 94.

Taxus baccata 'Stricta'

IRISH YEW. One of a popular group of evergreen shrubs and trees with flat sprays of dark green, needlelike foliage. Irish yew is a narrow, columnar plant eventually reaching 20 ft. tall. It needs room to grow but adds a strong formal look to the landscape. Like other yews, it tolerates repeated pruning and is often sheared to form a hedge. Female yews produce red berries, which are attractive but poisonous. Adapts to full sun, partial sun, or shade but must have well-drained soil. Once established, needs only occasional water. To maintain a formal look, shear back the new growth in spring, before it has matured. Prune individual branches as needed to maintain the desired shape. Page: 82.

Thymus praecox ssp. arcticus

MOTHER-OF-THYME, CREEPING THYME. A creeping perennial that forms low mats of wiry stems and tiny semievergreen leaves. Tolerates light foot traffic and smells good when you step on it. Clusters of pink, lavender, or white flowers bloom over a long season in midsummer. Grows 4 to 6 in. tall, 1 to 2 ft. wide. Look in the herb department of a nursery to find this plant. There are several other kinds of creeping thymes. 'Argenteus' and 'Aureus' variegated lemon thymes (*T.* x *citriodorus*, p. 29) have lemon-scented, silver- and yellow-variegated leaves, respectively. All make attractive, fragrant, tough ground covers for sites with full sun and well-drained soil. Need little water once established. Shear old stems close to the ground in fall to early spring. Plants may self-sow, but aren't weedy. Pages: 37, 38, 51, 81, 83.

Tipuana tipu

TIPU TREE. This large semi-evergreen or deciduous tree makes a useful lawn or shade tree. It grows 25 to 35 ft. tall and spreads twice as wide. Light green, finely divided leaves are topped with long clusters of yellow to apricot pea-like flowers from late spring to early summer, followed by large seedpods. Best grown where summers are warm and winters are mild. Foliage is damaged at 25°F. Pages: 35, 88.

Trachelospermum asiaticum

ASIAN JASMINE. This common ground cover is dense and low growing, forming a thick mat of small, shiny evergreen leaves. It grows less than 1 ft. tall and spreads to about 3 ft. Asian jasmine has few pest problems and only requires watering when it's dry and the leaves turn dull green. Shear as needed to keep tidy or mow each spring with the mower on the highest setting. Pages: 73, 75.

Thymus x *citriodorus* 'Aureus'
VARIEGATED LEMON THYME

Thymus praecox
ssp. *arcticus*
MOTHER-OF-THYME

Tipuana tipu
TIPU TREE

Trachelospermum
asiaticum
ASIAN JASMINE

Trachelospermum jasminoides
STAR JASMINE

Viburnum tinus 'Spring Bouquet'

Vitex agnus-castus CHASTE TREE

Trachelospermum jasminoides

STAR JASMINE. An evergreen vine with woody, twining stems lined with pairs of small, glossy green, oval leaves. Bears dangling clusters of cream-colored, sweet-smelling flowers in early summer. Climbs 10 to 15 ft. tall if given some type of support such as a fence or pillar. Can also be grown as a sprawling ground cover, 1 to 2 ft. high. Prune anytime to keep within bounds. If used as a ground cover, shear in spring to keep compact. Plant in full sun or partial shade. Water regularly. Page: 51.

Viburnum tinus 'Spring Bouquet'

'SPRING BOUQUET' VIBURNUM. Compact evergreen shrub with ragrant white flowers that emerge from pink buds. Blooms late fall to spring. Flowers are followed by shiny blue berries. Dark green leaves are borne on reddish stems. Grows 6 ft. tall and about 4 ft. wide. Plant in full sun or partial shade. Water regularly. Can be sheared as a low hedge. Mildew is a problem in coastal areas. Pages: 21, 97, 102.

Vinca minor

DWARF PERIWINKLE. An evergreen ground cover with small, glossy, leathery, dark green leaves. Gradually forms a thick mass of foliage about 6 in. high. In late spring it bears round lilac flowers. Grows best in partial or full shade. Can take drought but looks better with occasional water. Can be invasive. Shear plants to the ground every few years. Page: 17.

Vitex agnus-castus

CHASTE TREE. Tough deciduous shrub or small tree that can reach 20 to 25 ft. Generally grows with multiple trunks and has an open, spreading habit. Fan-shaped, divided leaves are dark green on top, grayish underneath. Showy flower spikes bear small, tubular, lavender-blue flowers in summer and attract many butterflies. Blooms best in warmer inland climates. Plant in full sun and water regularly for best flower display. Able to survive dry periods and isn't bothered by pests. Prune in winter to develop a tree shape; otherwise it will be shrubby and dense. Page: 28.

Water plants

Most big garden centers have a small collection of water plants. Mail-order water-garden specialists offer several dozen kinds. All grow best in full sun. Consult with a nursery specializing in water gardens to ensure the proper balance of plants to keep water clear and oxygenated. *Acorus gramineus* (p. 101) is a perennial with tufts of narrow, irislike leaves that grow 12 to 18 in. high. Flowers are not showy. *Canna* 'Tropicanna' (p. 101) grows from bulbous roots, producing upright stalks 5 to 6 ft. tall. Large leaves are gloriously striped with red, pink, yellow, and green. Stalks are topped with bright orange flowers in summer. Both acorus and 'Tropicanna' can be grown in pots covered by about 2 in. of water. (They are both common garden plants as well.) Oxygenating, or submerged, plants grow underwater; they help keep the water clear and provide oxygen, food, and shelter for fish. Anacharis (*Elodea canadensis*) is a popular oxygenator with tiny, dark green leaves.

Water lilies (*Nymphaea* species) are the most popular plant for pools and ponds. The best selection is available from specialty nurseries. There are two main groups of water lilies. Hardy water lilies survive outdoors from year to year and bloom in midsummer. They are usually the easiest to grow. Tropical water lilies need warm water and bloom over a longer season from summer through fall. They can be grown where citrus grows or can be treated as annuals. Both kinds are available in dwarf-size plants, suitable for small pools, with fragrant or scentless flowers in shades of white, yellow, and pink. Tropicals also come in shades of blue and purple. All water lilies need full sun. Plant the roots in a container of heavy, rich, garden soil, and set it in the pool so about 6 in. of water covers the soil. (See p. 173 for more on planting.)

Wisteria sinensis

CHINESE WISTERIA. A vigorous woody vine with deciduous compound leaves. Dangling clusters of very fragrant purple, lavender, or white flowers bloom in spring. It climbs by twining around a trellis, tree, or other support and can exceed 30 ft. Needs full sun to flower well, and well-drained soil. A young plant needs regular water and fertilizer. May not flower for several years after you plant it, but the lacy foliage is attractive meanwhile. Prune anytime to keep within bounds. Prune heavily in winter to keep open and to encourage blooming. Page: 81.

Zantedeschia aethiopica

CALLA LILY. This showy perennial creates a bright green clump of arrow-shaped leaves punctuated by dramatic, 8-inch long, pure white flowers for a long period of time in spring and summer. Grows 2 to 4 ft. tall and spreads wider. Calla lilies prefer full sun and rich, moist, slightly acidic soil. In very hot climates, plant them where they are protected from the afternoon sun. They can be planted from pots or rhizomes. Divide when clumps become crowded. Evergreen in mild climates. Page: 75.

Acorus gramineus
ACORUS

Canna 'Tropicanna'
CANNA

Nymphaea
WATER LILY

Zantedeschia aethiopica
CALLA LILLY

Guide *to* Installation

In this section, we introduce the hard but rewarding work of landscaping. Here you'll find information on all the tasks you need to install any of the designs in this book, organized in the order in which you'd most likely tackle them. Clearly written text and numerous illustrations help you learn how to plan the job; clear the site; construct paths, patios, ponds, fences, arbors, and trellises; prepare the planting beds; and install and maintain the plantings. Roll up your sleeves and dig in. In just a few weekends, you can create a landscape feature that will provide years of enjoyment.

Organizing Your Project

If your gardening experience is limited to mowing the lawn, pruning the bushes, and growing some flowers and vegetables, the thought of starting from scratch and installing a whole new landscape feature might be intimidating. But in fact, adding one of the designs in this book to your property is completely within reach, if you approach it the right way. The key is to divide the project into a series of steps and take them one at a time. This is how professional landscapers work. It's efficient and orderly, and it makes even big jobs seem manageable.

On this and the facing page, we'll explain how to think your way through a landscaping project and anticipate the various steps. Subsequent topics in this section describe how to do each part of the job. Detailed instructions and illustrations cover all the techniques you'll need to install any design from start to finish.

The step-by-step approach

Choose a design and adapt it to your site. The designs in this book address parts of the home landscape. In the most attractive and effective home landscapes, all the various parts work together. Don't be afraid to change the shape of beds; alter the number, kinds, and positions of plants; or revise paths and structures to bring them into harmony with their surroundings.

To see the relationships with your existing landscape, you can draw the design on a scaled plan of your property. Or you can work on the site itself, placing wooden stakes, pots, or whatever is handy to represent plants and structures.

Lay out the design on site. Once you've decided what you want to do, you'll need to lay out the paths and structures and outline the beds. Some people are comfortable pacing off distances and relying on their eye to judge sizes and relative positions. Others prefer to transfer the grid from the plan full size onto the site, using garden lime (a white powder available at nurseries) like chalk on a blackboard to "draw" a grid or outlines of planting beds.

Clear the site. (See pp. 160–161.) Sometimes you have to work around existing features—a nice big tree, a building or fence, a sidewalk—but it's usually easiest to start a new landscaping project by removing unwanted structures or pavement and killing, cutting down, or uprooting all the plants. This can generate

DIGGING POSTHOLES

AMENDING SOIL

a lot of debris to dispose of, but it's often worth the trouble to make a fresh start.

Make provisions for water. (See pp. 162–163.) In California, most landscape plants require more water than nature provides. A well-thought-out irrigation strategy and system can help you make the most of this increasingly precious natural resource. You'll need to plan its installation carefully. Some permanent parts of most watering systems need to be installed before the other landscape features. Additional parts are installed after the soil is prepared. And the final components are normally placed after planting.

Build the "hardscape." (See pp. 164–191.) Hardscape includes landscape structures such as fences, trellises, arbors, retaining walls, walkways, edging, and outdoor lighting. Install these elements before you start any planting.

Prepare the soil. (See pp. 192–195.) On most properties, it's uncommon to find soil that's as good as it should be for growing plants. Typically, the soil around a new house is shallow, compacted, and infertile. Some plants tolerate such poor conditions, but they don't thrive. To grow healthy, attractive plants, you need to improve the quality of the soil throughout the entire area that you're planning to plant.

Do the planting and add mulch. (See pp. 195–201.) Putting plants in the ground usually goes quite quickly and gives instant gratification. Mulching the soil makes the area look neat even while the plants are still small.

Maintain the planting. (See pp. 201–213.) Most plantings need regular watering and occasional weeding for the first year or two. After that, depending on the design you've chosen, you'll have to do some routine maintenance—watering, pruning, shaping, cutting back, and cleaning up—to keep the plants looking their best. This may take as little as a few hours a year or as much as an hour or two of your time every week throughout the growing season.

TRANSPLANTING

SETTING FLAGSTONES

Clearing the Site

The site you've chosen for a landscaping project may or may not need to be cleared of fences, old pavement, construction debris, and other objects. Unless your house is newly built, the site will almost certainly be covered with plants.

Before you start cutting plants down, try to find someone to identify them for you. As you walk around together, make a sketch that shows which plants are where, and attach labels to the plants, too. Determine if there are any desirable plants worth saving—mature shade trees that you should work around, shapely shrubs that aren't too big to dig up and relocate or give away, worthwhile perennials and ground covers that you could divide and replant, healthy sod that you could lay elsewhere. Likewise, decide which plants have to go—diseased or crooked trees, straggly or overgrown shrubs, weedy brush, invasive ground covers, tattered lawn.

You can clear small areas yourself, bundling the brush for pickup and tossing soft-stemmed plants on the compost pile, but if you have lots of woody brush or any trees to remove, you might want to hire someone else to do the job. A crew armed with power tools can turn a thicket into a pile of wood chips in just a few hours. Have them pull out the roots and grind the stumps, too. Save the chips; they're good for surfacing paths, or you can use them as mulch.

Working around a tree

If there are any large, healthy trees on your site, be careful as you work around them. It's okay to prune off some of a tree's limbs, as shown on the facing page, but respect its trunk and its roots. Keep heavy equipment from beneath the tree's canopy, and don't raise or lower the level of the soil there. Try never to cut or wound the bark on the trunk (don't nail things to a tree), because that exposes the tree to disease organisms. Plantings beneath existing California natives such as oak trees or madrones can endanger their health. Consult a certified arborist on ways to integrate these handsome, but sensitive, trees into your landscape and care for them properly.

Killing perennial weeds

Some common weeds that sprout back from perennial roots or runners are bindweed, blackberry, Bermuda grass, Johnson grass, nutsedge, and poison oak. Garden plants that can become weedy include bamboo, English ivy, ground ivy, pampas grass, broom, and mint. Once they get established, perennial weeds

Smothering weeds

This technique is easier than digging, particularly for eradicating large infestations, but much slower. First mow or cut the tops of the weeds as close to the ground as possible ❶. Then cover the area with sections from the newspaper, overlapped like shingles ❷, or flattened-out cardboard boxes and top with a layer of mulch, such as straw, grass clippings, tree leaves, wood chips, or other organic material spread several inches deep ❸.

Smothering works by excluding light, which stops photosynthesis. If any shoots reach up through the covering and produce green leaves, pull them out immediately. Wait a few months, until you're sure the weeds are dead, before you dig into the smothered area and plant there.

Where summers are hot, you can also kill weeds through a process called solarization. Till the weeds into the soil and moisten the area. Then cover the soil with a thick sheet of clear plastic, sealing its edges by burying them in a shallow trench. The heat generated underneath the plastic kills the weeds.

SMOTHERING WEEDS

❶ Smothering kills weeds by depriving them of light. Cut the tops off close to the ground.

❷ Cover with thick newspaper or cardboard.

❸ Top with several inches of mulch. Wait a few months to be sure weeds are dead, and then till rotted newspaper and mulch into the soil.

are hard to eliminate. You can't just cut off the tops, because the plants keep sprouting back. You need to dig the weeds out, smother them, or kill them with an herbicide, and it's better to do this before you plant a bed.

Digging. You can often do a good job of removing a perennial weed if you dig carefully at the base of the stems, find the roots, and follow them as far as possible, pulling out every bit of root that you find. Some plant roots go deeper than you can dig. Most plants will resprout from the bits that you miss, but these leftover sprouts are easy to pull.

Spraying. Herbicides are fast and effective weed killers. Ask at the nursery for those that break down quickly into more benign substances, and make sure the weed you're trying to kill is listed on the product label. Apply all herbicides as directed by the manufacturer. After spraying, you usually have to wait from one to four weeks for the weed to die. Some weeds need to be sprayed a second or third time before they give up.

Replacing turf

If you're planning to add a landscape feature where you now have lawn, you can "recycle" the turf to repair or extend the lawn elsewhere on your property.

The drawing below shows a technique for removing relatively small areas of strong, healthy turf for replanting. First, with a sharp shovel, cut it into squares or strips about 1 to 2 ft. square (these small pieces are easy to lift) ❶. Then slice a few inches deep under each square and lift the squares, roots and all, like brownies from a pan ❷. Quickly transplant the squares to a previously prepared site; water them well until the roots are established.

If you don't need the turf, or if it's straggly or weedy, leave it in place and kill the grass. Spraying with an herbicide kills most grasses within one to two weeks, but you may need to spray vigorous turf twice. Or cover it with a tarp or a sheet of black plastic for two to four weeks during the heat of summer (it takes longer in cool weather). Then dig or till the bed, shredding the turf, roots and all, and mixing it into the soil.

Removing large limbs

If there are large trees on your property now, you may want to remove some of the lower limbs so light can reach your plantings. Major pruning of large trees is a job for a professional arborist, but you can remove limbs smaller than 4 in. in diameter and less than 10 ft. above the ground yourself with a simple bow saw or pole saw.

Use the three-step procedure shown below to remove large limbs safely. First, saw partway through the bottom of the limb, approximately 1 ft. out from the trunk ❶. This keeps the bark from tearing down the trunk when the limb falls. Then make a corresponding cut down through the top of the limb ❷—be prepared to get out of the way when the limb drops. Finally, remove the stub ❸. Undercut it slightly or hold it as you finish the cut, so it doesn't fall away and peel bark off the trunk. Note that the cut is not flush with the trunk but is just outside the thick area at the limb's base, called the branch collar. Leaving the branch collar helps the wound heal quickly and naturally. Wound dressing is considered unnecessary today.

MOVING TURF

❶ With a sharp shovel, cut healthy turf into squares or strips of manageable size.

❷ Slice a few inches deep under each square, lift it, and place as soon as possible in a new spot.

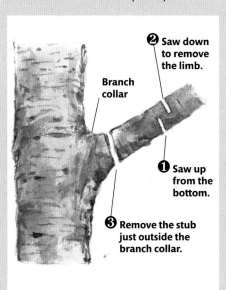

❷ Saw down to remove the limb.

Branch collar

❶ Saw up from the bottom.

❸ Remove the stub just outside the branch collar.

Water for Your Plants

California's long, dry summers and frequent droughts make watering a critical concern of gardeners here. Though some plants will survive long dry periods once established, almost all plants will need regular watering the first few years after planting. And most will need summer watering their entire life to look their best.

But there is more at stake than just the survival of plants. Water conservation is a daily obligation in California, where water is a valuable and limited resource. Outdoor landscapes use a large portion of urban water, so nothing should be wasted. During periods of drought, mandatory conservation is often strictly enforced.

So for the health of your plants and for the preservation of a valuable resource, make water conservation part of your landscape planning from the beginning. The box below outlines effective water-saving practices for home landscapes. (See p. 203 for more on when and how much to water.) You can also consult your local water department for advice about watering gardens and lawns.

Water-wise practices

Choose plants carefully. Many plants that require little water, including California natives, thrive in the state's dry summer climate and are increasingly available from local nurseries and garden centers.

Group plants with similar water needs. Position plants that require the most water near the house, where they can be more easily tended and watered. Use drought-tolerant plants farther from the house.

Plant in fall. This way, new plants will have the cooler, wetter winter and spring seasons to become established before facing the heat of summer.

Mulch plantings. A 2- to 3-in. layer of mulch reduces evaporation by keeping the soil cool and sheltering it from wind.

Create water-retaining basins. Use these to direct irrigation water to large plants. Make a low soil mound around the plant's perimeter, at its drip line. (Basins aren't necessary in drip-irrigated beds.)

Limit lawn size. Lawns demand lots of water. Reduce the size of your lawn by planting beds, borders, and less thirsty ground covers.

Water in the morning. Lower morning temperatures and less wind mean less water is lost to evaporation.

Adjust watering to conditions. Water less during cool weather in the spring and fall. Turn off automatic timers during the rainy season.

Install, monitor, and maintain an irrigation system. Even a simple drip system conserves water. Once it's installed, check and adjust the equipment on a regular basis. Be sure to inspect frequently for clogged emitters.

Watering systems

One of the best ways to conserve water is to use an efficient delivery system. The simplest watering systems—watering cans and handheld hoses—are also the most limited and inefficient. They can be adequate for watering new transplants or widely separated individual plants. But sprinkling plants in an entire bed with a hose and nozzle for even as long as an hour may provide less water than half an inch of rainfall. And wetting just the top few inches of soil this way encourages shallow root growth, making it necessary to water more frequently. To provide enough water to soak the soil to a depth of a foot or more, you need a system that can run untended for extended periods.

Hose-end sprinklers are easy to set up and leave to soak an area. But they're also inefficient: Water is blown away by wind. It runs off sloped or paved areas. It is applied unevenly, or it falls too far away from individual plants to be of use to them. And because sprinklers soak leaves as well as soil, the damp foliage may breed fungal diseases.

Low-volume irrigation. For garden beds and landscape plantings like those in this book, low-volume irrigation systems are the most efficient and offer the most flexibility and control. Frequently called "drip" irrigation systems, they deliver water at low pressure through a network of plastic pipes, hoses, and tubing and a variety of emitters and microsprinklers. Such systems are designed to apply water slowly and directly to the roots of targeted plants, so very little water is lost to runoff and evaporation or wasted on plants that don't need it. Because water is usually applied at soil level, the risk of foliar diseases is reduced. And because less soil is watered, weeds are also reduced.

Simple low-volume systems can be attached to ordinary outdoor faucets or garden hoses and controlled manually, just like a sprinkler. You can set up such a system in less than an hour. Sophisticated systems include (1) their own attachment

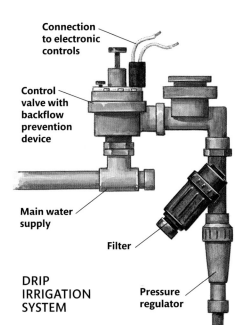

Connection to electronic controls

Control valve with backflow prevention device

Main water supply

Filter

Pressure regulator

DRIP IRRIGATION SYSTEM

Basic components of a drip irrigation system are shown here. Individual systems will vary. Several common types of emitters are shown; systems can incorporate others.

to your main water supply, (2) a network of valves and buried pipes that allow you to divide your property into zones, and (3) an electronic control device that can automatically water each zone at preset times for preset durations. Such systems often incorporate sprinkler systems for lawns.

A person with modest mechanical skills and basic tools can plan and install a low-volume irrigation system. Extensive multi-zoned systems (particularly those with their own attachment to the main water supply) are more difficult to design and install. If you tackle one, have a professional review your plans before you start. You can buy kits or individual system components from garden centers, nurseries, or specialty suppliers. (The main components of low-volume systems are outlined below.) Although most manufacturers provide helpful instructions, good criteria for choosing among different local suppliers are their knowledge of system design and installation and their ability to help you with both. A supplier may charge for this service, but good advice is worth the money.

Low-volume-system components. Any irrigation system connected to a domestic water supply needs a *backflow prevention device* (also called an antisiphon device) at the point of connection to the water supply to protect drinking water from contamination. Backflow devices are often mandated by city building codes, so check with local health or building officials to determine if a specific type of backflow prevention device is required.

Install a *filter* to prevent minerals and flakes that slough off metal water pipes from clogging the emitters. You'll need to clean the filter regularly. Between the filter and emitters, all hoses and tubing should be plastic, not metal.

Pressure regulators reduce the mains' water pressure to levels required by the system's low-volume emitters.

Supply lines deliver water from the source to the emitters. Some systems incorporate buried lines of rigid plastic pipe to carry water to plantings anywhere on the property. For aboveground use,

you'll need flexible tubing designed specifically for low-volume irrigation.

Emitters and *soaker hoses* deliver the water to the plants. A wide range of emitters are available for different kinds of plants and garden situations. Various drip fittings, bubblers, and microsprinklers can be plugged into the flexible plastic tubing. A single emitter or a group of emitters might serve individual or groups of plants. Soaker hoses and "ooze" tubes seep or drip water along their length. Consult with your supplier about which delivery systems best meet your plants' needs.

A *timer* or *electronic controller* helps ensure efficient water use. Unlike you, a controller won't forget and leave the water on too long. Used in conjunction with zoned plantings, these devices provide control and flexibility to deal with the specific water needs of groups of plants or even individual specimens.

Installation. Permanent irrigation equipment should be installed early in any project. Lay underground piping that crosses paths, patios, or similar landscape features after the site is cleared but before installing any of these permanent features. Lay pipes in planting areas after you have prepared the soil. That way, you won't damage the piping when digging or rototilling. Install underground pipe in trenches dug to the appropriate depth. Then temporarily cap the ends. Hook up the aboveground tubing and position emitters after planting.

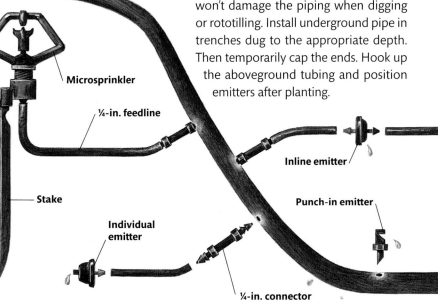

½-in. supply line

Microsprinkler

¼-in. feedline

Stake

Individual emitter

Inline emitter

Punch-in emitter

¼-in. connector

Making Paths and Walkways

Every landscape needs paths and walkways. A path can divide and define the spaces in the landscape, orchestrate the way the landscape is viewed, and even be a key element enhancing its beauty.

Whether it is a graceful curving garden path or a utilitarian slab leading to the garage, a walk has two main functional requirements: durability and safety. It should hold up through seasonal changes. It should provide a well-drained surface that is easy to walk on and to maintain.

A path's function helps determine its surface and its character. In general, heavily trafficked walkways leading to a door, garage, or shed need hard, smooth (but not slick) surfaces and should take you where you want to go fairly directly. A path to a backyard play area could be a strip of soft wood bark, easy on the knees of impatient children. A relaxed stroll in the garden might require only a hop-scotch collection of flat stones meandering from one prized plant to another.

Before laying out a walk or path, spend some time observing existing traffic patterns. If your path makes use of a route people already take (particularly children), they'll be more likely to stay on the path and off the lawn or flowers. Avoid areas that are slow to drain. When determining path width, consider whether the path must accommodate rototillers and wheelbarrows or two strollers walking abreast, or just provide steppingstone access for maintaining the plants.

Dry-laid paths

You can make a path by laying bricks or spreading wood chips on top of bare earth. While quick and easy, this method has drawbacks. Laid on the surface, with no edging to contain them, loose materials are soon scattered, and solid materials are easily jostled out of place. If the earth base doesn't drain well, the path will be a swamp after a rainstorm. And in California's higher-elevation cold-winter areas, repeated freezing and thawing expands and contracts the soil, moving path and walkway materials laid on it. The effect of this "frost heaving" is minimal on loose materials, but it can shift brick and stone significantly out of line.

The method we recommend—laying surface material on an excavated base of sand or gravel, or both—minimizes these problems. Water moves through sand and gravel quickly, and such a base "cushions" the surface materials from any freeze-thaw movement of the underlying soil. Excavation can place the path surface at ground level, where the surrounding soil or an edging can contain loose materials and keep hard materials from shifting.

The styles and materials discussed in this section can be laid on an excavated base of sand or gravel, alone or in combination.

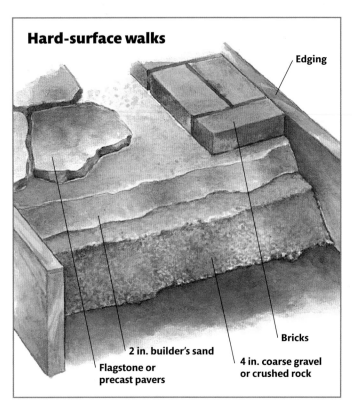

Hard-surface walks

Edging

2 in. builder's sand

Flagstone or precast pavers

Bricks

4 in. coarse gravel or crushed rock

Loose-surface paths

Edging

Water-permeable landscape fabric

Pea gravel, fine crushed rock, bark, or wood chips

4 in. coarse gravel or crushed rock

Choosing a surface

Walkways and paths can be made of either hard or soft material. Your choice of material will depend on the walkway's function, your budget, and your personal preferences.

Soft materials, including bark, wood chips, pine needles, and loose gravel, are best for informal and low-traffic areas. Inexpensive and simple to install, they settle, scatter, or decompose and must be replenished or replaced every few years.

Hard materials, such as brick, flagstone, and concrete pavers, are more expensive and time consuming to install, but they are permanent, requiring only occasional maintenance. (Compacted crushed stone can also make a hard-surface walk.) Durable and handsome, they're ideal for high-traffic, high-profile areas.

Bark, wood chips, and pine needles

Perfect for a natural look or a quick temporary path, these loose materials can be laid directly on the soil or, if drainage is poor, on a gravel bed. Bagged materials from a nursery or garden center will be cleaner, more uniform, and considerably more expensive than bulk supplies bought by the cubic yard. Check with local tree services to find the best prices on bulk material.

Gravel and crushed rock

Loose rounded gravel gives a bit underfoot, creating a soft but messy path. The angular facets of crushed stone eventually compact into a hard and tidier path that can, if the surrounding soil is firm enough, be laid without an edging. Gravel and stone type and color vary from area to area. Buy materials by the ton or cubic yard.

Concrete pavers

Precast concrete pavers are versatile, readily available, and often the least expensive hard-surface material. They come in a range of colors and shapes, including interlocking patterns. Precast edgings are also available. Most home and garden centers carry a variety of precast pavers, which are sold by the piece.

PRECAST PAVERS

Brick

Widely available in a range of sizes, colors, and textures, brick complements many design styles. When carefully laid on a well-prepared sand-and-gravel base, brick provides an even, safe, and long-lasting surface. If you buy used brick, pick the densest and hardest. Avoid brick with glazed faces; the glaze traps moisture and salts, which eventually damage the brick. If you live where it regularly freezes and thaws, buy bricks rated to withstand the weather conditions.

RUNNING BOND

TWO-BRICK BASKET WEAVE

HERRINGBONE

DIAGONAL HERRINGBONE

Flagstone

"Flagstone" is a generic term for stratified stone that can be split to form pavers. Limestone, sandstone, and bluestone are common paving materials. The surfaces of marble and slate are usually too smooth to make safe paving. Cut into squares or rectangles, flagstone can be laid as individual steppingstones or in interesting patterns. Flagstones come in a range of colors, textures, and sizes. Flags for walks should be at least 2 in. thick. Purchased by weight, surface area, or pallet load, flagstones are usually the most expensive paving choice.

CUT FLAGSTONE

CUT AND IRREGULAR FLAGSTONE

IRREGULAR FLAGSTONE

Drainage

Few things are worse than a path dotted with puddles or icy patches. To prevent these from forming, the soil around and beneath the path should drain well. The path's location and construction should ensure that rainwater does not collect on the surface. Before you locate a path, observe runoff and drainage on your property during and after heavy rains. Avoid routing a path through areas where water courses, collects, or is slow to drain.

While both loose and hard paving can sometimes be successfully laid directly on well-drained compacted soil, laying surface materials on a base of sand or gravel will help improve drainage and minimize frost heaving. Where rainfall is scant or drainage is good, a 4-in. base of either sand or gravel is usually sufficient. For most other situations, a 4-in. gravel bed topped with 2 in. of sand will work well. Very poorly drained soils may require more gravel, an additional layer of coarse rock beneath the gravel, or even drain tiles. If you suspect your site has serious drainage problems, consult a landscape architect or contractor.

Finally, keep water from pooling on a walk by making its surface higher in the center than at the edges. The center of a 4-ft.-wide walk should be at least ½ in. higher than its edges. If you're using a drag board to level the sand base, curve its lower edge to create this "crown." Otherwise crown the surface by eye.

Edgings

All walk surfaces need to be contained in some fashion along their edges. Where soil is firm or tightly knit by turf, neatly cut walls of the excavation can serve as edging. An installed edging often provides more effective containment, particularly if the walk surface is above grade. It also prevents damage to bricks or stones on the edges of paths. Walkway edgings are commonly made of 1- or 2-in.-thick lumber, thicker landscaping timbers, brick, or stone.

Wood edging

Wood should be rot-resistant redwood or cedar or or some other wood pressure-treated for ground-contact use. If you're working in loose soils, fix a deep wooden edging to support stakes with double-headed nails. When the path is laid, pull the nails, and fill and tamp behind the edging. Then drive the stakes below grade. In firmer soils, or if the edging material is not wide enough, install it on top of the gravel base. Position the top of the edging at the height of the path. Dimension lumber 1 in. thick is pliable enough to bend around gradual curves.

Treated dimensional lumber with support stakes

Landscape timbers with crossties laid on gravel base

Brick and stone edging

In firm soil, a row of bricks laid on edge and perpendicular to the length of the path adds stability. For a more substantial edging, stand bricks on end on the excavated soil surface; add the gravel base; and tamp the earth around the base of the bricks on the outside of the excavation. Stone edgings laid on end can be set in the same way. "End-up" brick or stone edgings are easy to install on curved walks.

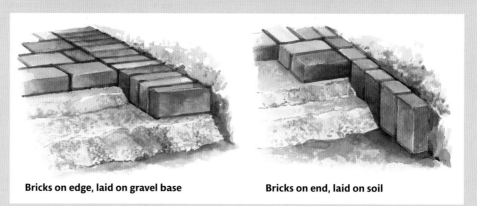

Bricks on edge, laid on gravel base

Bricks on end, laid on soil

Preparing the base

Having decided on location and materials, you can get down to business. The initial steps of layout and base preparation are much the same for all surface materials. Before you construct paths or walkways, check your irrigation plans. If underground water lines will cross any paths, be sure to lay the lines first.

Layout

Lay out straight sections with stakes and string ❶. You can plot curves with stakes and "fair" the curve with a garden hose, or you can outline the curve with the hose alone, marking it with lime or sand.

Excavation

The excavation depth depends on how much sand-and-gravel base your soil's drainage calls for, the thickness of the surface material, and its position above or below grade ❷. Mark the depth on a stake or stick and use this to check depth as you dig. Walking surfaces are most comfortable if they are reasonably level across their width. Check the bottom of the excavation with a level as you dig. If the walk cuts across a slope, you'll need to remove soil from the high side and use it to fill the low side to produce a level surface. If you've added soil or if the subsoil is loose, compact it by tamping.

Edging installation

Some edgings can be installed immediately after excavation; others are placed on top of the gravel portion of the base ❸. (See the sidebar "Edgings" on the opposite page.) If the soil's drainage permits, you can now lay soft materials, loose gravel, or crushed stone on the excavated, tamped, and edged soil base. To control weeds, and to keep bark, chips, or pine needles from mixing with the subsoil, you can spread water-permeable land-scape fabric over the excavated soil base.

Laying the base

Now add gravel (if required), rake it level, and compact it ❹. Use gravel up to 1 in. in diameter or ¼- to ¾-in. crushed stone, which drains and compacts well. You can rent a hand tamper (a heavy metal plate on the end of a pole) or a machine compactor if you have a large area to compact.

If you're making a loose-gravel or crushed-stone walk, add the surface material on top of the base gravel. (See "Loose materials" page 168.) For walks of brick, stone, or pavers, add a 2-in. layer of builder's sand, not the finer sand masons use for mixing mortar.

Rake the sand smooth with the back of a level-head rake. You can level the sand with a wooden drag board, also called a "screed" ❺. Nail together two 1x4s or notch a 1x6 to place the lower edge at the desired height of the sand, and run the board along the path edging. To settle the sand, dampen it thoroughly with a hose set on fine spray. Fill any low spots; rake or drag the surface level; and then dampen it again.

PREPARING THE BASE

❶ Lay out the path with stakes, string, garden hose, and lime.

❷ Dig out path between layout string and lime lines.

❸ Install the edging.

❹ Rake out gravel base.

Lay out free-form curved sections with garden hose and mark with lime.

Mark straight sections with 1x2 stakes and string.

Drag board

Edging

❺ Level sand base with a drag board.

Laying the surface

Whether you're laying loose or hard material, take time to plan your work. Provide access so delivery trucks can place material close to the worksite.

Loose materials

Install water-permeable landscape fabric over the gravel base to prevent gravel from mixing with the surface material. Spread bark or wood chips 2 to 4 in. deep. For a pine-needle surface, spread 2 in. of needles on top of several inches of bark or chips. Spread loose pea gravel about 2 in. deep. For a harder, more uniform surface, add 1/2 in. of fine crushed stone on top of the gravel. You can let traffic compact crushed-rock surfaces, or compact them by hand or with a machine.

Bricks and precast pavers

Take time to figure out the pattern and spacing of the bricks or pavers by laying them out on the lawn or driveway, rather than disturbing your carefully prepared sand base. When you're satisfied, begin in a corner, laying the bricks or pavers gently on the sand so the base remains even ❶. Lay full bricks first; then cut bricks to fit as needed at the edges. To produce uniform joints, space bricks with a piece of wood cut to the joint width. You can also maintain alignment with a straightedge or with a string stretched across the path between nails or stakes. Move the string as the work proceeds.

As you complete a row or section, bed the bricks or pavers into the sand base with several firm raps of a rubber mallet or a hammer on a scrap 2x4. Check with a level or straightedge to make sure the surface is even ❷. (You'll have to do this by feel or eye across the width of a crowned path.) Lift low bricks or pavers carefully and fill beneath them with sand; then reset them. Don't stand on the walk until you've filled the joints.

When you've finished a section, sweep fine, dry mason's sand into the joints, working across the surface of the path in all directions ❸. Wet thoroughly with a fine spray and let dry; then sweep in more sand if necessary. If you want a "living" walk, sweep a loam-sand mixture into the joints and plant small, tough, ground-hugging plants, such as thyme, in them.

Rare is the brick walk that can be laid without cutting something to fit. To cut brick, mark the line of the cut with a dark pencil all around the brick. With the brick resting firmly on sand or soil, score the entire line by rapping a wide mason's chisel called a "brickset" with a heavy wooden mallet or a soft-headed steel hammer as shown on the facing page. Place the brickset in the scored line across one face and give it a sharp blow with the hammer to cut the brick.

If you have a lot of bricks to cut, or if you want greater accuracy, consider renting a masonry saw. Whether you work by hand or machine, always wear safety glasses.

LOOSE MATERIALS

Cover gravel base with water-permeable landscape fabric and add 2 to 4 in. of bark or wood chips.

BRICKS AND PRECAST PAVERS

To turn square corners, align the edging board with a carpenter's square.

❶ Begin laying in a corner.

❷ Check the surface with a level or straightedge. Fill under low bricks; tamp down high ones. Use a plank to distribute your weight if you must work on the path.

❸ Sweep fine, dry sand into the joints to fix the bricks or pavers in place.

Stepping-stones

A stepping-stone walk set in turf creates a charming effect and is very simple to lay. You can use cut or irregular flagstones or field-stone, which is irregular in thickness as well as in outline. Arrange the stones on the turf; then set them one by one. Cut into the turf around the stone with a sharp flat shovel or trowel, and remove the stone; then dig out the sod with the shovel. Placing stones at or below grade will keep them away from mower blades. Fill low spots beneath the stone with earth or sand so the stone doesn't move when stepped on.

Cut around stepping-stone with shovel or trowel.

Remove sod and soil.

Set in place, filling with sand or soil to bed stone firmly.

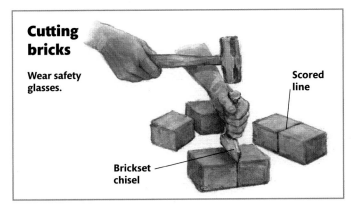

Cutting bricks

Wear safety glasses.

Scored line

Brickset chisel

Cutting flagstones

Wear safety glasses.

Scored line

Brickset

Wood batten

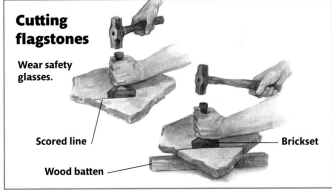

Flagstones

Install cut stones of uniform thickness as described for bricks and pavers. Working out patterns beforehand is particularly important—stones are too heavy to move around more than necessary. To produce a level surface with cut or irregular stones of varying thickness, you'll need to add or remove sand for each stone. Set the stone carefully on sand; then move it back and forth to work it into place ❶. Lay a level or straightedge over three or four stones to check the surface's evenness ❷. When a section is complete, fill the joints with sand or with sand and loam as described for bricks and pavers.

You can cut flagstone with a technique similar to that used for bricks. Score the line of the cut on the top surface with a brickset and hammer. Prop the stone on a piece of scrap wood, positioning the line of cut slightly beyond the edge of the wood. Securing the bottom edge of the stone with your foot, place the brickset on the scored line and strike sharply to make the cut.

FLAGSTONES

❶ Set flagstones in place carefully to avoid disturbing the sand base.

❷ Extend a straightedge over several stones to check the surface for evenness. Tap high spots to level.

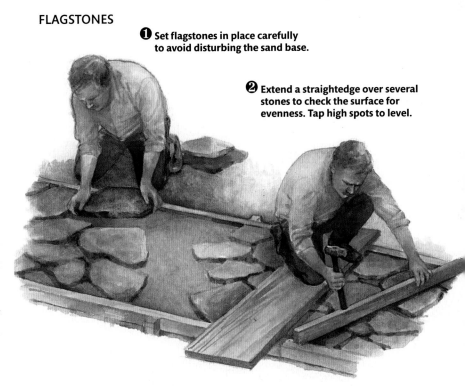

Laying a Patio

You can make a simple patio using the same techniques and materials we have discussed for paths. To ensure good drainage, an even surface, and durability, lay hard surfaces such as brick, flagstone, and pavers on a well-prepared base of gravel, sand, and compacted soil. (Crushed-rock and gravel surfaces likewise benefit from a sound base.) Make sure the surface drains away from any adjacent structure (house or garage); a drop-off of ¼ in. per foot is usually adequate. If the patio isn't near a structure, make it higher in the center to avoid puddles.

Establish the outline of the patio as described for paths; then excavate the area roughly to accommodate 4 in. of gravel,

2 in. of sand, and the thickness of the paving surface. (Check with a local nursery or landscape contractor to find out if local conditions require alterations in the type or amounts of base material.) Now grade the rough excavation to provide drainage, using a simple 4-ft. grid of wooden stakes as shown in the drawings.

Drive the first row of stakes next to the house (or in the center of a freestanding patio), leveling them with a 4-ft. builder's level or a smaller level resting on a straight 2x4. The tops of these stakes should be at the height of the top of the sand base (finish grade of the patio less the thickness of the surface material) ❶. Working from this row of stakes, establish another row about 4 to 5 ft. from the first. Make the tops of these stakes 1 in. lower than those of the first row, using a level and spacer block, as shown below. Continue adding rows of stakes, each 1 in. lower

LAYING A SIMPLE PATIO

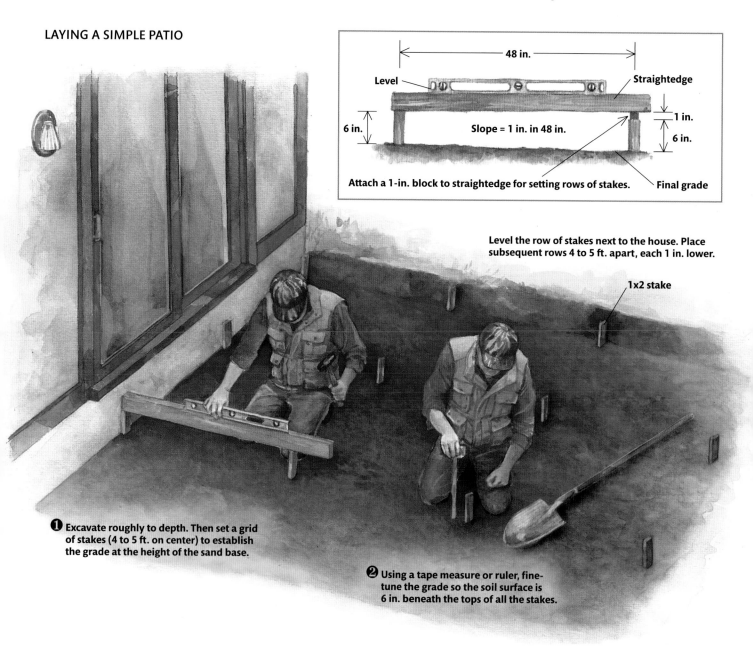

48 in.

Level   Straightedge

6 in.   Slope = 1 in. in 48 in.   1 in.   6 in.

Attach a 1-in. block to straightedge for setting rows of stakes.   Final grade

Level the row of stakes next to the house. Place subsequent rows 4 to 5 ft. apart, each 1 in. lower.

1x2 stake

❶ **Excavate roughly to depth. Then set a grid of stakes (4 to 5 ft. on center) to establish the grade at the height of the sand base.**

❷ **Using a tape measure or ruler, fine-tune the grade so the soil surface is 6 in. beneath the tops of all the stakes.**

than the previous row, until the entire area is staked. Then, with a measuring tape or a ruler and a shovel, fine-tune the grading by removing or adding soil until the excavated surface is 6 in. (the thickness of the gravel-sand base) below the tops of all the stakes ❷.

When installing the sand-and-gravel base, you'll want to maintain the drainage grade you've just established and produce an even surface for the paving material. If you have a good eye or a very small patio, you can do this by sight. Otherwise, you can use the stakes to install a series of 1x3 or 1x4 "leveling boards," as shown in the drawing below. (Before adding gravel, you may want to cover the soil with water-permeable landscape fabric to keep perennial weeds from growing; just cut slits to accommodate the stakes.)

Add a few inches of gravel ❸. Then set leveling boards along

each row of stakes, with the boards' top edges even with the top of the stakes ❹. Drive additional stakes to sandwich the boards in place (don't use nails). Distribute the remaining inch or so of gravel and compact it by hand or machine, then add the 2 in. of sand. Dragging a straight 2x4 across two adjacent rows of leveling boards will produce a precise grade and an even surface ❺. Wet the sand and fill low spots that settle.

You can install the patio surface as previously described for paths, removing the leveling boards as the bricks or pavers reach them ❻. Disturbing the sand surface as little as possible, slide the boards out from between the stakes and drive the stakes an inch or so beneath the level of the sand. Cover the stakes and fill the gaps left by the boards with sand, tamped down carefully. Then continue laying the surface. Finally, sweep fine sand into the joints.

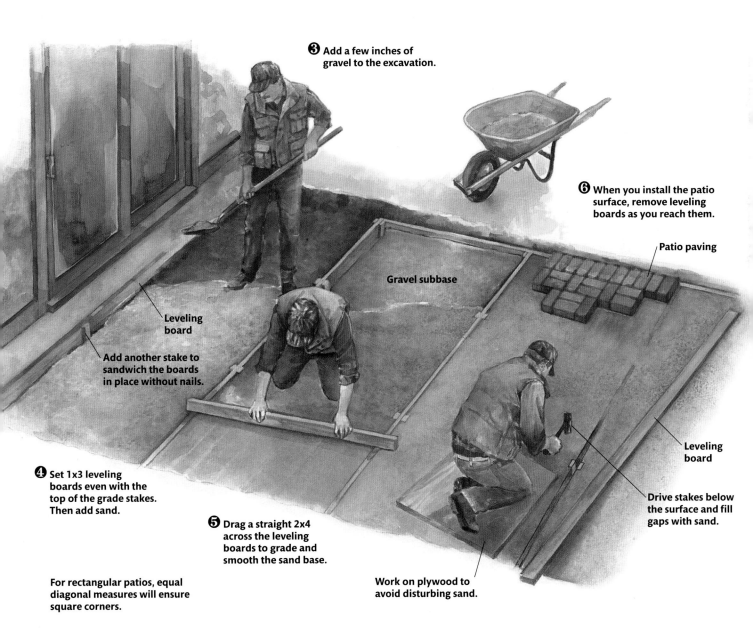

❸ Add a few inches of gravel to the excavation.

❻ When you install the patio surface, remove leveling boards as you reach them.

Patio paving

Gravel subbase

Leveling board

Add another stake to sandwich the boards in place without nails.

Leveling board

Drive stakes below the surface and fill gaps with sand.

❹ Set 1x3 leveling boards even with the top of the grade stakes. Then add sand.

❺ Drag a straight 2x4 across the leveling boards to grade and smooth the sand base.

For rectangular patios, equal diagonal measures will ensure square corners.

Work on plywood to avoid disturbing sand.

Installing a Pond

It wasn't so long ago that a garden pond like the one in this book required yards of concrete, an expert mason, and deep pockets. Today's strong, lightweight, and long-lasting synthetic liners and rigid fiberglass shells have put garden pools in reach of every homeowner. Installation does require some hard labor but little expertise: just dig a hole; spread the liner or seat the shell; install edging; and plant. We'll discuss installation of a pond with a liner in the main text; see below for installing a smaller, fiberglass pool.

Liner notes

More and more nurseries and garden centers are carrying flexible pond liners; you can also buy them from mail-order suppliers specializing in water gardens. Synthetic rubber liners are longer lasting but more expensive than PVC liners. (Both are much cheaper than rigid fiberglass shells.) Buy only liners specifically made for garden ponds—don't use ordinary plastic sheeting. Many people feel that black liners look best; blue liners tend to make the pond look like a swimming pool.

Before you dig

First, make sure you comply with any rules your town may have about water features. Then keep the following ideas in mind when locating your pond. Avoid trees whose shade keeps sun-loving water plants from thriving; whose roots make digging a chore; and whose flowers, leaves, and seeds clog the water, making it unsightly and inhospitable to plants or fish. Avoid the low spot on your property; otherwise your pond will be a catch basin for runoff. Select a level spot; the immediate vicinity of the pond

Small fiberglass pool

A fiberglass shell or half barrel 2 to 3 ft. in diameter and 2 to 3 ft. deep is ideal for the small pool on p. 102. Garden centers often stock pond shells in a variety of shapes.

Dig a hole about 6 in. wider on all sides than the shell. Hole depth should equal that of the shell plus 1 in. for a sand base and an allowance for the river rock that mulches the bed and surrounds the pool. To keep rocks out of the water, position the top edge of the shell or barrel so that it will be at the same height as the rock mulch. Compact the bottom of the hole and spread the sand; then lower the shell into place. Add temporary wedges or props if necessary to orient and level the shell. Slowly fill the shell with water, backfilling around it with sand or sifted soil so the fill keeps pace with the rising water level.

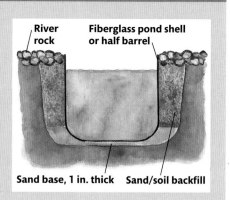

River rock   Fiberglass pond shell or half barrel

Sand base, 1 in. thick   Sand/soil backfill

A patio pond (pp. 100–101)

This pond is integrated with an adjacent patio and incorporates a gently sloping river-rock "shore." Concrete blocks support a flagstone walk and patio paving on three sides. The liner rests on a sand base and is covered with several inches of sand to cushion, and prevent damage from, the river rock and concrete blocks.

While the techniques on these pages will be useful in the pond's construction, check with your local building-code officials and consult with an experienced pond builder about its details. In particular, you need to ensure that the pond walls supporting the walkway and patio are properly constructed.

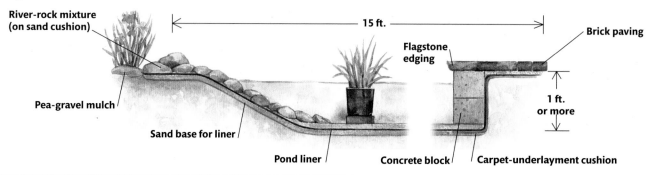

River-rock mixture (on sand cushion)

15 ft.

Brick paving

Flagstone edging

Pea-gravel mulch

1 ft. or more

Sand base for liner

Pond liner   Concrete block   Carpet-underlayment cushion

must be level, and starting out that way saves a lot of work. (Remember that you can use excavated soil to help level the site.)

Using graph paper, enlarge the outline of the pond provided on the site plan on p. 96 or p. 101, altering it as you wish. If you change the size or depth of the pond, or are interested in growing a wider variety of water plants or in adding fish, remember that a healthy pond must achieve a balance between the plants and fish and the volume, depth, and temperature of the water. Even if you're not altering size or pond plants and fish, it's a good idea to consult with a knowledgeable person at a nursery or pet store specializing in water-garden plants and animals.

Calculate the liner width by adding twice the maximum depth of the pool plus an additional 2 ft. to the width. Use the same formula to calculate the length. So, for a 2 x 7 x 15-ft. pond, the liner width would be 4 ft. + 7 ft. + 2 ft. (or 13 ft.). The length would be 4 ft. + 15 ft. + 2 ft. (or 21 ft.).

Water work

Unless you are a very tidy builder, the water you used to fit the liner will be too dirty to leave in the pond. (Spilled mortar can also make the water too alkaline for plants or fish.) Siphon or pump out the water; clean the liner; and refill the pond. If you're adding fish to the pond, you'll need to let the water stand for a week or so to allow any chlorine (which is deadly to fish) to dissipate. Check with local pet stores to find out if your water contains chemicals that require commercial conditioners to make the water safe for fish.

Installing the pond and plants is only the first step in water gardening. It takes patience, experimentation, and usually some consultation with experienced water gardeners to achieve a balance between plants, fish, and waterborne oxygen, nutrients, and waste that will sustain all happily while keeping algae, diseases, insects, and predators at acceptable levels.

Growing pond plants

One water lily, a few upright-growing plants, and a bundle of submerged plants (which help keep the water clean) are enough for a medium-size pond. An increasing number of nurseries and garden centers stock water lilies and other water plants. For a larger selection, your nursery or garden center may be able to recommend a specialist supplier.

These plants are grown in containers filled with heavy garden soil (not potting soil, which contains ingredients that float). You can buy special containers designed for aquatic plants, or simply use plastic pails or dishpans. Line basketlike containers with burlap to keep the soil from leaking out the holes. A water lily needs at least 2 to 3 gal. of soil; the more, the better. Most other water plants, such as dwarf papyrus, need 1 to 2 gal. of soil.

After planting, add a layer of gravel on the surface to keep soil from clouding the water and to protect roots from marauding fish. Soak the plant and soil thoroughly. Then set the container in the pond, positioning it so the water over the soil is 6 to 18 in. deep for water lilies, 0 to 6 in. for most other plants.

For maximum bloom, push a tablet of special water-lily fertilizer into the pots once or twice a month throughout the summer. Most water plants are easy to grow and carefree, although many are tropicals that die after a hard frost, so you'll have to replace them each spring.

PLANTING WATER PLANTS

Set water plants in a container of heavy garden soil. Then cover the surface with gravel to keep soil from floating away.

Gravel

1- to 3-gal. dishpan or special container

Heavy garden soil

Excavation

If your soil isn't too compacted or rocky, a good-size pond can be excavated with a shovel or two in a weekend ❶. If the site isn't level, you can grade it using a stake-and-level system like the one described on pp. 170–171 for grading the patio.

Of the two ponds with liners in the Portfolio section, the one on p. 96 is a more common design. The discussion and illustrations on these pages tell how to build a pond like it. The design on p. 101 (shown in cross section in the inset drawing on the facing page) is a more demanding construction project.

Outline the pond's shape with garden lime, establishing the curves with a garden hose or by staking out a large grid and plotting from the graph-paper plan. Many garden ponds have two levels. One end, often the widest, is 2 ft. deep to accommodate water lilies and other plants requiring deeper water, as well as fish. The other end is 12 to 16 in. deep for plants requiring shallower submersion. (You can also put plant pots on stacks of bricks to vary heights.) The walls will be less likely to crumble as you dig, and the liner will install more easily, if you slope the walls in about 3 to 4 in. for each foot of depth. Make them smooth, removing roots, rocks, and other sharp protrusions.

Excavate a relief around the perimeter to contain the liner overlap and the width and thickness of the stone edging. To receive runoff after a heavy rain, create an overflow channel, as shown in the drawing on the opposite page. This can simply be a 1- to 2-in. depression a foot or so wide spanned by one of the edging stones. Lengths of PVC pipe placed side by side beneath the stone will keep the liner in place. Position the overflow channel to open onto a lower area of lawn or garden adjacent to the pond or to a rock-filled dry well.

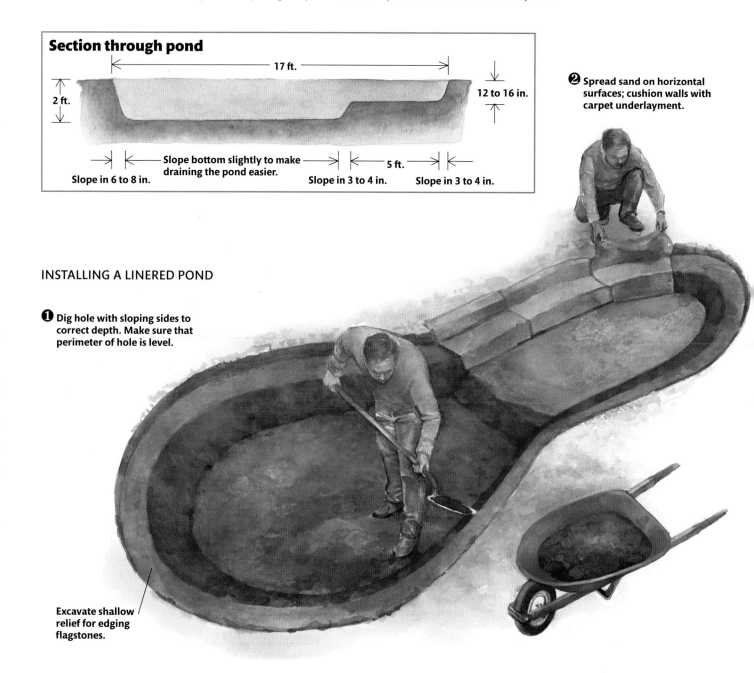

Section through pond

17 ft.

2 ft.

12 to 16 in.

Slope in 6 to 8 in.

Slope bottom slightly to make draining the pond easier.

Slope in 3 to 4 in.

5 ft.

Slope in 3 to 4 in.

❷ Spread sand on horizontal surfaces; cushion walls with carpet underlayment.

INSTALLING A LINERED POND

❶ Dig hole with sloping sides to correct depth. Make sure that perimeter of hole is level.

Excavate shallow relief for edging flagstones.

Fitting the liner

When the hole is complete, cushion the surfaces to protect the liner ❷. The drawing shows an inch-thick layer of sand on the bottom surfaces and carpet underlayment on the sloping walls. Fiberglass insulation also works well, as does heavy landscaping fabric.

Stretch the liner across the hole, letting it sag naturally to touch the walls and bottom but keeping it taut enough so it does not bunch up. Weight its edges with bricks or stones; then fill it with water ❸. The water's weight will push the liner against the walls, and the stones will prevent it from blowing around. As it fills, tuck and smooth out as many creases as you can. The weight of the water would make this difficult after the pond is full. If you stand in the pond to do so, take care not to damage the liner. Don't be alarmed if you can't smooth all the creases. Stop filling when the water is 2 in. below the rim of the pond, and cut the liner to fit into the overlap relief ❹. Hold it in place with a few long nails or large "staples" made from coat hangers while you install the edging.

Edging the pond

Finding and fitting flagstones so there aren't wide gaps between them is the most time-consuming part of this task. Cantilevering the stones an inch or two over the water will hide the liner somewhat.

The stones can be laid directly on the liner, as shown ❺. Add sand where necessary under the liner to level the surface so that the stones don't rock. Such treatment will withstand the occasional, careful traffic of pond maintenance. If you anticipate heavier traffic, you can bed the stones in 2 to 3 in. of mortar. It's prudent to consult with a landscape contractor about whether your intended use and soil require a footing for mortared stones.

Elevation detail of pond overflow

Flagstone edging, 12 in. or more wide

Cover pipe with flagstone.

Pond liner

To overflow area

PVC pipe, 1- or 2-in.-dia., about 12 in. long

Garden bed or lawn

1-in. layer of sand (horizontal surfaces)

Carpet underlayment (walls)

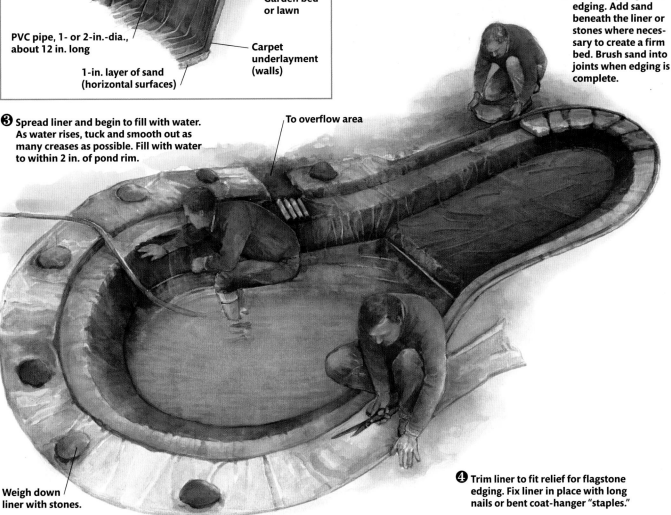

❺ Fit and lay flagstone edging. Add sand beneath the liner or stones where necessary to create a firm bed. Brush sand into joints when edging is complete.

❸ Spread liner and begin to fill with water. As water rises, tuck and smooth out as many creases as possible. Fill with water to within 2 in. of pond rim.

To overflow area

Weigh down liner with stones.

❹ Trim liner to fit relief for flagstone edging. Fix liner in place with long nails or bent coat-hanger "staples."

Building a Retaining Wall

Contours and sloping terrain can add considerable interest to a home landscape. But you can have too much of a good thing. Two designs in this book employ retaining walls to alter problem slopes. The wall shown on p. 60 eliminates a small but abrupt grade change, producing two almost level surfaces and the opportunity to install attractive plantings and a patio on them. On p. 68 a retaining wall helps turn a steep slope into a showpiece.

Retaining walls can be handsome landscape features in their own right. Made of cut stone, fieldstone, brick, landscape timbers, or concrete, they can complement the materials and style of your house or nearby structures. However, making a stable, long-lasting retaining wall of these materials can require tools and skills many homeowners do not possess.

For these reasons we've instead chosen retaining-wall systems made of precast concrete for designs in this book. Readily available in a range of sizes, sur-face finishes, and colors, these systems require few tools and no special skills to install. They have been engineered to resist the forces that soil, water, freezing, and thawing bring to bear on a retaining wall. Install these walls according to the manufacturer's specifications, and you can be confident that they will do their job for many years.

A number of systems are available in California through nurseries, garden centers, and local contracting suppliers. (Check the Yellow Pages.) But they all share basic design principles. Like traditional dry-stone walls, these systems rely largely on weight and friction to contain the soil. In many systems, interlocking blocks or pegs help align the courses and increase the wall's strength. In all systems, blocks must rest on a solid, level base. A freely draining backfill of crushed stone is essential to avoid buildup of water pressure in the retained soil, which can buckle even a heavy wall. (In hilly terrain or where drainage is a concern, experts often recommend installing drainage pipe to remove excess water from behind retaining walls.)

The construction steps shown here are typical of those recommended by most system manufacturers for retaining walls up to 3 to 4 ft. tall; be sure to follow the manufacturer's instructions for the system you choose. For higher walls, walls on loose soil or heavy clay soils, and walls retaining very steep slopes, it is prudent to consult with a landscape architect or contractor. (Some cities and towns have regulations for retaining walls and landscape steps. Be sure to check with local authorities before beginning work.)

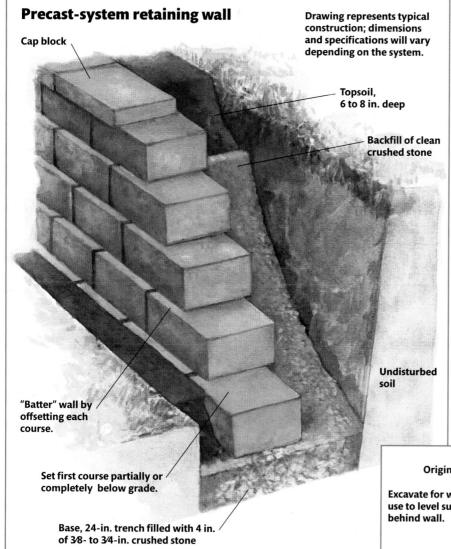

Precast-system retaining wall

Drawing represents typical construction; dimensions and specifications will vary depending on the system.

Cap block

Topsoil, 6 to 8 in. deep

Backfill of clean crushed stone

Undisturbed soil

"Batter" wall by offsetting each course.

Set first course partially or completely below grade.

Base, 24-in. trench filled with 4 in. of 3⁄8- to 3⁄4-in. crushed stone

Original slope

New grade level

Excavate for wall; use to level surface behind wall.

New grade

30–45° from plumb

Building a wall

Installing a wall system is just about as simple as stacking up children's building blocks. The most important part of the job is establishing a firm, level base. Start by laying out the wall with string and hose (for curves) and excavating a base trench.

As the boxed drawing shows, the position of the wall in relation to the base of the slope determines the height of the wall, how much soil you move, and the leveling effect on the slope. Unless the wall is very long, it is a good idea to excavate along the entire length and fine-tune the line of the wall before beginning

the base trench. Remember to excavate back far enough to accommodate the stone backfill. Systems vary, but a foot of crushed-stone backfill behind the blocks is typical. (For the two-wall design, build the bottom wall first, then the top.)

Systems vary in the width and depth of trench and type of base material, but in all of them, the trench must be level across its width and along its length. We've shown a 4-in. layer of ⅜- to ¾-in. crushed stone (blocks can slip sideways on rounded aggregate or pea gravel, which also don't compact as well). Depending on the system and the circumstances, a portion or all of the first course lies below grade, so the soil helps hold the blocks in place.

Add crushed stone to the trench, level it with a rake, and compact it with a hand tamper or mechanical compactor. Lay the first course of blocks carefully ❶. Check frequently to make sure the blocks are level across their width and

along their length. Stagger vertical joints as you stack subsequent courses. Offset the faces of the blocks so the wall leans back into the retained soil. Some systems design this "batter" into their blocks; others allow you to choose from several possible setbacks.

As the wall rises, shovel backfill behind the blocks ❷. Clean crushed rock drains well; some systems suggest placing a barrier of landscaping fabric between the rock and the retained soil to keep soil from migrating into the fill and impeding drainage.

Thinner cap blocks finish the top of the wall ❸. Some wall systems recommend cementing these blocks in place with a weatherproof adhesive. The last 6 to 8 in. of the backfill should be topsoil, firmed into place and ready for planting.

**BUILDING
A WALL**

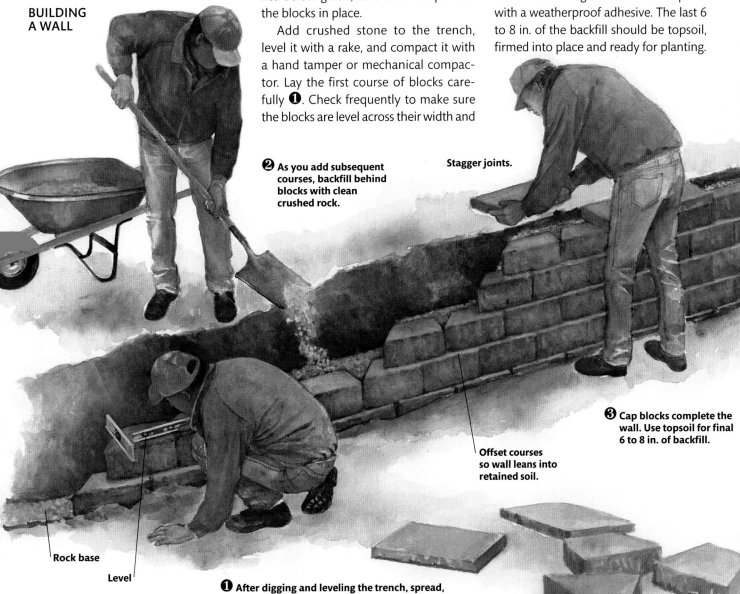

❷ **As you add subsequent courses, backfill behind blocks with clean crushed rock.**

Stagger joints.

❸ **Cap blocks complete the wall. Use topsoil for final 6 to 8 in. of backfill.**

Offset courses so wall leans into retained soil.

Rock base

Level

❶ **After digging and leveling the trench, spread, level, and compact the base materials; then lay the blocks. Check frequently to see that they are level across their width and length.**

Wall parallel with a slope: Stepped base

Construct walls running parallel to a slope in "steps," each with a level base.

Backfill so grade behind finishes level with top of wall.

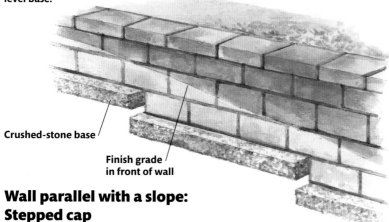

Crushed-stone base

Finish grade in front of wall

Wall parallel with a slope: Stepped cap

Sometimes the top of a wall needs to step up or down to accommodate grade changes in the slope behind.

Cap block

A "return" corner

Where you want the slope to extend beyond the end of the wall, make a corner that cuts into the slope.

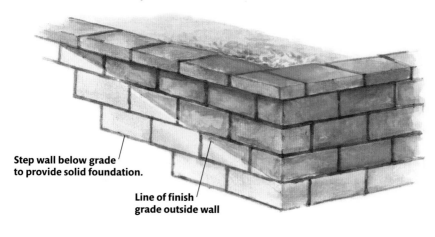

Step wall below grade to provide solid foundation.

Line of finish grade outside wall

Sloped sites

If your slope runs parallel with the length of the wall, you can "step" the bottom of the wall and make its top surface level, as shown in the drawing, top left. Create a length of level trench along the lowest portion of the site. Then work up the slope, creating steps as necessary. Add fill soil to raise the grade behind the wall to the level of the cap blocks.

Alternatively, you can step the top of the wall, as shown in the drawing, middle left. Here, the base of the wall rests on level ground, but the top of the wall steps to match the slope's decreasing height. This saves money and labor on materials and backfill, while producing a different look.

Retaining walls, such as the one shown on p. 60, are frequently placed perpendicular to the run of a slope. If you want to alter just part of the slope or if the slope continues beyond your property, you'll need to terminate the wall. A corner that cuts back into the slope, bottom left, is an attractive and structurally sound solution to this problem.

Constructing curves and corners

Wall-system blocks are designed so that curves, such as the one in the design on p. 68, are no more difficult to lay than straight sections. Corners may require that you cut a few blocks or use specially designed blocks, but they are otherwise uncomplicated. If your wall must fit a prescribed length between corners, consider working from the corners toward the middle (after laying a base course). Masons use this technique, which also helps to avoid exposing cut blocks at the corners.

You can cut blocks with a mason's chisel and mallet or rent a mason's saw. Chiseling works well where the block faces are rough textured, so the faces you cut blend right in. A saw is best for smooth-faced blocks and projects requiring lots of cutting.

Steps

Steps in a low retaining wall are not difficult to build, but they require forethought and careful layout. Systems differ on construction details. The drawing below shows a typical design where the blocks and stone base rest on "steps" cut into firm subsoil. If your soil is less stable or is recent fill, you should excavate the entire area beneath the steps to the same depth as the wall base and build a foundation of blocks, as shown in the boxed drawing.

These steps are independent of the adjacent "return" walls, which are vertical, not battered (stepped back). In some systems, steps and return walls are interlocked. To match a path, you can face the treads with the same stone, brick, or pavers, or you can use the system's cap blocks or special treads.

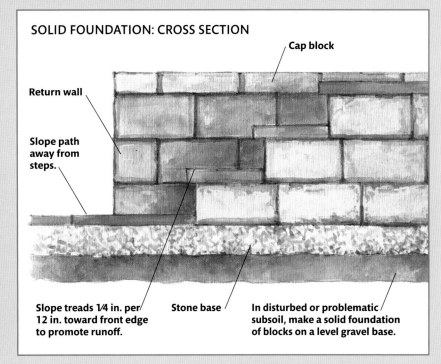

SOLID FOUNDATION: CROSS SECTION

Cap block

Return wall

Slope path away from steps.

Slope treads 1/4 in. per 12 in. toward front edge to promote runoff.

Stone base

In disturbed or problematic subsoil, make a solid foundation of blocks on a level gravel base.

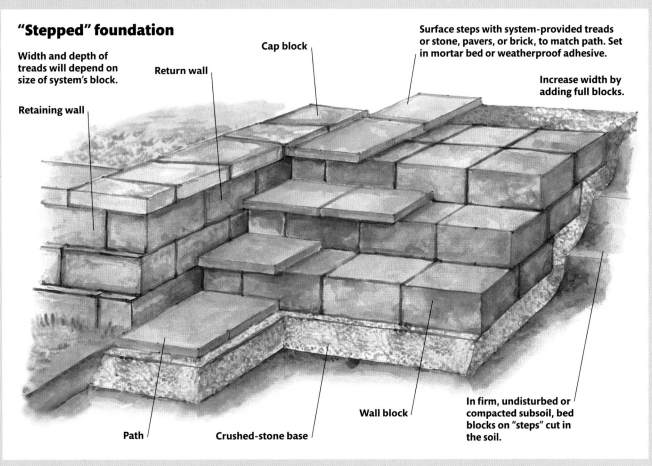

"Stepped" foundation

Width and depth of treads will depend on size of system's block.

Return wall

Cap block

Surface steps with system-provided treads or stone, pavers, or brick, to match path. Set in mortar bed or weatherproof adhesive.

Increase width by adding full blocks.

Retaining wall

Path

Crushed-stone base

Wall block

In firm, undisturbed or compacted subsoil, bed blocks on "steps" cut in the soil.

Fences, Arbors, and Trellises

Novices who have no trouble tackling a simple flagstone path often get nervous when it comes time to erect a fence, an arbor, or even a trellis. While such projects can require more skill and resources than others in the landscape, the ones in this book have been designed with less-than-confident do-it-yourself builders in mind. The designs are simple, the materials are read-ily available, and the tools and skills will be familiar to anyone accustomed to ordinary home maintenance.

First we'll introduce you to the tools and materials needed for the projects. Then we'll present the small number of basic opera-tions you'll employ when building them. Finally, we'll provide drawings and comments on each of the projects.

Tools and materials

Even the least-handy homeowner is likely to have most of the tools needed for these projects: claw hammer, crosscut handsaw, brace-and-bit or electric drill, adjustable wrench, combination square, measuring tape, carpenter's level, and sawhorses. You may even have Grandpa's old posthole dig-ger. Many will have a handheld power circular saw, which makes faster (though noisier) work of cutting parts to length. A cordless drill/screwdriver is invaluable if you're substituting screws for nails. If you have more than a few holes to dig, consider renting a gas-powered posthole dig-ger. A 12-in.-diameter hole will serve for 4x4 posts; if possi-ble, get a larger-diameter digger for 6x6 posts.

Materials

Of the materials offering strength, durability, and attractive-ness in outdoor settings, wood is the easiest to work and affords the quickest results. While almost all commercially available lumber is strong enough for landscape structures, most decay quickly when in prolonged contact with soil and water. Cedar, cypress, and redwood, however, contain natural preservatives and are excellent for landscape use. Alternatively, a range of softwoods (such as pine, fir, and hemlock) are pressure treated with preservatives and will last for many years. Parts of structures that do not come in contact with soil or are not continually wet can be made of ordinary construction-grade lumber, but unless they're reg-ularly painted, they will not last as long as treated or natu-rally decay-resistant material.

In addition to dimension lumber, several of the designs incorporate lattice, which is thin wooden strips crisscrossed to form patterns of diamonds or squares. Premade lattice is widely available in sheets 4 ft. by 8 ft. and smaller. Lattice comes in decay-resistant woods as well as in treated and untreated softwoods. Local supplies vary, and you may find lattice made of thicker or narrower material.

Fasteners

For millennia, even basic structures such as these would have been assembled with complicated joints. Today, with simple nailed, bolted, or screwed joints, a few hours' prac-tice swinging a hammer or wielding a cordless electric screwdriver is all the training necessary.

All these structures can be assembled using nails. But screws are stronger and, if you have a cordless screwdriver, make assembly easier. Buy common or box nails that are galvanized to prevent rust. Self-tapping screws ("deck" screws) require no pilot holes. For rust resistance, buy gal-vanized screws or screws treated with zinc dichromate.

Galvanized metal connectors are available to reinforce the joints used in these projects. For novice builders, con-nectors are a great help in aligning parts and making assem-bly easier. (Correctly fastened with nails or screws, the joints are strong enough without connectors.)

Finishes

Cedar, cypress, and redwood are handsome when left un-finished to weather, when treated with clear or colored stains, or when painted. Pressure-treated lumber is best painted or stained.

Outdoor stains are becoming increasingly popular. Clear or lightly tinted stains can preserve or enhance the rich reddish browns of cedar, cypress, and redwood. Stains also come in a range of colors that can be used like paint. Because they pen-etrate the wood rather than forming a film, stains don't form an opaque surface, but stains won't peel or chip like paint and are therefore easier to touch up and refinish.

When choosing a finish, take account of what plants are growing on or near the structure. It's a lot of work to remove yards of vines from a trellis or squeeze between a large shrub and a fence to repaint; consider an unfinished decay-resistant wood or an initial stain that you allow to weather.

Setting posts

Most of the projects are anchored by firmly set, vertical posts. In general, the taller the structure, the deeper the post should be set. Arbor posts should be at least 3 ft. deep. Corner and end posts of fences up to 6 ft. tall and posts supporting gates should also be 3 ft. deep. Intermediate fence posts can be set 2 ft. deep.

The length of the posts you buy depends, of course, on the depth at which they are set and their finished heights. When calculating lengths of arbor posts, remember that the tops of the posts must be level. The easiest method of achieving this is to cut the posts to length after installation. For example, buy 12-ft. posts for an arbor finishing at 8 ft. above grade and set 3 ft. in the ground. The convenience is worth the expense of the foot or so you cut off. The site and personal preference can determine whether you cut fence posts to length after installation or buy them cut to length and add or remove fill from the bottom of the hole to position them at the correct heights.

Arbor posts

When laying out the arbor, take extra care when positioning arbor posts. The corners of the structure must be right angles, and the sides must be parallel with one another. Locating the corners with batter boards and string is fussy but accurate. Make the batter boards by nailing 1x2 stakes to scraps of 1x3 or 1x4, and position them about 1 ft. from the approximate location of each post as shown in the boxed drawing at right. Locate the exact post positions with string; adjust the string so the diagonal measurements are equal, which ensures that the corners of the structure will be at right angles.

At the intersections of the strings, locate the postholes by eye or with a plumb bob ❶. Remove the strings and dig the holes; then reattach the strings to position the posts exactly ❷. Plumb and brace the posts carefully. Check positions with the level and by measuring between adjacent posts and across diagonals. Diagonal braces between adjacent posts will stiffen them and help align their faces ❸. Then add concrete ❹ and let it cure for a day.

To establish the height of the posts, measure up from grade on one post, then use a level and straightedge to mark the heights of the other posts from the first one. Where joists will be bolted to the faces of the posts, you can install the joists and use their top edges as a handsaw guide for cutting the posts to length.

SETTING ARBOR POSTS

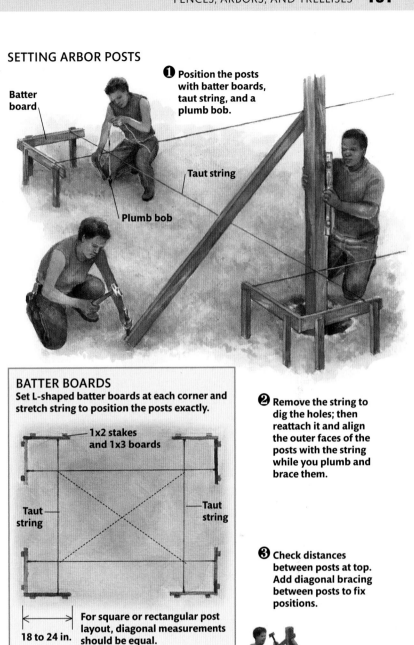

❶ Position the posts with batter boards, taut string, and a plumb bob.

Batter board

Taut string

Plumb bob

BATTER BOARDS
Set L-shaped batter boards at each corner and stretch string to position the posts exactly.

1x2 stakes and 1x3 boards

Taut string

Taut string

18 to 24 in.

For square or rectangular post layout, diagonal measurements should be equal.

❷ Remove the string to dig the holes; then reattach it and align the outer faces of the posts with the string while you plumb and brace them.

❸ Check distances between posts at top. Add diagonal bracing between posts to fix positions.

❹ Cement posts in place.

Fence posts

Lay out and set the end or corner posts of a fence first, then add the intermediate posts. Dig the holes by hand or with a power digger ❶. To promote drainage, place several inches of gravel at the bottom of the hole for the post to rest on. Checking with a carpenter's level, plumb the post vertically and brace it with scrap lumber nailed to stakes ❷. Then add a few more inches of gravel around the post's base.

If your native soil compacts well, you can fix posts in place with tamped earth. Add the soil gradually, tamping it continu-ously with a heavy iron bar or 2x4. Check regularly with a level to see that the post doesn't get knocked out of plumb. This technique suits rustic or informal fences, where misalignments caused by shifting posts aren't noticeable or damaging.

For more formal fences, or where soils are loose or fence panels are buffeted by winds or snow, it's prudent to fix posts in concrete ❸. Mix enough concrete to set the two end posts; as a rule of thumb, figure one 80-lb. bag of premixed concrete per post. As you shovel it in, prod the concrete with a stick to settle it, particularly if you've added rubble to extend the mix. Build

SETTING A FENCE POST

❷ Plumb the post, checking on adjacent faces with a level. Hold it in position with stakes and braces.

❶ Position the end or corner posts; then dig holes for them.

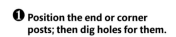

Post ——

Slope top surface for drainage.

3 ft. (typical)

Concrete and rubble (shown), or tamped earth

Coarse gravel

1 ft. (typical)

❸ Fill the hole with concrete and rubble.

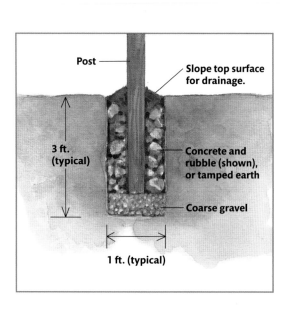

the concrete slightly above grade and slope it away from the post to aid drainage.

Once the end posts are set, stretch a string between the posts. (The concrete should cure for 24 hours before you nail or screw rails and panels in place, but you can safely stretch string while the concrete is still wet.) Measure along the string to position the intermediate posts; drop a plumb bob from the string at each intermediate post position to gauge the center of the hole below ❹. Once all the holes have been dug, again stretch a string between the end posts, near the top. Set the intermediate posts as described previously; align one face with the string and plumb adjacent faces with the carpenter's level ❺. Check positions of intermediate posts a final time with a measuring tape.

If the fence is placed along a slope, the top of the slats or panels can step down the slope or mirror it (as shown in the bottom drawing at left). Either way, make sure that the posts are plumb, rather than leaning with the slope.

❹ Stretch a string between the tops of the two end posts. Then locate positions of intermediate posts with a plumb bob.

❺ After digging the holes, stretch a string between the end posts to align intermediate posts. Use a level to plumb adjacent faces.

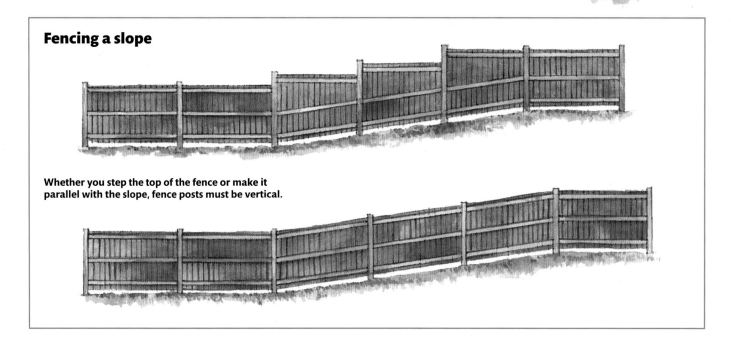

Fencing a slope

Whether you step the top of the fence or make it parallel with the slope, fence posts must be vertical.

Joints

The components of the fences, arbors, and trellises used in this book are attached to the posts and to each other with the simple joints shown below. Because all the parts are made of dimensioned lumber, the only cuts you'll need to make are to length. For strong joints, cut ends as square as you can, so the mating pieces make contact across their entire surfaces. If you have no confidence in your sawing, many lumberyards will cut pieces to length for a modest fee.

Beginners often find it difficult to keep two pieces correctly positioned while trying to drive a nail into them, particularly when the nail must be driven at an angle, called "toenailing." If you have this problem, consider assembling the project with screws, which draw the pieces together, or with metal connectors, which can be nailed or screwed in place on one piece and then attached to the mating piece.

For one of the designs, you need to attach lattice panels to posts. The panels are made by sandwiching store-bought lattice

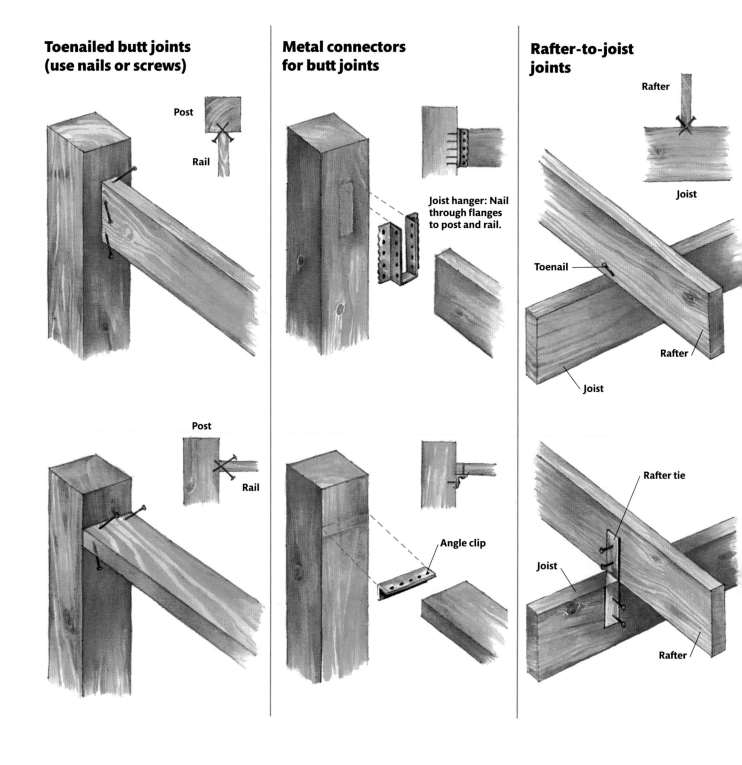

Toenailed butt joints (use nails or screws)

Post

Rail

Post

Rail

Metal connectors for butt joints

Joist hanger: Nail through flanges to post and rail.

Angle clip

Rafter-to-joist joints

Rafter

Joist

Toenail

Rafter

Joist

Rafter tie

Joist

Rafter

between frames of dimension lumber (construction details are given on the following pages). While the assembled panels can be toenailed to the posts, novices may find that the job goes easier using one or more types of metal connector, as shown in the drawing at below right. Attach the angle clips or angle brackets to the post; then position the lattice panel and fix it to the connectors. For greatest strength and ease of assembly, attach connectors using self-tapping screws driven by a cordless or electric screwdriver or drill-driver.

In the following pages, we'll show construction details of the fences, arbors, and trellises presented in the Portfolio of Designs. (The page number indicates the design.) Where the basic joints discussed here can be used, we have shown the parts but left choice of fasteners to you. Typical fastenings are indicated for other joints. We have kept the constructions shown here simple and straightforward. They are not the only possibilities, and we encourage experienced builders to adapt and alter constructions as well as designs to suit differing situations and personal preferences.

Frame corner with metal connector

Attaching framed lattice panels to posts

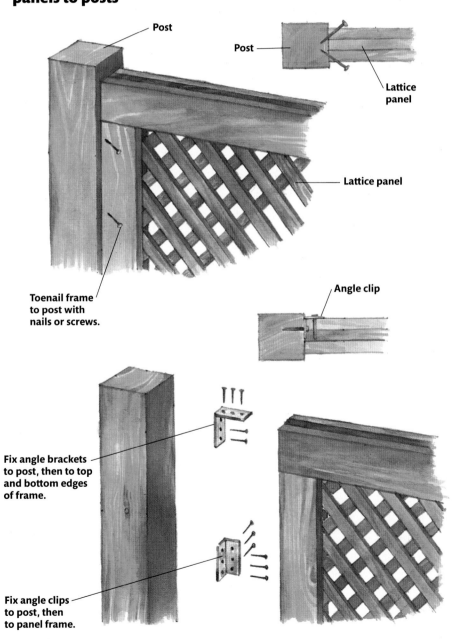

Post

Post

Lattice panel

Lattice panel

Toenail frame to post with nails or screws.

Angle clip

Fix angle brackets to post, then to top and bottom edges of frame.

Fix angle clips to post, then to panel frame.

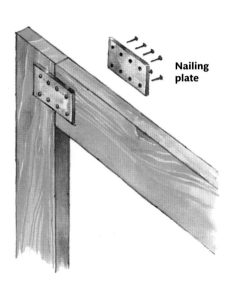

Nailing plate

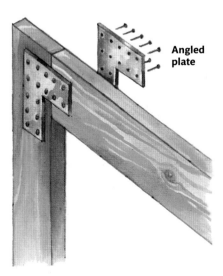

Angled plate

Homemade lattice trellis
(pp. 66–67 and 50–51)

The trellis shown here supports climbing plants to make a vertical garden of a blank wall (or tall fence). The design can be altered to fit walls of different sizes, while keeping its pleasing proportions. The 32-in.-wide modules are simpler to make than a single large trellis. Hung on L-hangers, they're easy to remove when you need to paint the wall or fence behind. For the design on p. 67, the trellis is 8 ft. tall and requires four sections. The design on p. 51 uses six sections (three on the wall and three on the fence) and is 6 ft. tall.

Start by cutting all the pieces to length. (Here we'll call the horizontal members "rails" and the vertical members "stiles.") Working on a large flat surface, nail or screw the two outer stiles to the top and bottom rails, checking the corners with a framing square. The 2x2 rails provide ample material to house the L-hangers.

Carefully attach the three intermediate stiles, then the 1x2 rails. Cut a piece of scrap 6 in. long to use as a spacer. Fix the L-shaped hangers to the wall or fence. Buy hangers long enough to hold the trellis several inches away from the surface, allowing air to circulate behind the foliage.

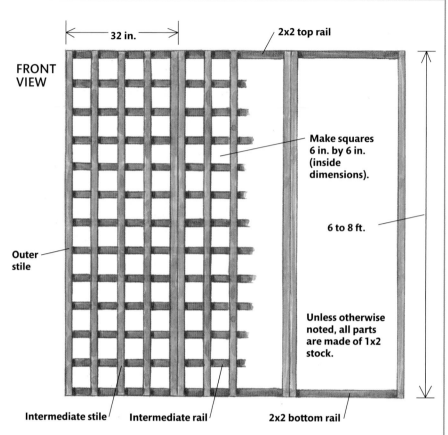

FRONT VIEW

32 in.

2x2 top rail

Make squares 6 in. by 6 in. (inside dimensions).

6 to 8 ft.

Unless otherwise noted, all parts are made of 1x2 stock.

Outer stile

Intermediate stile

Intermediate rail

2x2 bottom rail

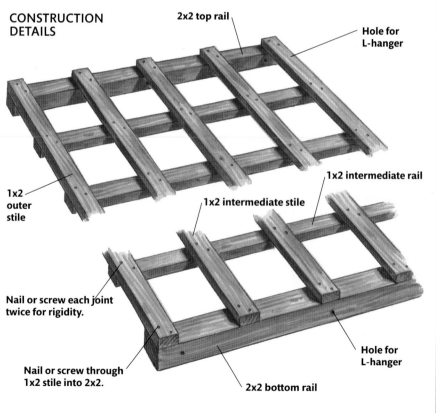

CONSTRUCTION DETAILS

2x2 top rail

Hole for L-hanger

1x2 outer stile

1x2 intermediate rail

1x2 intermediate stile

Nail or screw each joint twice for rigidity.

Nail or screw through 1x2 stile into 2x2.

Hole for L-hanger

2x2 bottom rail

TRELLIS HANGER DETAIL

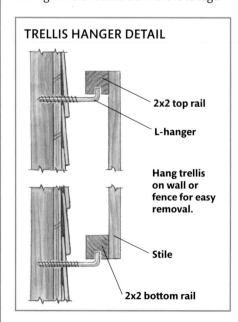

2x2 top rail

L-hanger

Hang trellis on wall or fence for easy removal.

Stile

2x2 bottom rail

Hideaway arbor
(pp. 49, 92)

This cozy enclosure shelters several comfortable chairs or a bench and supports vines to shade the occupants.

Its rustic posts and rafters, made from peeled logs and tree stakes, create a setting of comfortable informality perfectly in tune with the surrounding plantings. Tree stakes are used to support newly planted trees. Peeled posts and tree stakes are available from nurseries, garden centers, or landscape contractors.

The arbor is easy to construct. Set the posts in cement (see pp. 180–183). Then bolt the 4x4 beams to the tops of the posts, boring clearance and pilot holes first. You can toenail 4x4 ties between beams to keep the structure rigid while you add the stake rafters, but the finished arbor would be sturdy enough without them. Fix the stake rafters in place with galvanized spikes or long deck screws, as shown in the detail drawing. Bore pilot holes for spikes and screws to prevent splitting the rafters and to make the fasteners easier to drive.

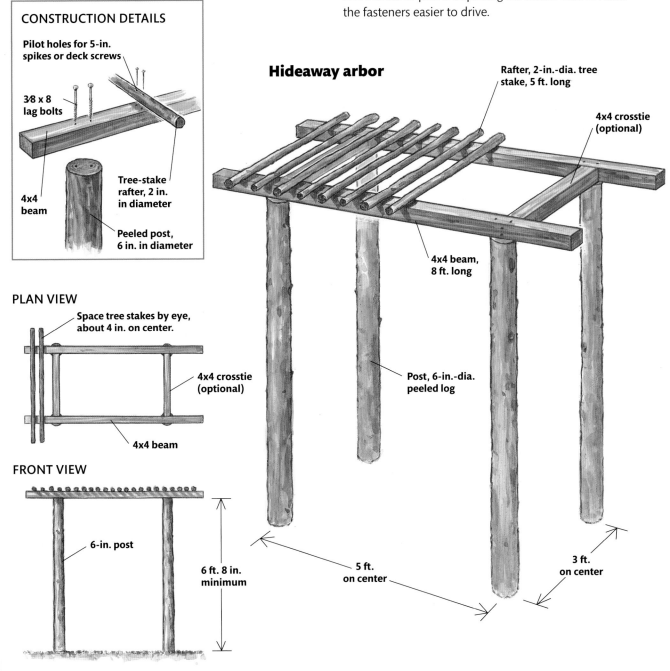

CONSTRUCTION DETAILS

Pilot holes for 5-in. spikes or deck screws

3⁄8 x 8 lag bolts

4x4 beam

Tree-stake rafter, 2 in. in diameter

Peeled post, 6 in. in diameter

Hideaway arbor

Rafter, 2-in.-dia. tree stake, 5 ft. long

4x4 crosstie (optional)

4x4 beam, 8 ft. long

Post, 6-in.-dia. peeled log

PLAN VIEW

Space tree stakes by eye, about 4 in. on center.

4x4 crosstie (optional)

4x4 beam

FRONT VIEW

6-in. post

6 ft. 8 in. minimum

5 ft. on center

3 ft. on center

Patio arbor and sun screen
(pp. 80–81 and 72–73)

This simple structure offers relief from the sun on a portion of a backyard patio. The closely spaced 2x4 rafters form a sun screen, while allowing air circulation. Adapt rafter spacing and orientation to accommodate your site. In the design on pp. 80–81, the arbor supports wisteria vines, which provide additional cooling shade as well as a pleasant leafy ambiance.

If you're building the patio and arbor at the same time, set the 6x6 posts (see pp. 180–183) before you lay the patio surface. If you're adding the arbor to an existing patio, you'll need to break through the paving to set the posts or pour footings to support surface attachments. Consult local building officials or a landscape contractor for advice on how best to proceed.

Once the posts are set, fix the 2x8 beams to pairs of posts with carriage bolts. Nail the 2x8s in place; then make the bolt holes by boring through the 2x8s and the post with a long electrician's bit. Fix the long 2x6 joists and the 2x4 rafters in place with metal connectors. Metal connectors fixed with screws will stand up best to the vigorous growth of wisteria.

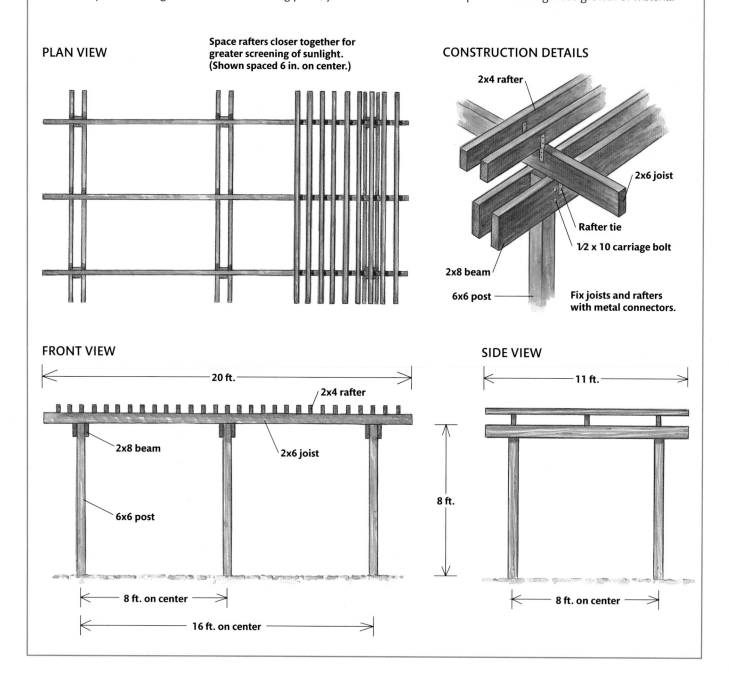

PLAN VIEW

Space rafters closer together for greater screening of sunlight. (Shown spaced 6 in. on center.)

CONSTRUCTION DETAILS

2x4 rafter

2x6 joist

Rafter tie

1/2 x 10 carriage bolt

2x8 beam

6x6 post

Fix joists and rafters with metal connectors.

FRONT VIEW

20 ft.

2x4 rafter

2x8 beam

2x6 joist

6x6 post

8 ft. on center

16 ft. on center

SIDE VIEW

11 ft.

8 ft.

8 ft. on center

Passageway arbor
(pp. 48–49)

Draped with hardenbergia, this shallow arbor welcomes visitors to a small stroll garden situated in a narrow side yard. Once you have gathered the materials together, you should need no more than an afternoon to build the arbor.

Set the posts first, as described on pp. 180–183. The hefty 6x6 posts shown here add presence to the arbor, but cheaper, easier-to-handle 4x4s will make an equally sturdy structure. Cut the joists and rafters to length. The 60° angles on their ends can easily be cut with a handsaw. Bolt or nail the joists in place. Then toenail the short rafters to the joists or attach them with metal connectors.

In addition to the posts, you can provide other supports for the hardenbergia to twine around. Strands of coarse rope or cord work well when stretched between the large screw eyes fixed to the rafters and the base of the posts, as shown here. The vines soon hide the rope or cord from view.

CONSTRUCTION DETAILS

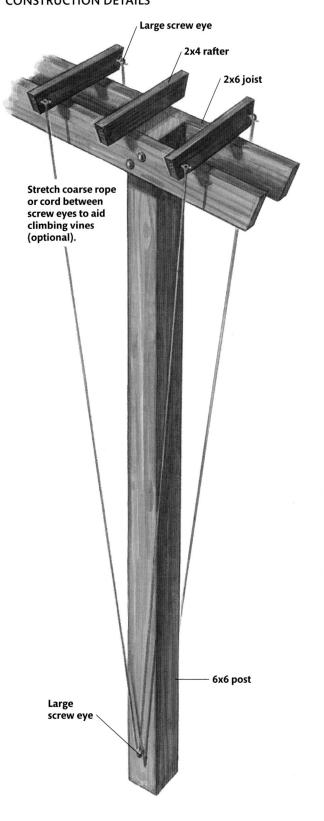

Large screw eye

2x4 rafter

2x6 joist

Stretch coarse rope or cord between screw eyes to aid climbing vines (optional).

6x6 post

Large screw eye

PLAN VIEW

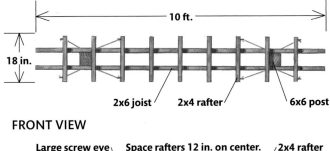

10 ft.

18 in.

2x6 joist   2x4 rafter   6x6 post

FRONT VIEW

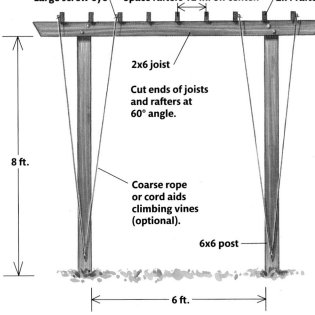

Large screw eye   Space rafters 12 in. on center.   2x4 rafter

2x6 joist

Cut ends of joists and rafters at 60° angle.

8 ft.

Coarse rope or cord aids climbing vines (optional).

6x6 post

6 ft.

Entry arbor and fence
(pp. 44–47)

This arbor makes an event of the passage from sidewalk to front door or from one part of your property to another. Two versions are shown in the Portfolio. One features the arbor alone; the other adds a picket fence.

Hefty 6x6 posts provide real presence here; the 12-footers you'll need are heavy, so engage a couple of helpers to save your back. As with the previous arbor, once the posts are set, the job is easy. You can toenail the 3x6 beams to the tops of the posts and the 2x4 rafters to the beams. (Or you can fix them with long spikes or lag screws, 10 in. and 8 in. long, respectively. This job is easier if you drill pilot holes, with bits slightly thinner than the spikes.) Attach the 2x2 cross rafters with screws or nails. If you can't buy 3x6s, you can nail two 2x6s together face to face.

Sandwich lattice between 1x3s to make the side panels and fix them between posts with nails, screws, or metal connectors. Alternating the corner overlap, as shown on the drawing, makes a stronger frame.

The fence forms small enclosures on either side of the arbor before heading off across the property. To match the arbor, use 6x6 posts for the enclosures; then switch to 4x4s if you wish, spacing them no farther apart than 8 ft.

You can purchase ready-made lengths of picket fence, but it is easy enough to make yourself. Set the posts; then cut and fit 2x4 rails on edge between them. Space 1x3 picket slats 1½ in. apart. The drawing on the facing page shows large round wooden finials atop the fence posts; you can buy various types of ready-made finials, or you could work a heavy bevel around the top end of the posts themselves.

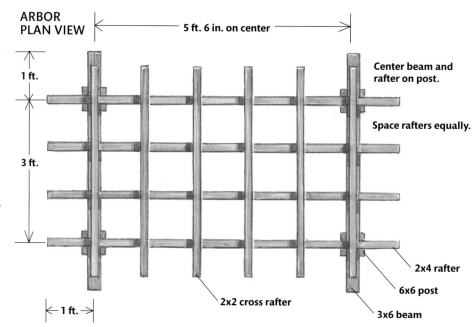

ARBOR PLAN VIEW

5 ft. 6 in. on center

1 ft.

3 ft.

1 ft.

Center beam and rafter on post.

Space rafters equally.

2x4 rafter

6x6 post

3x6 beam

2x2 cross rafter

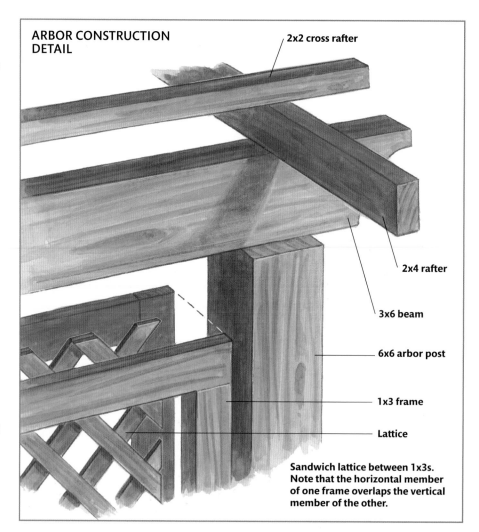

ARBOR CONSTRUCTION DETAIL

2x2 cross rafter

2x4 rafter

3x6 beam

6x6 arbor post

1x3 frame

Lattice

Sandwich lattice between 1x3s. Note that the horizontal member of one frame overlaps the vertical member of the other.

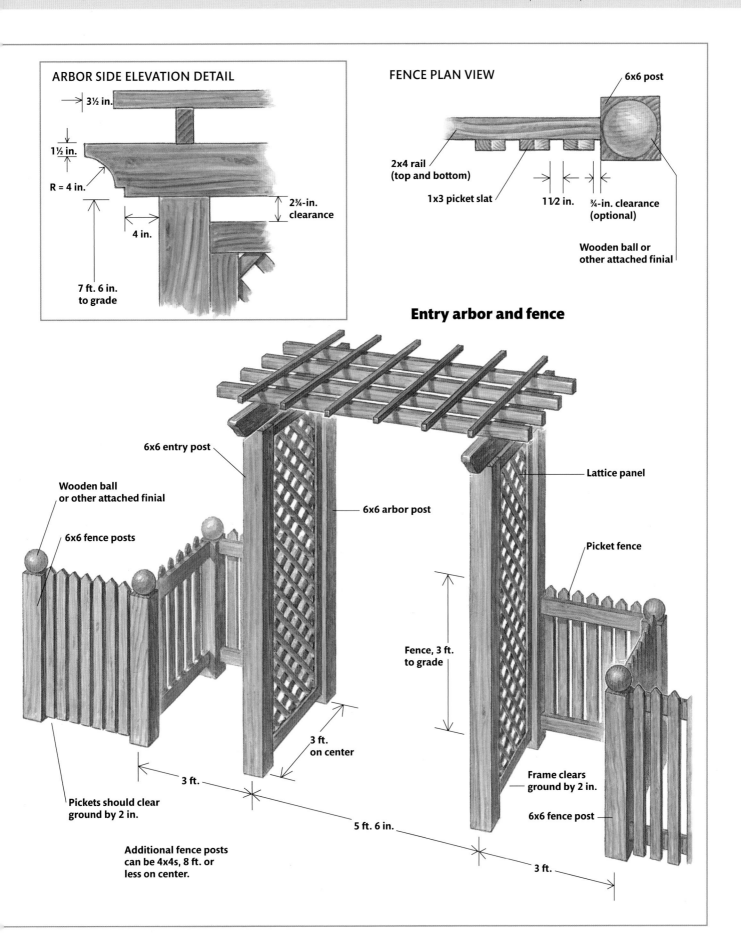

ARBOR SIDE ELEVATION DETAIL

3½ in.

1½ in.

R = 4 in.

4 in.

2¾-in. clearance

7 ft. 6 in. to grade

FENCE PLAN VIEW

6x6 post

2x4 rail (top and bottom)

1x3 picket slat

1½ in.

¾-in. clearance (optional)

Wooden ball or other attached finial

Entry arbor and fence

6x6 entry post

Wooden ball or other attached finial

6x6 fence posts

Lattice panel

6x6 arbor post

Picket fence

Fence, 3 ft. to grade

3 ft. on center

Frame clears ground by 2 in.

6x6 fence post

3 ft.

Pickets should clear ground by 2 in.

5 ft. 6 in.

3 ft.

Additional fence posts can be 4x4s, 8 ft. or less on center.

Preparing the Soil for Planting

The better the soil, the better the plants. Soil quality affects how fast plants grow, how big they get, how good they look, and how long they live. But on many residential lots, the soil is shallow and infertile. Unless you're lucky enough to have a better-than-average site where the soil has been cared for and amended over the years, perhaps for use as a vegetable garden or flower bed, you should plan to improve your soil before planting in it.

If you were planting just a few trees or shrubs, you could prepare individual planting holes for them and leave the surrounding soil undisturbed. However,

for nearly all the plantings in this book, digging individual holes is impractical, and it's much better for the plants if you prepare the soil throughout the entire area that will be planted. (The major exception is when you're planting under a tree, which is discussed on p. 194.)

For most of the situations shown in this book, you could prepare the soil with hand tools—a spade, digging fork, and rake. The job goes faster, though, if you use a rototiller, and a rototiller is better than hand tools for mixing amendments into the soil. Unless you grow vegetables, you probably won't use a rototiller often enough to justify buying one yourself, but

you can easily borrow or rent a rototiller or hire someone with a tiller to come and prepare your site.

Loosen the soil

After you've removed any sod or other vegetation from the designated area (see pp. 160–161), the first step is digging or tilling to loosen the soil ❶. Do this on a day when the soil is moist—not so wet that it sticks to your tools or so dry that it makes dust. Start at one end of the bed and work back and forth until you reach the other end. Try to dig down at least 8 in., or deeper if possible. If the ground is very compacted, you'll have to make repeated passes with a tiller to reach 8 in. deep. Toss aside any large rocks, roots, or debris that you encounter. When you're working near a house or other buildings, watch out for buried wires, cables, and pipes. Most town and city governments have a number you can call to request that someone help you locate buried utilities.

After this initial digging, the ground will likely be very rough and lumpy. Whump the clods with the back of a digging fork or make another pass with the tiller. Continue until you've reduced all the clumps to the size of apples.

Once you've loosened the existing soil and dug it as deeply as possible, you may need to add topsoil to fill in low spots, refine the grade, or raise the planting area above the surrounding grade for better drainage or to make it easier to see a favorite plant. Unless you need just a small amount, order topsoil by the cubic yard. Consult the staff at your local nursery to find a reputable supplier of topsoil.

Add organic matter

Common soil (and purchased topsoil, too) consists mainly of rock and mineral fragments of various sizes—which are mostly coarse and gritty in sandy soil, and dust-fine in clay soil. One of the best

Common fertilizers and soil amendments

The following materials serve different purposes. Follow soil-test recommendations or the advice of an experienced gardener in choosing which amendments and fertilizers would be best for your soil. If so recommended, you can apply two or three of these at the same time, using the stated rate for each one.

Material	Description	Amount for 100 sq. ft.
Compost	Amendment. Decomposed or aged plant parts and animal manures	1 cu. yd.
Wood by-products	Amendment. Finely ground bark or sawdust, composted or not. Add nitrogen to non-composted material.	1 cu. yd.
All-purpose fertilizer	Synthetic fertilizer containing various amounts of nitrogen, phosphorus, and potassium	According to label
Organic fertilizer	Derived from a variety of organic materials. Provides nutrients in slow-release form.	According to label
Composted manure	Weak nitrogen fertilizers. Bagged steer manure is common.	6–8 lb.

things you can do to improve any kind of soil for landscape and garden plants is to add some organic matter.

Organic materials used in gardening and landscaping are derived from plants and animals and include ground bark, peat moss, compost, and composted manures. Organic matter can be bought in bags or in bulk at nurseries and many municipal recycling centers. If possible, purchase only composted or aged material to amend your soil. Fresh manure can "burn" plant roots. Fresh bark and sawdust can "steal" nitrogen from the soil as they decay. If you buy uncomposted materials, ask at your nursery how best to use them as amendments (some require supplemental nitrogen).

How much organic matter should you use? Compost or aged material can be spread 2 to 3 in. thick across the entire area you're working on ❷. At this thick-

PREPARING THE SOIL FOR PLANTING

ness, a cubic yard (about one heaping pickup-truck load) of bulk material will cover 100 to 150 sq. ft. If you're working on a large area and need several cubic yards of organic matter, have it delivered and dumped close to your project area. You can spread a lot of material in just a few hours if you don't have to cart it very far. Composted and aged manures, such as the bagged steer manure sold at nurseries, contain higher concentrations of nitrogen and should be applied at much lower rates than other composts. They are more commonly used as slow-release fertilizers than as soil-improving amendments.

Add fertilizers and mineral amendments

Organic matter improves the soil's texture and helps it retain water and nutrients, but these materials usually lack essential nutrients. To provide the nutrients that plants need, you typically need to use organic or synthetic fertilizers and powdered minerals. It's most helpful if you mix these materials into the soil before you do any

planting, putting them down into the root zone as shown in the drawing ❸. But you can also sprinkle them on top of the soil in subsequent years to maintain a planting.

Getting a sample of soil tested is the most accurate way to determine how much of which nutrients is needed. (To locate a soil-testing lab, look in the Yellow Pages or ask your Cooperative Extension Service.) Less precise, but often adequate, is seeking the advice of nursery staff. Test results or a good adviser will point out any significant deficiencies in your soil, but large deficiencies are uncommon. Most soil just needs a moderate, balanced dose of nutrients.

The key thing is to avoid using too much of any fertilizer or mineral. Don't guess at this; measure and weigh carefully. Calculate your plot's area. Follow your soil-test results or instructions on a commercial product's package. If necessary weigh out the appropriate amount, using a kitchen or bathroom scale. Apply the material evenly across the plot with a spreader or by hand.

❶ Use a spade, digging fork, or tiller to dig at least 8 in. deep and break the soil into rough clods. Discard rocks, roots, and debris. Watch out for underground utilities.

❷ Spread a 2- to 3-in. layer of organic matter on top of the soil.

❸ Sprinkle measured amounts of fertilizer and mineral amendments evenly across the entire area, and mix thoroughly into the soil.

Mix and smooth the soil

Finally, use a digging fork or tiller and go back and forth across the bed again until the added materials are mixed thoroughly into the soil and everything is broken into nut-size or smaller lumps ❹. Then use a rake to smooth the surface ❺.

At this point, the soil level may look too high compared with adjacent pavement or lawn, but don't worry. It will settle a few inches over the next several weeks and end up close to its original level.

Working near trees

Plantings under the shade of stately old trees can be cool lovely oases, like the ones shown on pp. 104–107. But to establish the plants, you'll need to contend with the tree's roots. Contrary to popular belief, most tree roots are in the top few inches of the soil, and they extend at least as far away from the trunk as the limbs do. Always try to disturb as few roots as possible when planting beneath established trees. To do so, it's often best to dig individual planting holes. Avoid cutting large roots. To start ground covers and perennials, you can add up to 6 inches of soil under the canopy of many established trees. Keep the new soil and any mulch away from the trunk. Covering roots with too much soil can starve them of oxygen, damaging or killing them; soil or mulch next to the trunk can rot the bark.

Plantings beneath existing native oaks and madrones are normally problematic because the additional water needed to maintain the planting may damage or kill these trees. If you're uncertain about whether or how to plant beneath any established tree, or if your landscape plans call for significant grade changes beneath them, consult with a certified arborist.

❹ Use a tiller or digging fork to mix everything together, again working as deep as possible.

❺ Finish by smoothing the surface with a rake.

Making neat edges

All but the most informal landscapes look best if you define and maintain neat edges between the lawn and any adjacent plantings. There are several ways to do this, varying in appearance, effectiveness, cost, and convenience. In California, attractive, easy-to-install edges include cut, brick or stone, and plastic strip. If you plan to install an edging, put it in after you prepare the soil but before you plant the bed.

Cut edge

Lay a hose or rope on the ground to mark the line where you want to cut. Then cut along the line with a sharp spade or edging tool. Lift away any grass that was growing into the bed (or any plants that were running out into the lawn). Use a rake or hoe to smooth out a shallow trench on the bed side of the cut. Keep the trench empty; don't let it fill up with mulch.

Pros and cons: Free. Good for straight or curved edges, level or sloped sites. You have to recut the edge every four to eight weeks during the growing season, but you can cut 50 to 100 ft. in an hour or so. Don't cut the trench too deep; if a mower wheel slips into it, you may scalp the lawn. Crabgrass and other weeds may sprout in the exposed soil; if this happens, hoe or pull them out.

Brick mowing strip

Dig a trench about 8 in. wide and 4 in. deep around the edge of the bed. Fill it halfway with sand; then lay bricks on top, setting them level with the soil on the lawn side. You'll need three bricks per foot of edging. Sweep extra sand into any cracks between the bricks. In cold-winter areas, you'll probably need to reset a few frost-heaved bricks each spring. You can substitute cut stone blocks or concrete pavers for bricks.

Pros and cons: Good for straight or curved edges on level or gently sloped sites. Looks good in combination with brick walkways or brick houses. Fairly easy to install and maintain. Some kinds of grass and plants will grow under, between, or over the bricks.

Plastic strip edging

Garden centers and home-improvement stores sell heavy-duty plastic edging in strips 5 or 6 in. wide and 20 or 50 ft. long. To install it, use a sharp tool to cut straight down through the sod around the edge of the bed. Hold the edging so the round lip sits right at soil level, and drive the stakes through the bottom of the edging and into the undisturbed soil under the lawn. Stakes, which are supplied with the edging, should be at least 8 in. long and set about 3 ft. apart.

Pros and cons: Good for straight or curved edges, but only on relatively level sites. Neat and carefree when well installed, but installation is a two- or three-person job. If the lip isn't set right on the ground, you're likely to hit it with the mower blade. Liable to shift or heave unless it's very securely staked. Hard to drive stakes in rocky soil. Some kinds of grass and ground covers can grow across the top of the edging.

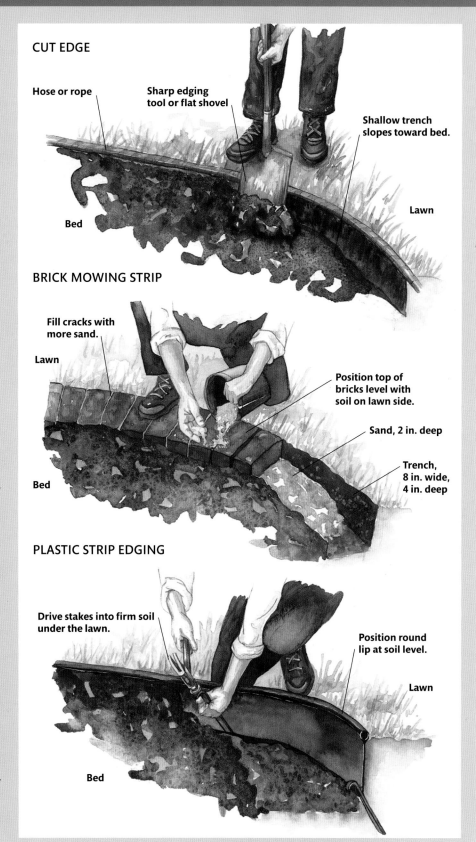

CUT EDGE

Hose or rope

Sharp edging tool or flat shovel

Shallow trench slopes toward bed.

Lawn

Bed

BRICK MOWING STRIP

Fill cracks with more sand.

Lawn

Position top of bricks level with soil on lawn side.

Sand, 2 in. deep

Trench, 8 in. wide, 4 in. deep

Bed

PLASTIC STRIP EDGING

Drive stakes into firm soil under the lawn.

Position round lip at soil level.

Lawn

Bed

Buying Plants

Once you have chosen and planned a landscape project, make a list of the plants you want and start thinking about where to get them. You'll need to locate the kinds of plants you're looking for, choose good-quality plants, and get enough of them to fill your design area.

Where and how to shop

You may already have a favorite place to shop for plants. If not, look in the Yellow Pages under the headings "Nurseries," "Nurserymen," and "Garden Centers," and choose a few places to visit. Take your shopping list, find a salesperson, and ask for help. The plants in this book are commonly available in most parts of California, but you may not find everything you want at one place. The salesperson may refer you to another nursery, offer to special-order plants, or recommend similar plants that you could use as substitutes.

If you're buying too many plants to carry in your car or truck, ask about delivery—it's usually available and sometimes free. Some nurseries offer to replace plants that fail within a limited guarantee period, so ask about that, too.

The staff at a good nursery or garden center will normally be able to answer most of the questions you have about which plants to buy and how to care for them. If you can, go shopping on a rainy weekday when business is slow so staff will have time to answer your questions.

Don't be lured by the low prices of plants for sale at supermarkets or stores that sell plants for only a few months unless you're sure you know exactly what you're looking for and what you're looking at. The staff at these stores rarely have the time or knowledge to offer you much help, and the plants are often disorganized, unlabeled, and stressed by poor care.

If you can't find a plant locally or have a retailer order it for you, you can always order it yourself from a mail-order nursery. Most mail-order nurseries produce good plants and pack them well, but if you haven't dealt with a business before, be smart and place a minimum order first. Judge the quality of the plants that arrive; then decide whether or not to order larger quantities from that firm.

Timing

It's a good idea to plan ahead and start shopping for plants before you're ready to put them in the ground. That way, if you can't find everything on your list, you'll have time to keep shopping around, place special orders, or choose substitutes. Most nurseries will let you "flag" an order for later pickup or delivery, and they'll take care of the plants in the meantime. Or you can bring the plants home; just remember to check the soil in the containers every day and water if needed.

Choosing healthy plants

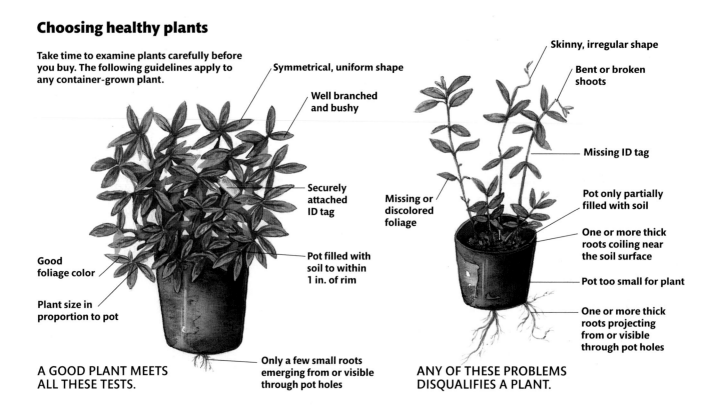

Take time to examine plants carefully before you buy. The following guidelines apply to any container-grown plant.

Symmetrical, uniform shape

Well branched and bushy

Securely attached ID tag

Pot filled with soil to within 1 in. of rim

Good foliage color

Plant size in proportion to pot

Only a few small roots emerging from or visible through pot holes

A GOOD PLANT MEETS ALL THESE TESTS.

Skinny, irregular shape

Bent or broken shoots

Missing ID tag

Missing or discolored foliage

Pot only partially filled with soil

One or more thick roots coiling near the soil surface

Pot too small for plant

One or more thick roots projecting from or visible through pot holes

ANY OF THESE PROBLEMS DISQUALIFIES A PLANT.

Choosing particular plants

The Planting Process

If you need, for example, five azaleas and the nursery or garden center has a whole block of them, how do you choose which five to buy? Because the sales staff may be too busy to help you decide, you may need to choose by yourself.

Most plants today are grown in containers, so it's possible to lift them one at a time and examine them from all sides. Following the guidelines shown in the drawings below, evaluate each plant's shape, size, health and vigor, and root system.

Trees and shrubs are sometimes sold "balled-and-burlapped," that is, with a ball of soil and roots wrapped tightly in burlap. For these plants, look for strong limbs with no broken shoots, an attractive profile, and healthy foliage. Then press your hands against the burlap-covered root ball to make sure that it feels firm, solid, and damp, not loose or dry. (If the ball is buried within a bed of wood chips, carefully pull the chips aside; then push them back after inspecting the plant.)

To make the final choice when you're considering a group of plants, line them up side by side and select the ones that are most closely matched in height, bushiness, and foliage color. If your design includes a hedge or mass planting where uniformity is very important, it's a good idea to buy a few extra plants as potential replacements in case of damage or loss. It's easier to plan ahead than to find a match later. Plant the extras in a spare corner so you'll have them if you need them.

Sometimes a plant will be available in two or more sizes. Which is better? That depends on how patient you are. The main reason for buying bigger plants is to make a landscape look impressive right away. If you buy smaller plants and set them out at the same spacing, the planting will look sparse at first, but it will soon catch up. A year after planting, you can't tell if a perennial came from a quart- or gallon-size pot: they will look the same. For shrubs, the difference between one pot size and the next larger one usually represents one year's growth.

Throughout most of California, the cooler weather of fall or early spring makes those times best for planting. In fall, new plants have the upcoming wet season to become established before the onset of hot summer weather. Frost-tender plants such as citrus, on the other hand, are best planted in spring after the threat of cold temperatures has passed. Most nurseries also have a wider selection of perennials, trees, and shrubs in fall and spring.

Although it's handy to plant a whole bed at once, you can divide the job, setting out some plants in fall and adding the rest in spring, or vice versa. If possible, do the actual planting on a cloudy day or evening when rain is forecast. On the following pages we'll give an overview of the process and discuss how to handle individual plants. If you're installing an irrigation system, remember that some of the components may need to be put in place after the soil is prepared but before planting.

Try to stay off the soil

Throughout the planting process, do all you can by reaching in from outside the bed. Stepping on the newly prepared bed compacts the soil and makes it harder to dig planting holes. Use short boards or scraps of plywood as temporary steppingstones if you do need to step on the soil. As soon as you can decide where to put them, lay permanent steppingstones for access to plants that need regular maintenance.

Check placement and spacing

The first step in planting is to mark the position of each plant. It's easy to arrange most of the plants themselves on the bed; use empty pots or stakes to represent plants too heavy to move easily. Follow the site plan for the design, checking the spacing with a yardstick as you place the plants.

Then step back and take a look. What do you think? Should you make any adjustments? Don't worry if the planting looks a little sparse. It *should* look that way at first. Plants almost always get bigger than you can imagine when you're first setting them out. And it's almost always better to wait for them to fill in rather than having to prune and thin a crowded planting in a few years. (You might fill between young plants with low-growing annuals, as suggested in the box on p. 198.)

PLANTING POINTERS

When working on top of prepared soil, kneel on a piece of plywood to distribute your weight.

Use empty pots or stakes to mark positions of plants not yet purchased or too heavy to move frequently.

Moving through the job

When you're satisfied with the arrangement, mark the position of each plant with a stake or stone, and set the plants aside out of the way, so you won't knock them over or step on them as you proceed. Start planting in order of size. Do the biggest plants first, then move on to the medium-size and smaller plants. If all the plants are about the same size, start at the back of the bed and work toward the front, or start in the center and work to the edges.

Position trees and shrubs to show their best side

Most trees and shrubs are slightly asymmetric. There's usually enough irregularity in their branching or shape that one side looks a little fuller or more attractive than the other sides do. After you've set a tree or shrub into its hole, step back and take a look. Then turn it partway, or try tilting or tipping it a little to one side or the other. Once you've decided which side and position looks best, start filling in the hole with soil. Stop and check again before you firm the soil into place.

The fine points of spacing

When you're planting a group of the same kind of plants, such as perennials or ferns, it normally looks best if you space them informally, in slightly curved or zigzag rows, with the plants in one row offset from those of the next row. Don't arrange plants in a straight row unless you want to emphasize a line, such as the edge of a bed. After planting, step back and evaluate the effect. If you want to adjust the placement or position of any plant, now is the time to do so.

Rake, water, and mulch

Use a garden rake to level out any high and low spots that remain after planting. Water enough to settle the soil into place around the roots. Mulch the entire planting area with 1 to 3 in. of composted bark, wood chips, or other organic matter. Mulch is indispensable for controlling weeds and regulating the moisture and temperature of the soil. If you're running out of time, you don't have to spread the mulch right away, but try to get it done within a week or so after planting.

Using annuals as fillers

The plants in our designs have been spaced so they will not be crowded at maturity. Buying more plants and spacing them closer may fill things out faster, but in several years (for perennials; longer for shrubs) you'll need to remove plants or prune them frequently.

If you want something to fill the gaps between young plants for that first year or two, use some annuals. The best annual fillers are compact plants that grow only 6 to 10 in. tall. These plants will hide the soil or mulch and make a colorful carpet. Avoid taller annuals, because they can shade or smother your permanent plantings. And don't forget, filler plants will need water.

The following annuals are all compact, easy to grow, readily available, and inexpensive. Seeds of those marked with a symbol (✿) can be sown directly in the garden. For the others, buy six-packs or flats of plants. Thin seedlings or space plants 8 to 12 in. apart.

Annual phlox ✿: Red, pink, or white flowers. Good for hot dry sites.
China pink ✿: Red, pink, white, or bicolor flowers. Blooms all summer.
Dusty miller: Silvery foliage, often lacy-textured. No flowers.
Edging lobelia: Dark blue, magenta, or white flowers. Likes afternoon shade.

Flossflower: Fluffy blue, lavender, or white flowers. Choose dwarf types.
Garden verbena: Bright red, pink, purple, or white flowers.
Globe candytuft ✿: Pink or white flowers. Best in cool weather.
Moss rose: Bright flowers in many colors. Ideal for hot dry sites.
Pansy and viola: Multicolored flowers. Grow best in cool weather.
Sweet alyssum ✿: Fragrant white or lilac flowers. Blooms for months. Prefers cool weather.
Wax begonia: Rose, pink, or white flowers. Good for shady sites but takes sun if watered regularly.

Planting Basics

Most of the plants that you buy for a landscaping project today are grown and sold in individual plastic containers, but large shrubs and trees may be balled-and-burlapped. Mail-order plants may come bare-root. And ground covers are sometimes sold in flats. In any case, the basic concern is the same: be careful what you do to a plant's roots. Spread them out; don't fold or coil them or cram them into a tight hole. Keep them covered; don't let the sun or air dry them out. And don't bury them too deep; set the top of the root ball level with the surrounding soil.

Planting container-grown plants

The steps are the same for any plant, no matter what size container it's growing in. Dig a hole that's a little wider than the container but not quite as deep ❶. Check by setting the container into the hole—the top of the soil in the container should be slightly higher than the surrounding soil. Dig several holes at a time, at the positions that you've already marked out.

Remove the container ❷. With one hand, grip the plant at the base of its stems or leaves, like pulling a ponytail, while you tug on the pot with the other hand. If the pot doesn't slide off eas-ily, don't pull harder on the stems. Try whacking the pot against a hard surface; if it still doesn't slide off, use a strong knife to cut or pry it off.

Examine the plant's roots ❸. If there are any thick, coiled roots, unwind them and cut them off close to the root ball, leaving short stubs. If the root ball is a mass of fine, hairlike roots, use the knife to cut three or four slits from top to bottom, about 1 in. deep. Pry the slits apart and tease the cut roots to loosen them. This cutting or slitting may seem drastic, but it's actually good for the plant because it forces new roots to grow out into the surrounding soil. Work quickly. Once you've taken a plant out of its container, get it in the ground as soon as possible. If you want to prepare several plants at a time, cover them with an old sheet or tarp to keep the roots from drying out.

Set the root ball into the hole ❹. Make sure that the plant is positioned right, with its best side facing out, and that the top of the root ball is level with or slightly higher than the surface of the bed. Then add enough soil to fill in the hole, and pat it down firmly.

PLANTING CONTAINER-GROWN PLANTS

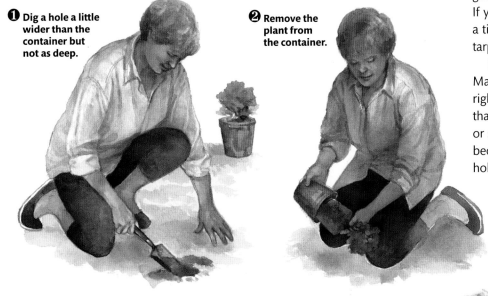

❶ Dig a hole a little wider than the container but not as deep.

❷ Remove the plant from the container.

❸ Unwind any large, coiled roots and cut them off short. Cut vertical slits through masses of fine roots.

❹ Position the plant in the hole and fill in around it with soil.

Planting a balled-and-burlapped shrub or tree

Nurseries often grow shrubs and trees in fields, and then dig them with a ball of oot-filled soil and wrap a layer of burlap snugly around the ball to keep it intact. The problem is that even a small ball of soil is very heavy. A root ball that is a foot wide is a two-person job. For larger root balls, ask the nursery to deliver and plant it. Here's how to proceed with plants that are small enough that you can handle them.

Dig a hole several inches wider than the root ball but not quite as deep as the root ball is high. Firm the soil so the plant won't sink. Set the plant into the hole, and lay a stick across the top of the root ball to make sure it's at or a little higher than grade level. Be sure to cut or untie any twine that wraps around the trunk. Fold the burlap down around the sides of the ball. Don't try to pull the burlap out altogether—roots can grow out through it, and it will eventually decompose. Fill soil all around the sides of the ball and pat it down firmly. Spread only an inch of soil over the top of the ball.

The top of the ball should be level with the surrounding soil. Cut twine that wraps around the trunk. Fold down the burlap, but don't remove it.

Planting bare-root plants

Mail-order nurseries sometimes dig perennials, roses, and other plants when the plants are dormant, cut back the tops, and wash all the soil off the roots, to save space and weight when storing and shipping them. If you receive a plant in bare-root condition, unwrap it, trim away any roots that are broken or damaged, and soak the roots in a pail of water for several hours.

To plant, dig a hole large enough that you can spread the roots across the bottom without folding them. Start covering the roots with soil, then lay a stick across the top of the hole and hold the plant against it to check the planting depth, as shown in the drawing. Raise or lower the plant if needed in order to bury just the roots, not the buds. Add more soil, firming it down around the roots, and continue until the hole is full.

Dig a hole wide enough that you can spread out the roots. A stick helps position the plant at the correct depth as you fill the hole with soil.

Planting ground covers from flats

Sometimes ground covers are sold in flats of 25 or more rooted cuttings. Start at one corner, reach underneath the soil, and lift out a portion of the flat's contents. Work quickly because the roots are exposed. Tease the cuttings apart, trying not to break off any roots, and plant them individually. Then lift out the next portion and continue planting.

Remove a clump of little plants, tease their roots apart, and plant them quickly.

Planting bulbs

Plant spring-blooming bulbs in October and November. If the soil in the bed was well prepared, you can use a trowel to dig holes for planting individual bulbs; where you have room, you can dig a wider hole or trench for planting a group of bulbs all at once. The perennials, ground covers, shrubs, and trees you planted earlier in the fall or in the spring will still be small enough that you won't disturb their roots. As a rule of thumb, plant small (grape- or cherry-size) bulbs about 2 in. deep and 3 to 5 in. apart, and large (walnut- or egg-size) bulbs 4 to 6 in. deep and 6 to 10 in. apart.

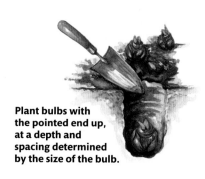

Plant bulbs with the pointed end up, at a depth and spacing determined by the size of the bulb.

Planting on a hillside

Successful planting on a hillside depends on keeping the bare soil and young plants from blowing or washing away while they establish themselves. Here are some tips. Rather than amending all the soil, prepare individual planting holes. Work from the top of the slope to the bottom. Push one or more wooden shingles into the slope just below a plant to help hold it in place. Mulch with heavier materials, such as wood chips, that won't wash or blow away. If the soil is loose, spread water-permeable landscape fabric over it to help hold it in place; slit the fabric and insert plants through the openings. Water with drip irrigation, which is less likely to erode soil than sprinklers are.

Confining perennials

Yarrow, bee balm, artemisia, and various other perennials, grasses, and ferns are described as invasive because they spread by underground runners. To confine these plants to a limited area, install a barrier when you plant them. Cut the bottom off a 5-gal. or larger plastic pot, bury the pot so its rim is above the soil, and plant the perennial inside. You'll need to lift, divide, and replant part of the perennial every second or third year.

Position rim above soil surface.

Remove bottom of pot.

Basic Landscape Care

The landscape plantings in this book will grow increasingly carefree from year to year as the plants mature, but of course you'll always need to do some regular maintenance. This ongoing care may require as much as a few hours a week during the season or as little as a few hours a year. You'll have to control weeds, use mulch, water as needed, and do spring and fall cleanups. Trees, shrubs, and vines may need staking or training at first and occasional pruning or shearing afterward. Perennials, ground covers, and grasses may need to be cut back, staked, deadheaded, or divided. Performing these tasks, which are explained on the following pages, is sometimes hard work, but for many gardeners it is enjoyable labor, a chance to get outside in the fresh air. Also, spending time each week with your plants helps you identify and address problems before they become serious.

Mulches and fertilizers

Covering the soil in all planted areas with a layer of organic mulch does several jobs at once: it improves the appearance of your garden while you're waiting for the plants to grow, reduces the number of weeds that emerge, retards water loss from the soil during dry spells, moderates soil temperatures, and adds nutrients to the soil as it decomposes. Inorganic mulches such as landscape fabric and gravel also provide some of these benefits, but their conspicuous appearance and the difficulty of removing them if you ever want to change the landscape are serious drawbacks.

Many materials are used as mulches; the box on p. 202 presents the most common, with comments on their advantages and disadvantages. Consider appearance, availability, cost, and convenience when you're comparing different products. Most garden centers have a few kinds of bagged mulch materials, but for mulching large areas, it's easier and cheaper to have a nursery or other supplier deliver a truckload of bulk mulch. A landscape looks best if you see the same mulch throughout the entire planting area, rather than a patchwork of different mulches. You can achieve a uniform look by spreading a base layer of homemade compost, hay, or other inexpensive material and topping that with a neater-looking material such as bark chips or shredded bark.

It takes at least a 1-in. layer of mulch to suppress weeds, but there's no need to spread it more than 3 in. deep. As you're spreading it, don't put any mulch against the stems of any plants, because that can lead to disease or insect problems. Put most of the mulch between plants, not right around them. Check the mulch during your spring and fall cleanups. Be sure it's pulled back away from the plant stems. Rake the surface of the mulch lightly to loosen it, and top it up with a fresh layer if the old material has decomposed.

Fertilizer

Decomposing mulch frequently supplies enough nutrients to grow healthy plants, but using fertilizer helps if you want to boost the plants—to make them grow faster, get larger, or produce more flowers. Young plants or those growing in poor soils also benefit from occasional applications of fertilizer. There are dozens of fertilizer products on the market—liquid and granular, fast-acting and slow-release, organic and synthetic. All give good results if applied as directed. And observe the following precautions: Don't overfertilize, don't fertilize when the soil is dry, and don't fertilize tender plants after late summer, because they need to slow down and finish the season's growth before cold weather comes.

Mulch materials

Bark products

Bark nuggets, chipped bark, shredded bark, ground bark, and composted bark, usually from conifers, are available in bags or in bulk. All are attractive, long lasting, medium-price mulches.

Chipped tree trimmings

The chips available from utility companies and tree services are a mixture of wood, bark, twigs, and leaves. These chips cost less than pure bark products (you may be able to get a load for free), but they don't look as good and you have to replace them more often, because they decompose fast.

Sawdust and shavings

These are cheap or free at sawmills and woodshops. They make good path coverings, but they aren't ideal mulches, because they tend to pack down into a dense, water-resistant surface. Sawdust can also blow around.

Hulls and shells

Ground coconut hulls, cocoa hulls, and nut shells can be picked up at food-processing plants and are sometimes sold at garden centers. They're all attractive, long lasting mulches. Price varies from free to quite expensive, depending on where you get them.

Tree leaves

A few big trees may supply all the mulch you need, year after year. You can just rake the leaves onto a bed in fall, but it's better to chop them up with the lawn mower, pile them in compost bins for the winter, and spread them where needed in late spring. Pine needles likewise make good mulch, especially for rhododendrons, azaleas, and other acid-loving shrubs. You can spread pine needles in fall, because they cling together and don't blow around.

Grass clippings

A 1- to 2-in. layer of dried grass clippings makes an acceptable mulch that decomposes within a single growing season. Don't pile clippings too thick, though. If you do, the top surface dries and packs into a water-resistant crust, and the bottom layer turns into nasty slime.

Hay and straw

Farmers sell hay that's unsuitable for fodder as "mulch" hay. Hay is cheap but likely to include weed seeds. Straw—the stems of grain crops such as wheat—is usually seed-free but more expensive. Both hay and straw are more suitable for mulching vegetable gardens than landscape plantings because they decompose quickly and must be renewed each year. They also tend to attract rodents.

Gravel

A mulch of pea gravel or crushed rock, spread 1 to 2 in. thick, helps keep the soil cool and moist, and many plants grow very well with a gravel mulch. However, compared with organic materials such as bark or leaves, it's much more tiring to apply a gravel mulch in the first place; it's harder to remove leaves and litter that accumulate on the gravel or weeds that sprout up through it; it's annoying to dig through the gravel if you want to replace or add plants later; and it's tedious to remove the gravel itself, should you ever change your mind about having it there. Gravel mulches also reflect heat and can make a yard hotter than normal.

Landscape fabrics

Various types of synthetic fabrics, usually sold in rolls 3 to 4 ft. wide and 20, 50, or 100 ft. long, can be spread over the ground as a weed barrier. Unlike plastic, these fabrics allow water and air to penetrate into the soil. A topping of gravel, bark chips, or other mulch can anchor the fabric and hide it from view. If you're planting small plants, you can spread the fabric and insert the plants through X-shaped slits cut in the fabric where needed. You can plant larger plants first, then cut and snug the fabric around them. Drip irrigation is best laid on top of the fabric, to make it easier to see clogs and leaks. It's also useful to lay fabric under paths, although it can be difficult to secure the fabric neatly and invisibly along the edges of adjacent planting beds. Removing fabric—if you change your mind—is a messy job. However, there are newer biodegradable fabrics that break down after a few years.

Clear or black plastic

Don't even think about using any kind of plastic sheeting as a landscape mulch. The soil underneath a sheet of plastic gets bone-dry, while water accumulates on top. Any loose mulch you spread on plastic won't stay in an even layer. No matter how you try to secure them, the edges of plastic sheeting always pull loose, appear at the surface, degrade in the sun, and shred into tatters.

Watering

To use water efficiently and effectively it is helpful to know how to gauge when and how much your plants need and how to ensure that your system supplies it.

Deciding whether water is needed

Many experienced gardeners can judge whether a plant needs water simply by looking at its leaves. But drooping or dull leaves can be caused by pests, disease, and overwatering as well as by water stress. A surer way to decide whether you need to water is to examine the soil. If the top 3 to 4 in. is dry, most annuals, perennials, and shallow-rooted shrubs such as azaleas will need to be watered. Most trees and larger shrubs need water if the top 6 to 8 in. is dry. To check soil moisture, you can get down on your hands and knees and dig. But digging in an established planting can be awkward as well as harmful to crowded roots.

A less invasive method of checking moisture is to use a paint stirrer or similar piece of unfinished, light-colored wood like a dipstick. Push it down through the mulch and 6 to 8 in. into the soil. Leave it there for an hour or so, and pull it out to see if moisture has discolored the wood. If so, the soil is moist enough for plants. It is also helpful to make a habit of monitoring rainfall. Also, listen to the weather reports, marking a calendar to keep track of rainfall amounts.

Pay attention to soil moisture or rainfall amounts all year long, because plants can suffer from dryness in any season, not just in the heat of summer. Water whenever the soil is dry. As for time of day, it's best to water early in the morning when the wind is calm, evaporation is low, and plant foliage will have plenty of time to dry off before nightfall (wet leaves at night can promote some foliar diseases). Early morning (before 5 a.m.) is also when most urban and suburban neighborhoods have plenty of water pressure.

How much to water

Determining how much water to apply and how often to apply it is one of gardening's greatest challenges. Water too much and plants drown. Water too little and they dry out and die. For most gardeners, gauging how much water a plant or bed needs is an art more than a science. The key to watering enough but not too much is to be a good observer. Examine your soil often, keep an eye on your plants, and make adjustments with the weather.

New plantings, even those of drought-tolerant plants, require frequent watering during the first year until the plants are established. In the heat of summer, new plantings may require water twice a week or more.

Established landscape plants vary in their water needs. (The descriptions for most of the plants in the Plant Profiles include water requirements.) When you do water, it is always best to water deeply, wetting a large portion of the plant's root zone. Shallow watering encourages shallow rooting, and shallow-rooted plants dry out fast and need watering more frequently. Furthermore, a water-stressed plant is also more susceptible to disease and insect damage. As a rule of thumb, water most perennials to a depth of 12 to 18 in.; water most shrubs 2 to 3 ft. deep and most trees 3 to 4 ft. deep. (Lawns, in contrast, should be watered 6 to 8 in. deep, but they require frequent watering.)

Determining how much water will be required to penetrate to these depths depends on your soil. Water moves through different soils at different speeds. In general, 1 in. of water will soak about 4 to 5 in. deep in clay soil, 6 to 7 in. deep in loam, and 10 to 12 in. in sandy soil.

Different watering systems, from hose-end sprinklers to automated drip systems, deliver water at different rates. Manufacturers often provide these rates in the product descriptions. You can determine the delivery rate for a sprinkler by setting tuna-fish cans in the area it covers and timing how long it takes to deposit an inch of water in one or more cans.

Whatever your system, you'll need to know how long it has to run for water to penetrate to the desired depths in your soil. As we've said, digging to determine water penetration is often impractical. To gauge penetration to a foot or so deep, you can use wooden "dipsticks" as described previously. (Insert the sticks after you've watered.) For a rough gauge of deeper penetration, you can push a ¼- to ½-in.-diameter iron bar into the soil. The bar will move easily through wet soil. When it encounters dry soil, it will become harder to push or it will feel different as you push. Run your system and time it as you check penetration depths.

CHECKING SOIL MOISTURE

Stick a paint stirrer or similar piece of light-colored, unfinished wood down through the mulch and into the soil. Pull it up after an hour. If the bottom of the stick looks and feels damp, the soil is moist enough for plants.

Controlling weeds

Weeds are not much of a problem in established landscapes. Once the "good" plants have grown big enough to merge together, they tend to crowd or shade out all but the most persistent undesirable plants. But weeds can be troublesome in a new landscape unless you take steps to prevent and control them.

There are two main types of weeds: those that mostly sprout up as seedlings and those that keep coming back from perennial roots or runners. Try to identify and eliminate any perennial weeds before you start a landscaping project (see p. 88). Then you'll only have to deal with new seedlings later, which is a much easier job.

Annual and perennial weeds that commonly grow from seeds include Bermuda grass, bindweed, crabgrass, dandelions, oxalis, plantain, purslane, and spurge. Trees and shrubs such as cherry laurel, Chinese elm, privet, mimosa, cottonwood, and Scotch broom produce weedy seedlings, too. For any of these weeds that grow from seeds, the strategy is twofold: try to keep the weed seeds from sprouting, and eliminate any seedlings that do sprout as soon as you see them, while they are still small.

Almost any patch of soil includes weed seeds that are ready to sprout whenever that soil is disturbed. Preparing the soil for planting will probably cause an initial flush of weeds, but you'll never see that many weeds again if you leave the soil undisturbed in subsequent years. You don't have to hoe, rake, or cultivate around perennial plantings. Leave the soil alone, and fewer weeds will appear. Using mulch helps even more; by shading the soil, it prevents weed seeds from sprouting. And if weed seeds blow in and land on top of the mulch, they'll be less likely to germinate there than they would on bare soil.

Pull or cut off any weeds that appear while they're young and small, just a few inches tall. Don't let them mature and go to seed. Most weed seedlings emerge in late spring and early summer. If you get rid of them then, you won't see many more seedlings for the rest of the growing season.

Using herbicides

Two kinds of herbicides can be very useful and effective in maintaining home landscapes, but only if used correctly. You have to choose the right product for the job and follow the directions on the label regarding dosage and timing of application exactly.

Preemergent herbicides. Sold in granular or liquid form, these herbicides are designed to prevent weed seeds, particularly crabgrass and other annual weeds, from sprouting. Make the first application in early fall before the first rain. You'll probably need to make another application in spring before hot-weather season.

WEEDS THAT SPROUT FROM SEEDS

Simple root systems can be easily pulled while still small.

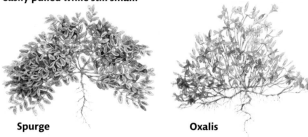

Spurge   Oxalis

WEEDS THAT SPROUT BACK FROM PERENNIAL ROOTS OR RUNNERS

Connected by underground runners, the shoots of these weeds need to be pulled repeatedly, smothered with a thick mulch, or killed with an herbicide.

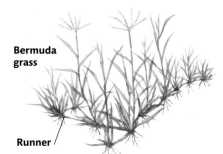

Bermuda grass

Runner

Use a disposable, sponge-type paintbrush to apply the herbicide selectively, painting only the weeds. Prepare the solution as directed for spray application. Use only enough to wet the leaves, so none drips off.

USING HERBICIDES ON PERENNIAL WEEDS

Ready-to-use spot-weeder sprays are convenient, but you must aim carefully. Try using a sheet of cardboard as a backdrop to protect desirable plants from herbicide drift.

Caring for Woody Plants

Make sure the herbicide you buy is registered for use around the kinds of ground covers, perennials, shrubs, or other plants you have. Granular forms are often used in smaller areas, liquid in larger areas. Apply them exactly as described on the product label. Wear heavy rubber gloves that are rated for use with farm chemicals, not household rubber gloves.

Postemergent herbicides. These chemicals are used to kill growing plants. Some kill only the aboveground parts of a plant; others are absorbed into the plant and kill it, roots and all. Postemergent herbicides are typically applied as sprays, which you can buy ready-to-use or prepare by mixing a concentrate with water. Look for those that break down quickly, and read the label carefully for registered applications, specific directions, and safety instructions.

Postemergent herbicides work best if applied when the weeds are growing vigorously. You usually have to apply enough to thoroughly wet the plant's leaves, and do it during a spell of dry weather. Applying an herbicide is an effective way to get rid of a perennial weed that you can't dig or pull up, but it's really better to do this before you plant a bed, as it's hard to spray herbicides in an established planting without getting some on your good plants. (Some postemergent herbicides are more selective, affecting only certain types of plants.) Aim carefully, shielding nearby plants as shown in the drawing, left, and don't spray on windy days. Brushing or sponging the herbicide on the leaves is slower than spraying, but you're sure to avoid damaging adjacent plants.

Using postemergent herbicides in an established planting may be the only way to get rid of a persistent perennial weed. For young weed seedlings, it's usually easier to pull them by hand.

A well-chosen garden tree, such as the ones recommended in this book, grows naturally into a pleasing shape, won't get too large for its site, is resistant to pests and diseases, and doesn't drop messy pods or other litter. Once established, these trees need very little care from year to year.

Regular watering is the most important concern in getting a tree off to a good start. Don't let it suffer from drought for the first few years. To reduce competition, don't plant ground covers or other plants within 2 ft. of the tree's trunk. Just spread a thin layer of mulch there.

Arborists now dismiss other care ideas that once were common practice. According to current thinking, you don't need to fertilize a tree when you plant it (in fact, unless they show obvious signs of deficiency or grow poorly, most landscape trees never need fertilizing). Keep pruning to a minimum at planting time; remove only dead or damaged twigs, not healthy shoots. Finally, research has shown that tree trunks grow stronger when they're not supported by stakes. However, most newly planted trees need some support, usually for no more than a year. It is very important that the supported trunk be allowed a certain amount of movement. Be sure to ask your nursery about proper staking for your tree.

Pruning basics

Proper pruning keeps plants healthy and looking their best. There are two basic types of pruning cuts: heading and thinning. Heading cuts are made along the length of a branch or stem, between its tip and its base. These cuts induce vigorous growth in the dormant buds below the cut. Such growth is useful for filling in hedges and rejuvenating shrubs and perennials. But heading can drastically change the appearance of a plant, even destroying its natural shape. Heading can also produce weakly attached branches in trees and shrubs.

Thinning cuts remove stems and branches at their origin (the plant's crown or where the branch attaches to the trunk or a larger limb). Unlike heading, thinning does not produce vigorous growth. Instead, thinning opens the plant's interior to light and air, which improves its health. And, by reducing congested growth, thinning often enhances the natural appearance of the plant. In most cases, thinning is the preferred pruning technique, especially for trees and shrubs.

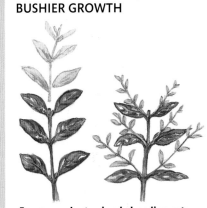

BUSHIER GROWTH

For many plants, simple heading cuts can produce fuller, bushier growth. Cut off the ends of stems to induce growth from lower buds.

Pruning roses

Roses are vigorous, fast-growing shrubs that need regular pruning to keep them shapely and attractive. Most of this pruning is done in winter to early spring, just as the buds start to swell but before the new leaves start to unfold. Always use sharp pruning shears and cut back to a healthy bud, leaving no stub. Right after pruning is a good time to add fresh mulch around the plant.

Prune hybrid tea roses to keep them neat, compact, and continuously producing long-stemmed flowers. Remove skinny or weak stems plus a few of the oldest stems (their bark is tan or gray instead of green) by cutting them off at their base. Prune off any shoots that got frozen or broken during the winter, remove old or weak shoots and crossing or crowded stems, and trim back any asymmetric or unbalanced shoots. Don't be afraid of cutting back too hard; it's better to leave just a few strong shoots than a lot of weak ones. If you cut old stems off at ground level, new ones will grow to replace them. Cut damaged or asymmetric stems back partway and they will branch out.

Hybrid tea roses bloom on new growth, so if you prune in early spring you aren't cutting off any flower buds. During the growing season, make a habit of removing the flowers as soon as they fade. This keeps the plant neat and makes it bloom longer and more abundantly. At least once a week, locate each faded flower, follow down its stem to the first or second five-leaflet leaf, and prune just above one of those leaves. (Follow the same steps to cut roses for a bouquet.)

Climbing roses are pruned differently than hybrid teas. In late winter, remove weak, dead, or damaged shoots by cutting them back to the ground or to healthy wood. Select the healthiest stems for a main framework, and tie them securely to a support. Shorten all side shoots on these stems to two buds. Shoots growing from these buds will produce flowers.

Climbing roses need regular attention throughout the summer, because their stems (also called canes) can grow a foot or more in a month. Check regularly and tie this new growth to the trellis while it's still supple and manageable. When the canes grow long enough to reach the top of the trellis or arbor, cut off their tips and tie the canes horizontally to induce production of flowering side shoots. Remove spent roses by cutting the stems back to the nearest healthy five-leaflet leaf.

Shrub roses, floribundas, and other landscape roses can be pruned with hedge shears. Simply cut back one-third to one-half the growth in winter and remove diseased or damaged canes. You can also remove spent flowers with hedge shears.

PRUNING A HYBRID TEA ROSE

In late winter or early spring, remove old, weak, or damaged shoots; stems that are crossing or crowded; and stems that stick out too far and look asymmetric. Don't be afraid to cut a lot away.

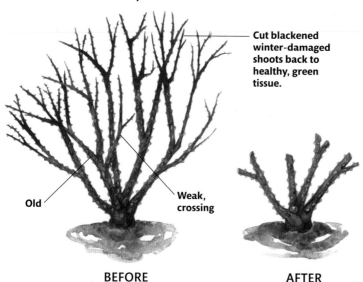

Cut blackened winter-damaged shoots back to healthy, green tissue.

Old

Weak, crossing

BEFORE

AFTER

REMOVING FLOWERS

Roses can look messy as they fade. Cut off by pruning the stem back to the first healthy five-leaflet leaf.

Five-leaflet leaf

Shaping young trees

As a tree grows, you can affect its shape by pruning once a year, usually in winter. Take it easy, though. Don't prune just for the sake of pruning; that does more harm than good. If you don't have a good reason for making a cut, don't do it. Follow these guidelines:

▎ **Use sharp pruning shears, loppers, or saws,** which make clean cuts without tearing the wood or bark.

▎ **Cut branches back** to a healthy shoot, leaf, or bud, or cut back to the branch collar at the base of the branch, as shown at right. Don't leave any stubs; they're ugly and prone to decay.

▎ **Remove any dead or damaged** branches and any twigs or limbs that are very spindly or weak.

▎ **Where two limbs cross over or rub** against each other, save one limb—usually the thicker, stronger one—and prune off the other one.

▎ **Prune or widen narrow crotches.** Places where a branch and trunk or two branches form a narrow V are weak spots, liable to split apart as the tree grows. Where the trunk of a young tree exhibits such a crotch or where either of two shoots could continue the growth of a branch, prune off the weaker of the two. Where you wish to keep the branch, insert a piece of wood as a spacer to widen the angle, as shown in the drawings below. Leave the spacer in place for a year or so.

One trunk or several?

If you want a young tree to have a single trunk, identify the leader or central shoot and let it grow straight up, unpruned. The trunk will grow thicker faster if you leave the lower limbs in place for the first few years, but if they're in

WHERE TO CUT

When removing the end of a branch, cut back to a healthy leaf, bud, or side shoot. Don't leave a stub. Use sharp pruning shears to make a neat cut that slices the stem rather than tears it.

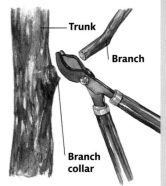

Trunk

Branch

Branch collar

When removing an entire branch, cut just outside the slightly thickened area, called the branch collar, where the branch grows into the trunk.

the way, you can remove them. At whatever height you choose—usually about 8 ft. off the ground if you want to walk or see under the tree—select the shoots that will become the main limbs of the tree. Be sure they are evenly spaced around the trunk, pointing outward at wide angles. Remove any lower or weaker shoots. As the tree matures, the only further pruning required will be an annual checkup to remove dead, damaged, or crossing shoots.

Several of the trees in this book, including crape myrtle, redbud, Japanese maple, and saucer magnolia, are often grown with multiple trunks, for a graceful, clumplike appearance. When buying a multiple-trunk tree, choose one with trunks that diverge at the base. Prune multiple-trunk trees as previously described for single-trunk trees. Remove some of the branches that are growing toward the center of the clump, so the center doesn't get too dense and tangled.

AVOIDING NARROW CROTCHES

A tree's limbs should spread wide, like outstretched arms. If limbs angle too close to the trunk or to each other, there isn't room for them to grow properly and they may split apart after a few years, ruining the tree.

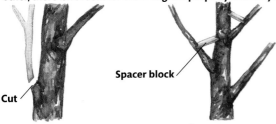

Spacer block

Cut

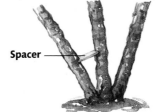

Spacer

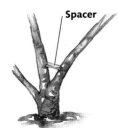

Spacer

Single-trunk trees: Correct narrow crotches on a young tree by removal or by widening the angle with a wooden spacer block. Choose well-spaced shoots to become the main limbs of a shade tree.

Multiple-trunk trees: Whether the stems of a multiple-trunk tree emerge from the ground or from a single trunk near the ground, widen angles if necessary to keep the trunks from touching.

Pruning shrubs

Shrubs are generally carefree plants, but they almost always look better if you do some pruning at least every other year. As a minimum, remove dead twigs from time to time, and if any branches are broken by storms or accidents, remove them as soon as convenient, cutting back to a healthy bud or branch or to the plant's crown. Also, unless the shrub produces attractive seedpods or berries, it's a good idea to trim off the flowers after they fade.

Beyond this routine pruning, some shrubs require more attention. (The entries in Plant Profiles, pp. 114–155, give more information on when and how to prune particular shrubs.) Basically, shrub pruning falls into three categories: selective pruning, severe pruning, and shearing. (See the drawings, below right.)

Selective pruning means using pruning shears to head back or thin individual shoots in order to refine the shape of the bush and maintain its vigor, as well as limit its size. This job takes time but produces a very graceful and natural-looking bush. Cut away weak or spindly twigs and any limbs that cross or rub against each other, and head all the longest shoots back to a healthy, outward-facing bud or to a pair of buds. You can do selective pruning on any shrub, deciduous or evergreen, at any time of year.

Severe pruning means using pruning shears or loppers to cut away most of a shrub's top growth, leaving just short stubs or a gnarly trunk. This kind of cutting back is usually done once a year in late winter or early spring. Although it seems drastic, severe pruning is appropriate in several situations.

It makes certain fast-growing shrubs, such as bigleaf hydrangea and butterfly bush, flower more profusely. It keeps others, such as spirea and 'Powis Castle' artemisia, compact and bushy.

One or two severe prunings done when a shrub is young can make it branch out at the base, producing a bushier specimen or a fuller hedge plant. Nurseries often do this pruning as part of producing a good plant, and if you buy a shrub that's already bushy, you don't need to cut it back yourself. Older shrubs that have gotten tall and straggly sometimes respond to a severe pruning by sprouting out with renewed vigor, sending up lots of new shoots that bear plenty of foliage and flowers. This strategy doesn't work for all shrubs, though—sometimes severe pruning kills a plant. Don't try it unless you know it will work (check with a knowledgeable person at a nursery) or are willing to take a chance.

Shearing means using hedge shears or an electric hedge trimmer to trim the surface of a shrub, hedge, or tree to a neat, uniform profile, producing a solid mass of greenery. Both deciduous and evergreen shrubs and trees can be sheared; those with small, closely spaced leaves and a naturally compact growth habit usually look best. A good time for shearing most shrubs is late spring, after the new shoots have elongated but before the wood has hardened, but you can shear at other times of year. You may have to shear some plants more than once a year.

If you're planning to shear a plant, start when it is young and establish the shape—cone, pyramid, flat-topped hedge, or whatever. Looking at the profile, always make the shrub wider at the bottom than on top; otherwise the lower limbs will be shaded and won't be as leafy. Shear off as little as needed to maintain the shape as the shrub grows. Once it gets as big as you want it, shear as much as you have to to keep it that size.

Selective pruning. Remove weak, spindly, bent, or broken shoots (red). Where two branches rub on each other, remove the weakest or the one that's pointing inward (orange). Cut back long shoots to a healthy, outward-facing bud (blue).

Severe pruning. In late winter or early spring, before new growth starts, cut all the stems back close to the ground.

Shearing. Trim with hedge clippers to a neat profile.

Making a hedge

To make a hedge that's dense enough that you can't see through it, choose shrubs that have many shoots at the base. If you can only find skinny shrubs, prune them severely the first spring after planting to stimulate bushier growth.

Hedge plants are set in the ground as described on pp. 199–200 but are spaced closer together than they would be if planted as individual specimens. This helps create the hedge-like look. We took that into account in creating the designs and plant lists for this book; just follow the spacings recommended in the designs. If you're impatient for the hedge to fill in, you can space the plants closer together, but don't put them farther apart.

A hedge can be sheared, pruned selectively, or left alone, depending on how you want it to look. Slow-growing, small-leaved plants such as boxwood and box-leaf euonymus make rounded but natural-looking hedges with no pruning at all, or you can shear them into any profile you choose and make them perfectly neat and uniform. (Be sure to keep them narrower at the top.) Choose one style and stick with it. Once a hedge is established, you can neither start nor stop shearing it without an awkward transition that may last a few years before the hedge looks good again.

Getting a vine off to a good start

Nurseries often sell jasmine, clematis, wisteria, and other vines as young plants with a single stem fastened to a stake. To plant the vine, remove the stake and cut off the stem right above the lowest pair of healthy leaves, usually about 4 to 6 in. above the soil ❶. This forces the vine to send out new shoots low to the ground. As soon as those new shoots have begun to develop (usually a month or so after planting), cut them back to their first pairs of leaves ❷. After this second pruning, the plant will become bushy at the base. Now, as new shoots form, use sticks or strings to direct them toward the base of the support they are to climb ❸.

Once they're started, twining vines such as the ones named at left can scramble up a lattice trellis, although it helps if you tuck in any stray ends. The plants can't climb a smooth surface, however. To help them cover a fence with wide vertical slats or a porch post, you have to provide something the vine can wrap around. Screw a few eyebolts to the top and bottom of such a support and stretch wire, nylon cord, or polypropylene rope between them. (The wires or cords should be a few inches out from the fence, not flush against it.)

Clinging vines can climb any surface by means of their adhesive rootlets and need no further assistance or care.

So-called climbing roses don't really climb at all by themselves—you have to fasten them to a support. Twist-ties are handy for this job. Roses grow fast, so you'll have to tie in the new shoots every few weeks from spring to fall.

After the first year, most vines need annual spring pruning to remove any dead, damaged, or straggly stems. If vines grow too long, you can cut them back anytime and they will branch out from below the cut.

STARTING A VINE

❶ At planting, cut just above the first pair of healthy leaves.

❷ Then cut new shoots back to the first pair of leaves.

❸ Severe initial pruning forces the vine to branch at the base. Tie shoots from these branches to cover the trellis fully and evenly.

Caring for Perennials

Perennials are simply plants that send up new growth year after year. A large group, perennials include flowering plants such as daylilies and purple coneflower as well as grasses, ferns, and hardy bulbs. Although some perennials need special conditions and care, most of the ones in this book are adaptable and easygoing. Get them off to a good start by planting them in well-prepared soil, adding a layer of mulch, watering as often as needed throughout the first year, and keeping weeds away. After that, keeping perennials attractive and healthy typically requires just a few minutes per plant each year.

Routine annual care

Some of the perennials that are used as ground covers, such as ajuga, lilyturf, mondo grass, and vinca, need virtually no care. On a suitable site, they'll thrive for decades even if you pay them almost no attention at all.

Most garden perennials, though, look and grow better if you clean away the old leaves and stems at least once a year. When to do this depends on the type of plant. Perennials such as daylily, dwarf fountain grass, hosta, and Siberian iris have leaves and stalks that turn tan or brown after they're frosted in fall. Cut these down to the ground in late fall or early spring; either time is okay.

Perennials such as Shasta daisy, geranium, blue fescue grass, dianthus, coralbells, and phlox have foliage that is more or less evergreen, depending on the severity of the winter. For those plants, wait until after they've bloomed or until the fall; then cut back any leaves or stems that are discolored or shabby-looking. Don't leave cuttings lying on the soil, because they may contain disease spores. To avoid contaminating your compost, send diseased stems or leaves to the dump.

Right after you've cleared away the dead material is a good time to renew the mulch on the bed. Use a fork, rake, or cultivator to loosen the existing mulch, and add some fresh mulch if needed. Also, if you want to sprinkle some granular fertilizer on the bed, do that now, when it's easy to avoid getting any on the plants' leaves. Fertilizing perennials is optional, but it does make them grow bigger and bloom more than they would otherwise.

Remove faded flowers

Removing flowers as they fade (called "deadheading") makes the garden look neater, prevents unwanted self-sown seedlings, and often stimulates a plant to continue blooming longer than it would if you left it alone, or to bloom a second time later in the season. (This is true for shrubs and annual plants as well as for perennial plants.)

Pick large flowers such as daisies, daylilies, irises, and lilies one at a time, snapping them off by hand. Use pruning shears on perennials such as garden penstemon, phlox, and yarrow that produce tall stalks crowded with lots of small flowers, cutting the stalks back to the height of the foliage. Use hedge shears on bushy plants that are covered with lots of small flowers on short stalks, such as salvia, 'Moonbeam' coreopsis, dianthus, evergreen candytuft, and 'Homestead Purple' verbena, cutting the stems back by about one-half their length.

Instead of removing them, you may want to let the flowers remain on purple coneflower, Siberian iris, 'Autumn Joy' sedum, and the various grasses. These plants all bear conspicuous seedpods or seed heads on stiff stalks that remain standing and look interesting throughout the fall and winter.

Pruning and shearing perennials

Some perennials that bloom in summer or fall respond well to being pruned earlier in the growing season. Mexican sage, chrysanthemum, garden phlox, and 'Autumn Joy' sedum all form tall clumps of stems topped with lots of little flowers. Unfortunately, tall stems are liable to flop over in stormy weather, and even if they don't, too-tall clumps can look leggy or top-heavy. To prevent floppiness, prune these plants when the stems are about 1 ft. tall. Remove the weakest stems from each clump by cutting them off at the ground; then cut all the remaining, strong stems back by about one-third. Pruning in this way keeps these plants shorter, stronger, and bushier, so you don't have to bother with stakes to keep them upright.

Germander and 'Powis Castle' artemisia are grown more for their foliage than for their flowers. You can use hedge shears to keep them neat, compact, and bushy, shearing off the tops of the stems once or twice in spring and summer.

PRUNING A PERENNIAL

Prune to create neater, bushier clumps of some summer- and fall-blooming perennials such as garden phlox, chrysanthemums, and 'Autumn Joy' sedum. When the stalks are about 1 ft. tall, cut them all back by one-third. Remove the weakest stalks at ground level.

Dividing perennials

Most perennials send up more stems each year, forming denser clumps or wider patches. Dividing is the process of cutting or breaking apart these clumps or patches. This is an easy way to make more plants to expand your garden, to control a plant that might otherwise spread out of bounds, or to renew an old specimen that doesn't look good or bloom well anymore.

Most perennials can be divided as often as every year or two if you're in a hurry to make more plants, or they can go for several years if you don't have any reason to disturb them. Fall is the best time to divide most perennials, but you can also do it in early spring.

There are two main approaches to dividing perennials, as shown in the drawings at right. You can leave the plant in the ground and use a sharp spade to cut it apart, like slicing a pie, and then lift out one chunk at a time. Or you can dig around and underneath the plant and lift it out all at once, shake off the extra soil, and lay the plant on the ground or a tarp where you can work with it.

Some plants, such as ajuga, yarrow, and some ferns, are easy to divide. They almost fall apart when you dig them up. Others, such as agapanthus, daylily, and most grasses, have very tough or tangled roots and you'll have to wrestle with them, chop them with a sharp butcher knife, pry them apart with a strong screwdriver or garden fork, or even cut through the roots with a hatchet or pruning saw. However you approach the job, before you insert any tool, take a close look at the plant right at ground level, and be careful to divide between, not through, the biggest and healthiest buds or shoots. Using a hose to wash loose mulch and soil away makes it easier to see what you're doing.

Don't make the divisions too small; they should be the size of a plant that you'd want to buy, not just little scraps. If you have more divisions than you need or want, choose just the best-looking ones to replant and discard or give away the others. Replant new divisions as soon as possible in freshly prepared soil. Water them right away, and water again whenever the soil dries out over the next few weeks or months, until the plants are growing again.

Divide hardy bulbs such as daffodils and crocuses every few years. Dig clumps after bloom but before the foliage turns yellow. Shake the soil off the roots, pull the bulbs apart, and replant them promptly, setting them as deep as they were buried before.

DIVIDING PERENNIALS

You can divide a clump or patch of perennials by cutting down into the patch with a sharp spade, like slicing a pie or a pan of brownies, then lifting out the separate chunks.

Or you can dig up the whole clump, shake the extra soil off the roots, then pull or pry it apart into separate plantlets.

Problem Solving

Some plants are much more suscep-tible than others to damage by severe weather, pests, or diseases. In this book, we've recommended plants that are gen-erally trouble-free, especially after they have had a few years to get established in your garden. But even these plants are subject to various mishaps and problems. The challenge is learning how to distin-guish which problems are really serious and which are just cosmetic, and decid-ing how to solve—or, better yet, prevent—those problems that are serious.

Pests, large and small

Deer and rabbits are liable to be a prob-lem if your property is surrounded by or adjacent to fields or woods. You may not see them, but you can't miss the dam-age they do—they bite the tops off or eat whole plants of agapanthus, daylilies, and many other perennials. Deer also eat the leaves and stems of maples, azaleas, and many other trees and shrubs. Com-mercial or homemade repellents that you spray on the foliage may be helpful if the animals aren't too hungry and you use them often. (See the box, below, for thoughts on deer-proof plants.) But in the long run, the only solution is to fence out deer and to trap and remove smaller animals.

Squirrels are cute but naughty. They normally don't eat much foliage, but they do eat some kinds of flowers and several kinds of bulbs. They also dig up new transplants, and they plant nuts in your flower beds and lawns. Meadow voles and field mice can kill trees and shrubs by stripping the bark off the trunk, usually near the ground. Gophers eat the roots of shrubs, trees, and perennials. Moles don't eat plants, but their digging makes a mess of a lawn or flower bed. Persistent trap-ping is the most effective way to control all of these little critters. (You can protect the roots of some plants from gophers by planting the plants in wire cages sold at many nurseries.)

Aphids, beetles, caterpillars, grubs, grasshoppers, spider mites, scale insects, slugs, snails, weevils, and countless other pests can cause minor or devastating dam-age in a home landscape. Most plants can afford to lose part of their foliage or sap without suffering much of a setback, so don't panic if you see a few holes chewed in a leaf. However, whenever you suspect that insects or related pests are attacking one of your plants, try to catch one of them in a glass jar and get it identified, so you can decide what to do.

Indentify, then treat

Don't jump to conclusions and start spraying chemicals on a supposedly sick plant before you know what (if anything) is actually wrong with it. That's waste-ful and irresponsible, and you're likely to do the plant as much harm as good. Pinpointing the exact cause of a problem is difficult for even experi-enced gardeners, so save yourself frustration and seek out expert help from the beginning.

If it seems that there's something wrong with one of your plants—for exam-ple, if the leaves are discolored, have holes in them, or have spots or marks on them—cut off a sample branch, wrap it in damp paper towels, and put it in a plastic bag (so it won't wilt). Take the sample to the nursery or garden center where you bought the plant, and ask for help. If the nursery can't help, contact the nearest office of your state's Cooperative Extension Service or a public gar-den in your area and ask if they have a staff member who can diagnose plant problems.

Meanwhile, look around your property and around the neighborhood, too, to see if any other plants (of the same or different kinds) show similar symp-toms. If a problem is widespread, you shouldn't have much trouble finding someone who can identify it and tell you what, if anything, to do. If only one plant is affected, it's often harder to diagnose the problem, and you may just have to wait and see what happens to it. Keep an eye on the plant, continue with watering and other regular maintenance, and see if the problem gets worse or goes away. If nothing more has happened after a few weeks, stop worrying. If the problem continues, intensify your search for expert advice.

Plant problems stem from a number of causes: insect and animal pests, diseases, and poor care, particularly in winter. Remember that plant problems are often caused by a combination of these; all the more reason to consult with experts about their diagnosis and treatment.

Deer-proof plants?

Planting from lists of deer-proof plants often results in disappoint-ment. What's deer-proof in one area may not be in another. And if deer are really hungry, they'll eat almost anything. If you live in an area where deer are common, check with local nurseries for planting solutions or stroll through your neighborhood to see what's nibbled and what's not.

DEER-CONTROL FENCING

Deer have been known to jump very tall fences. Experience shows that a wide midheight fence is one of the best ways to keep deer out. This fence is suitable for a larger property. It is about 6 ft. wide and 5 ft. high and consists of angled poles fixed to posts spaced about 10 ft. apart. Attach wires at 12-in. intervals to the poles. For advice on deer fences that work best in your area, consult your Cooperative Extension service.

There are several new kinds of insecticides that are quite effective but much safer to use than the older products. For example, insecticidal soap, a special kind of detergent, quickly kills aphids and other soft-bodied insects, but it's nontoxic to mammals and birds and it breaks down quickly, leaving no harmful residue. Horticultural oil, a highly refined mineral oil, is a good control for scale insects, which frequently infest gardenias, camellias, and other broad-leaved evergreens. Most garden centers stock these and other relatively safe insecticides.

Before using any insecticide, study the fine print on the label to make sure that the product is registered to control your particular pest. Carefully follow the directions for how to apply the product, or it may not work.

Diseases

Several types of fungal, bacterial, and viral diseases can attack garden plants, causing a wide range of symptoms such as disfigured or discolored leaves or petals, powdery or moldy-looking films or spots, mushy or rotten stems or roots, and overall wilting. As with insect problems, if you suspect that a plant is infected with a disease, gather a sample of the plant and show it to someone who can identify the problem before you do any spraying.

In general, plant diseases are hard to treat, so it's important to take steps to prevent problems. These steps include choosing plants adapted to your area, choosing disease-resistant plants, spacing plants far enough apart so that air can circulate between them, and removing dead stems and litter from the garden.

Perennials that would otherwise be healthy are prone to fungal infections during spells of humid weather, especially if the plants are crowded together or if they have flopped over and are lying on top of each other or on the ground. If your garden has turned into a jungle, look closely for moldy foliage, and if you find any, prune it off and discard (don't compost) it. It's better to cut the plants back severely than to let the disease spread. Plan to avoid repeated problems by dividing the perennials, replanting them farther apart, and pruning them early in the season so they don't grow so tall and floppy again. Crowded shrubs are also subject to fungal problems in the summer and should be pruned so that air can flow around them.

Winter damage

Even though most of California enjoys mild, if not glorious, winters, occasional cold spells that damage normally hardy plants are not uncommon. After a cold spell, wait until at least midsummer to assess the severity of the damage. At that time, new growth will tell you just how far back a plant has been killed and you can prune out limbs that are brown and dead.

Glossary

Amendments. Organic materials or minerals used to improve the soil. Peat moss, perlite, and compost are commonly used.

Annual. A plant that grows from seed, flowers, produces new seeds, and dies during a single growing season; a perennial plant treated like an annual in that it is grown for only a single season's display and then removed.

Balled-and-burlapped. Describes a tree or shrub dug out of the ground with a ball of soil intact around the roots; the ball is then wrapped in burlap and tied for transport.

Bare-root. Describes a plant dug out of the ground and then shaken or washed to remove the soil from the roots.

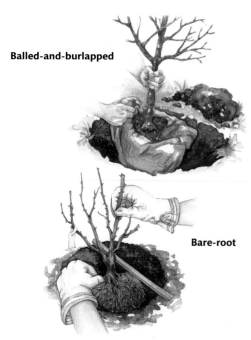

Balled-and-burlapped

Bare-root

Compound leaf. A leaf consisting of two or more leaflets branching from the same stalk.

Container-grown. Describes a plant raised in a pot that is removed before planting.

Crown. The part of a plant where the roots and stem meet, usually at soil level.

Cultivar. A cultivated variety of a plant, often bred or selected for some special trait such as double flowers, compact growth, cold hardiness, or disease and pest resistance.

Deadheading. Removing spent flowers during the growing season to improve a plant's appearance, prevent seed formation, and stimulate the development of new flowers.

Deciduous. Describes a tree, shrub, or vine that drops all its leaves in winter.

Division. Propagation of a plant by separating it into two or more pieces, each piece possessing at least one bud and some roots. Plants commonly divided include perennials, bulbs, grasses, and ferns.

Division

Drainage. Movement of water through soil. If water poured into a foot-deep hole drains completely in a few hours, the drainage is good.

Drip line. The circle of soil beneath a tree mirroring the circumference of the tree's canopy. This area benefits from direct rainfall and "drip" from leaves. Because many of the tree's feeder roots are found along the drip line and beyond, this area is the best for fertilizing and watering.

Dry-laid. Describes a masonry path or wall that is installed without mortar.

Edging. A barrier that serves as the border between lawn and a planting bed.

Edgings may be shallow trenches or barriers of plastic, brick, or boards.

Exposure. The characterization of a site according to the sun, wind, and temperature acting upon it.

Formal. Describes a style of landscaping that features symmetrical layouts, with beds and walks related to adjacent buildings, and often with plants sheared to geometric or other shapes.

Foundation planting. Traditionally, a narrow border of evergreen shrubs planted around the foundation of a house. Contemporary foundation plantings often include deciduous shrubs, grasses, perennials, and other plants as well.

Frost heaving. A disturbance or uplifting of soil, pavement, or plants caused when moisture in the soil freezes and expands.

Full shade. Describes a site that receives no direct sun during the growing season.

Full sun. Describes a site that receives at least eight hours of direct sun each day during the growing season.

Garden soil. Soil specially prepared for planting to make it loose enough for roots and water to penetrate easily. Usually requires digging or tilling and the addition of some organic matter.

Grade. The angle and direction of the ground's slope in a given area.

Ground cover. A plant providing continuous cover for an area of soil. Commonly a low, spreading foliage plant such as candytuft, vinca, or ajuga.

Habit. The characteristic shape of a plant, such as upright, mounded, columnar, or vase-shaped.

Hardiness. A plant's ability to survive the winter temperatures in a given region without protection.

Brick mowing strip

Hardscape. Parts of a landscape constructed from materials other than plants, such as walks, walls, and trellises made of wood, stone, or other materials.

Herbicide. A chemical used to kill plants. Preemergent herbicides are used to kill weed seeds as they sprout, and thus to prevent weed growth. Postemergent herbicides kill plants that are already growing.

Hybrid. A plant with two parents that belong to different varieties, species, or genera.

Interplant. To use plants with different bloom times or growth habits in the same bed to increase the variety and appeal of the planting.

Invasive. Describes a plant that spreads quickly, usually by runners, and mixes with or dominates adjacent plantings.

Landscape fabric. A synthetic fabric, sometimes water-permeable, spread under paths or mulch to serve as a weed barrier.

Lime, limestone. Mineral compounds applied to soil to lower its pH, rendering it less acid and thereby allowing plants to absorb nutrients better. Limestone also supplies calcium that plants need.

Loam. Soil rich in organic matter and with mineral particles in a range of sizes. Excellent for many garden plants.

Microclimate. A small-scale "system" of factors affecting plant growth on a particular site, including shade, temperature, rainfall, and so on.

Mowing strip. A row of bricks or paving stones set flush with the soil around the edge of a bed, and wide enough to support one wheel of the lawn mower.

Mulch. A layer of organic or other materials spread several inches thick around the base of plants and over open soil in a bed. Mulch conserves soil moisture, smothers weeds, and moderates soil temperatures. Where winters are cold, mulches help protect plants from freezing. Common mulches include compost, shredded leaves, straw, lawn clippings, gravel, newspaper, and landscape fabric.

Native. Describes a plant that is or once was found in the wild in a particular region and was not imported from another area.

Nutrients. Elements needed by plants. Found in the soil and supplied by fertilizers, nutrients include nitrogen, phosphorus, potassium, calcium, magnesium, sulfur, iron, and other elements, in various forms and compounds.

Organic matter. Partially or fully decomposed plant and animal matter. Includes leaves, trimmings, and manure.

Peat moss. Partially decomposed mosses and sedges. Dug from boggy areas, peat moss is often used as an organic amendment for garden soil.

Perennial. A plant with a life span of more than one year. Woody plants such as trees and shrubs are perennials, in addition to the "herbaceous perennials" more commonly cited, which have no woody tissue that persists from year to year.

Pressure-treated lumber. Softwood lumber treated with chemicals that protect it from decay.

Propagate. To produce new plants from seeds or by vegetative means such as dividing plant parts, taking root cuttings, and grafting stems onto other plants.

Retaining wall. A wall built to stabilize a slope and keep soil from sliding or eroding downhill.

Rhizome. A horizontal underground stem from which roots and shoots emerge. Some swell to store food. Branched rhizomes (those of iris, for instance) can be divided to produce new plants.

Root ball. The mass of soil and roots dug with a plant when it is removed from the ground; the soil and roots of a plant grown in a container.

Rosette. A low, flat cluster or crown of overlapping leaves.

Selective pruning. Using pruning shears to remove or cut back individual shoots in order to refine the shape of a shrub, maintain its vigor, or limit its size.

Severe pruning. Using pruning shears or loppers to cut away most of a shrub's top growth, leaving just short stubs or a gnarly trunk.

Shearing. Using hedge shears or an electric hedge trimmer to shape the surface of a shrub, hedge, or tree and produce a smooth, solid mass of greenery.

Specimen plant. A plant placed for individual display.

Spike. An elongated flower cluster on which individual flowers are attached directly to the main stem or are on very short stalks attached to the main stem.

Tender. Describes a plant that is damaged by cold weather in a particular region.

Underplanting. Growing short plants, such as ground covers, under a taller plant, such as a shrub.

Variegated. Describes foliage with color patterns in stripes, specks, or blotches that occur naturally or result from breeding.

Index

NOTE: Page numbers in **bold italic** refer to illustrations.

Photo Credits

Front Cover: *main image* Saxon Holt, design: Brandon Tyson; *top left* Jerry Pavia; *top right & center* Richard Shiell

Back Cover: *both* Saxon Holt

page 1: Saxon Holt

page 7: Jerry Pavia

pages 14–15: Saxon Holt

page 19: *top* Jerry Pavia; *center & bottom* Saxon Holt

page 23: *both* Saxon Holt

page 27: *top left* Jerry Pavia; *top right* Charles Mann; *bottom right* Charles Mann, design: Nancy Wagoner; *bottom left* Saxon Holt

page 30: *top & center* Saxon Holt; *bottom* Charles Mann, design: Greg Trutza

page 34: *top left* Charles Mann, design: Tina Rousselot; *top right* Saxon Holt; *bottom* Charles Mann, design: Steve Martino

page 39: *top & bottom right* Saxon Holt; *left* Charles Mann

page 42: *top left* Charles Mann, design: Joan Brink; *top right* Saxon Holt; *bottom* Saxon Holt, design: Jaquie Tomke-Bosch Garden

page 47: *top left & bottom* Saxon Holt; *top right* Jerry Pavia

page 51: *top* Saxon Holt; *bottom right* Saxon Holt, design: Sharon Osmund; *bottom left* Jerry Pavia, courtesy of Chozen Gardens, design: Roger's Gardens Colorscapes

page 54: *both* Saxon Holt, *bottom* design: Diana Stratton

page 58: *top* Charles Mann, design: Dulcy Mahar; *center & bottom* Saxon Holt

page 62: *top* Saxon Holt, courtesy of Gemes Garden; *center* Saxon Holt; *bottom* Jerry Pavia

page 66: *top & center* Jerry Pavia; *bottom* Saxon Holt, design: Keeyla Meadows

page 71: *top* Jerry Pavia; *bottom* Saxon Holt

page 75: *top* Jerry Pavia; *center & bottom* Saxon Holt

page 79: *top* Jerry Pavia; *bottom* Saxon Holt

page 82: *top* Saxon Holt, design: Suzanne Arca; *center* Saxon Holt; *bottom* Jerry Pavia

page 87: *both* Saxon Holt

page 91: *all* Saxon Holt

page 94: *top left* Jerry Pavia; *top right* Charles Mann; *bottom* Saxon Holt

page 99: *all* Jerry Pavia

page 103: *top left* Charles Mann, design: Joan Brink; *top right* Jerry Pavia; *bottom* Saxon Holt, design: Chris Jacobson

page 107: *both* Saxon Holt, *top* courtesy of Reid Garden

page 110: *top left & bottom* Saxon Holt; *top right* Charles Mann

pages 112–113: Charles Mann, design: Dulcy Mahar

page 114: *top left* Michael & Lois Warner/Photos Horticultural; *top right* Charles Mann; *bottom* Galen Gates

page 115: *top left & bottom right* Charles Mann; *top right & bottom left* Rita Buchanan; *center* Thomas Eltzroth; *bottom right* ; *bottom left*

page 116: *top left, bottom left & bottom right* Jerry Pavia; *top right* Charles Mann; *bottom center* Thomas Eltzroth

page 117: *top* Charles Mann; *top center right* Thomas Eltzroth; *top center left & bottom* Jerry Pavia; *bottom center* Saxon Holt

page 118: *top, top middle & bottom middle* Charles Mann; *bottom* Jerry Pavia

page 119: *top left* Rita Buchanan; *top right* Thomas Eltzroth; *center* Richard Shiell; *bottom* Jerry Pavia

page 120: *top left & bottom left* Jerry Pavia; *middle left* Richard Shiell; *bottom center & bottom right* Saxon Holt

page 121: *top both* Charles Mann; *bottom all* Jerry Pavia

page 122: *top left & bottom* Thomas Eltzroth; *top center & right* Charles Mann

page 123: *top left & bottom left* Thomas Eltzroth; *top right, center & bottom right* Saxon Holt

page 124: *top, center & bottom left* Charles Mann; *bottom center* Jerry Pavia; *bottom right* Saxon Holt

page 125: *top left & bottom right* Jerry Pavia; *top right* Charles Mann; *middle right* Richard Shiell; *bottom left* Saxon Holt

page 126: *top* Saxon Holt; *bottom right & left* Jerry Pavia; *bottom middle* Lance Walheim

page 127: *top left & bottom* Charles Mann; *top center* Carole Ottesen; *top right* Saxon Holt; *center both* Jerry Pavia

page 128: *top* Saxon Holt; *middle* Galen Gates; *bottom both* Jerry Pavia

page 129: *top & middle left* Jerry Pavia; *middle right* Thomas Eltzroth; *bottom right* Saxon Holt; *bottom left* Charles Mann

page 130: *top all* Jerry Pavia; *bottom* Saxon Holt

page 131: *top left* Charles Mann; *top right* Thomas Eltzroth; *middle & bottom all* Jerry Pavia

page 132: *top* Richard Shiell; *bottom right* Jerry Pavia; *bottom left* Charles Mann

page 133: *top left* Rita Buchanan; *top right* Saxon Holt; *center & bottom* Charles Mann

page 134: *top both* Charles Mann; *bottom* Saxon Holt

page 135: *top left & middle both* Saxon Holt; *top right* Charles Mann; *bottom* Jerry Pavia

page 136: *top left* Galen Gates; *top center & right* Saxon Holt; *bottom* Charles Mann

page 137: *top left* Cheryl Richter; *top right* Charles Mann; *middle right* Richard Shiell; *middle left* Stephen Pategas; *bottom* Saxon Holt

page 138: *top left* Lauren Springer; *top right* Charles Mann; *middle right* Jerry Pavia; *middle left* Saxon Holt; *bottom* Rita Buchanan

page 139: *top left* Thomas Eltzroth; *top right, center & bottom left* Richard Shiell; *bottom right* Jerry Pavia

page 140: *left* Dency Kane; *center* Charles Mann; *right* Cheryl Richter

page 141: *top left & bottom* Jerry Pavia; *top right* Carole Ottesen

page 142: *top both & bottom left* Charles Mann; *bottom right* Jerry Pavia

page 143: *top left* Stephen Pategas; *top middle* Saxon Holt; *top right* Richard Shiell; *bottom* Thomas Eltzroth

page 144: *top left* Jerry Pavia; *top right & bottom* Charles Mann

page 145: *top left & top right* Thomas Eltzroth; *top center* Saxon Holt; *middle* Jerry Pavia; *bottom* Charles Mann

page 146: *top left & bottom* Richard Shiell; *top center* Michael Dirr; *top right* Saxon Holt

page 147: *top both* Thomas Eltzroth; *bottom both* Jerry Pavia

page 148: *top & bottom right* Jerry Pavia; *bottom left* Saxon Holt; *bottom center* Neil Soderstrom

page 149: *top* Richard Shiell; *middle* Jerry Pavia; *bottom* Charles Mann

page 150: *top, left center & bottom left* Charles Mann; *right center* Jerry Pavia; *bottom right* Saxon Holt

page 151: *top, bottom left & center* Charles Mann; *bottom right* Jerry Pavia

page 152: *top left* Charles Mann; *top right & bottom right* Saxon Holt; *bottom left* Susan A. Roth

page 153: *top left* Saxon Holt; *top right* Jerry Pavia; *bottom right* Greg Grant; *bottom left* Stephen Pategas

page 154: *left & center* Jerry Pavia; *right* Saxon Holt

page 155: *top left & bottom left* Jerry Pavia; *top right* Richard Shiell; *bottom right* Saxon Holt

pages 156–157: Charles Mann, design: Joan Brink

Have a home gardening, decorating, or improvement project?

Look for these and other fine Creative Homeowner books wherever books are sold

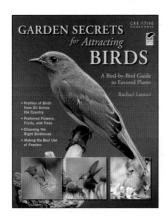

GARDEN SECRETS FOR ATTRACTING BIRDS
Provides information to turn your yard into a mecca for birds.

Over 250 photographs and illustrations.
160 pp.
8½" × 10⅝"
$14.95 (US)
BOOK #: CH274561

CHAR-BROIL'S EVERYBODY GRILLS!
More than 200 recipes for delicious grilled, barbecued, and smoked dishes.

Over 250 photographs.
304 pp.
8½" × 10⅞"
$24.95 (US)
BOOK #: CH253001

CHAR-BROIL'S AMERICA GRILLS!
222 Flavorful recipes that will fire up your appetite.

Over 250 photographs.
304 pp.
8½" × 10⅞"
$24.95 (US)
BOOK #: CH253050

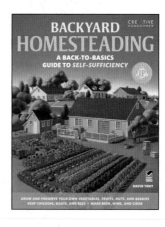

BACKYARD HOMESTEADING
How to turn your yard into a small farm.

Over 235 photographs.
256 pp.
8½" × 10⅞"
$16.95 (US)
BOOK #: CH274800

DECORATING: THE SMART APPROACH TO DESIGN
A go-to how-to guide on decorating, explaining fundamental design principles, for real people.

Over 375 photographs.
288 pp.
8½" × 10⅞"
$21.95 (US)
BOOK #: CH279680

EASY CLOSETS
Introduces homeowners to the variety of closet types and closet systems available.

Over 275 photographs.
160 pp.
8½" × 10⅞"
$14.95 (US)
BOOK #: CH277135

For more information and to order direct, go to **www.creativehomeowner.com**